CONTEMPORARY CAPITALISM

CONTEMPORARY CAPITALISM

JOHN STRACHEY

RANDOM HOUSE · NEW YORK

First Printing
© Copyright, 1956, by John Strachey
All rights reserved under International
and Pan-American Copyright Conventions
Library of Congress Catalog Card Number: 56–7075
Manufactured in the United States of America
by H. Wolff, New York

to the Labour Movement

CONTENTS

ACKNOWLEDGMENTS

It is a somewhat delicate matter to make adequate acknowledgment to all those who have assisted in the revision of a controversial work such as this. However specifically the author may repudiate the suggestion that his friends are responsible for anything he has written, attempts may be made to associate them with his inaccuracies, his errors, or, simply, his opinions. But perhaps there is safety in numbers. No one could really think that all the men and women who have helped me could have any element of responsibility for anything written herein, for their opinions are so different, and, let me assure the reader, their suggestions have been so diverse.

The following practising economists have given me unstinted help, reading and re-reading the whole typescript, instructing and informing me: Mrs. Joan Robinson, Dr. Thomas Balogh and Mr. Colin Clark. In addition Mr. Dudley Seers has twice read and criticised drafts of Chapter 7.

Of my fellow-working politicians in the House of Commons, the following have read and criticised the draft typescript at various stages: Mr. R. L. S. Crossman, Mr. Hugh Gaitskell, Mr. Douglas Jay and Mr. Reginald Paget. Again the book's mistakes and limitations are its author's alone: but if it proves to have some contact with practical politics that will be largely because it has been written and re-written, revised and re-revised, under the cross-fire of the criticisms which these hard-pressed men of affairs have had the generosity and disinterest to devote to it.

Of those who are laymen, in respect both of practising economics and practising politics, but whose help may be all the more valuable on that account, Mr. Victor Gollancz has read the typescript as a friend and as a critic rather than as a publisher and has made highly important suggestions. Mr. Peter Shore both read and criticised my book while he was producing a book of his own, a particularly generous act as between authors. Mr. Euan Cooper-Willis, my sister, my son and my wife have all been pressed into service, and not without substantial benefits to the book. Finally my secretary, Miss C. K. Edgley, has done prodigies of typing and re-typing.

I do not know why so many people have been willing to do so much. Perhaps it means that they think that I have been at least trying to do something of value.

Contemporary Capitalism is the first volume of a projected series of studies on the principles of democratic socialism.

John Strachey

London
March, 1956

CONTEMPORARY CAPITALISM

INTRODUCTION

Socialist thinking must begin with the study of capitalism. This is as true for the evolutionary as for the revolutionary tradition, for the Webbs as for Marx. It is this which marks the distinction between the attempt genuinely to comprehend and control the development of human society and mere dreaming. This is the distinction between what has been called "scientific" and "utopian" socialism. What is to be can only emerge from what is.

Renewed attempts to assess the nature of contemporary capitalism are overdue. Capitalist society in 1956 is a very different thing from what it was 100 years ago when the socialist *critique* of it was first undertaken, or even from what it was 50 years ago when most of the current socialist conceptions of it were first formulated. Socialists will not succeed very well in their task of social transformation until and unless they form a clear idea of what capitalism has become and is becoming.

THE POSSIBLE

Moreover, there is a more immediately practical necessity for re-assessments of the society in which we live. Without them the best-intentioned, the most idealistic, the most heroic, political activities may, and frequently do, end in frustration or catastrophe. For politics, as we are tediously informed, is the art of the possible. What else could it be? The point is to discover what is possible and what is not. And for that an estimate of the nature and tendencies of our economic system is first of all indispensable.

If this were questioned it would only be necessary to imagine what Ricardo called "strong cases," or extreme examples. For instance, if we adopted the "strong case" that contemporary capitalism has now solved all its problems and overcome all its difficulties, then clearly one kind of politics would become "the possible" and another "the impossible." Conversely, if we adopted the "strong case" that capitalism had exhausted all its possibilities of existence and must immediately collapse, then quite different politics would be respectively "possible" and "impossible." The first thing to do, then, is to delimit the politics which are likely to constitute "the possible" for, say, most of the remainder of our century and in our part of the world. For it may prove practicable to make that delimitation a good deal narrower than would be represented by choosing one or other of the above "strong cases."

This book is, then, one of political economy, in the most old-fashioned sense of that term. It has little in common, that is to say, with the view that economics can be a precise science. It is directed rather to the point of interaction between economic and political forces, to the point, in particular, at which the effects of political democracy interact with the innate tendencies of highly developed capitalist economics.

THE ECONOMIC FACTOR

The fact that the study begins at the economic end of the social complex may be thought to imply a particular view of the nature, workings and inter-connections of human society. And so it does. It implies, that is to say, a conviction that the economic, political and all other aspects of society are inter-connected: that they interact in a way which it is just beginning to be possible to understand. But it does not imply that the economic aspect of society is the unique determinant of all the rest. On this famous issue, it implies no more and no less than this: that the way in which men get their livings—the techniques, in the broadest sense of that term, by which at any given time and place they produce the wherewithal of life—profoundly affects, and is profoundly affected by, the economic, social and political relationships in which they find themselves involved. For, whether they know it or not, they have entered into those relationships (which in the last resort are relationships of power: of the power of one man, or one group, over another) largely at least, in order to operate the techniques available to them.

It is my undiminished conviction that this fact of a comprehensible inter-connection and interaction between the different aspects of society is the still but dimly apprehended clue to the social labyrinth. (The issue will be discussed in a later volume of this study.) But it may be largely a question of personal habit of mind whether or not the explorer enters that labyrinth by the path of economic analysis, for he will soon find that political, sociological, ideological, moral, religious and all other factors may be as much "causes" of the development which he studies as are the economic. Still, to my mind at least, the economic factor is the most get-at-able, the least illusive. So surely it is prudent to lay hold upon it first of all, before we get lost in the baffling elaboration of the social structure. The economic substructure of society is only the skeleton on which hang the flesh, blood, connective tissues, nerves, sense organs and brain of the body social. Certainly the skeleton is not the only, or even in many respects the most important, part of the human body; but it would be a rash anatomist who did not begin with the bones of his subject.

MARXISM

In this connection it may be useful to define the place of Marxism in this study. The method of presentation in a number of chapters is to compare the analysis made by one or other of the eminent economists who have studied the capitalist system, not only with reality as it has in fact unfolded, but also with the analysis made by Marx or by his successors. This treatment involves close attention to Marxism; in this volume to Marxian economics, in subsequent volumes to Marxian historical and sociological theory.

Two reasons justify such attention to the Marxist system. The first is that Marxism is today the exclusive method of social analysis, the official philosophy—indeed, the only permitted method of thought—of some third of the human race. This would in itself be enough to make it ridiculous to attempt to comprehend contemporary social reality without comprehending Marxism. For it would be to fall into one of the errors of a crude and oversimplified version of Marxism itself to suppose that a mental system so widespread, so fanatically held, and so dogmatic, would not itself become a factor in the total situation, reacting upon and modifying the social reality which it seeks to elucidate. Therefore, even if Marxism were an almost wholly false doctrine, with little or no contact with reality, an ignorance of it would still render almost valueless any study of the contemporary world scene. And how many painstaking studies are more or less completely vitiated by such an ignorance?

Nevertheless there is a still more important reason for the study of Marxism as part of any attempt to make sense of the world. It is simply this: Of all the "mental systems" which have hitherto been offered for the elucidation of human society, Marxism does, on the whole, less violence to reality than any other, which may not be saying much. We may leave on one side for the present the question of whether *any* such mental system is in the long run a help or a hindrance. Perhaps such systems, in fact, pass through a sort of life cycle of growth and decay, becoming, to use Marxian language, first a facility for, and later a fetter on, social analysis. In this connection we shall take up the question of why Marxism, which should be, and professes to be, a *method,* and not a "system," which professes indeed to be a method of the greatest flexibility, has been allowed to degenerate into, precisely, a system of the greatest rigidity.

Nevertheless, if we compare the degree of insight which, in the light of experience, we now know that Marx achieved, with the achievement of any other single sociologist, we shall be filled with respect. True, that respect should take the form of the most rigorous criticism which we can possibly make of every aspect of Marxism. The reader will find that we shall deal especially fully with those of Marx's predictions which the real development of events has falsified. For this is the sole means by which everything which is lively and true in Marxism can be preserved. But to suppose that contemporary reality, in either its economic or its sociological aspect, could be fruitfully studied without taking into the most careful account, at every step, what Marx and his major successors thought and wrote, would be simply to waste the time of both reader and writer. For these reasons, it is gratifying to be able to pay the tribute of rigorous criticism to the genius of that eminent Victorian, Karl Marx. While, then, the first subject of this study is contemporary capitalism, its second and more theoretical subject is Marxism and its contemporary development.

For Marxism contains astringent truths about human society in general, and about the society in which we live in particular; it contains truths which are hard to take because they ask us to strip off illusions which are for many their comfort in a terrifying world. It would be tragic indeed if those truths, once seen, were to be lost sight of. An attempt is made, then, to take a modest step in the indispensable process of re-integrating Marxism with the Western cultural tradition from which it derives, but from which it has widely diverged. The aim is to see Marxism neither as an anathematised heresy, nor yet a gospel, but as one, partial, brilliant, rich, prejudiced, but precious, contribution to our cultural heritage.

THE MENACE OF A THEORY AND THE NECESSITY OF THEORY

Nevertheless it must be acknowledged that immense dangers are inherent in the use of any method as sweeping and comprehensive as Marx's. He who would bend the bow of Odysseus must have strong muscles, or he may not only fail to shoot the arrow, but may also break his back. It is easy to fall into a Procrustean paring and lopping of reality to fit the needs of any vast and complicated mental system. The teachings of its author may have been not so much mastered as succumbed to.

The profoundly anti-theoretical tradition of British sociological thought in general, and of the British labour movement in particular, has always been acutely aware of such dangers. It is felt that no man ever did, nor could, construct a mental system which would fit social reality. Only those ideas and institutions which have been built up piece by piece, and largely unconsciously, as the coral insect constructs its gigantic monuments; only those ideas and institutions which have been formed by ceaseless, minute adjustment to social reality have proved, it is felt, to be in any way useful. All grand theories and systems are seen as mere stumbling-blocks to true insight.

Such has always been the mental climate of this country, made explicit in the British empirical tradition. Nor has recent experience done anything but confirm that tradition. For the evidence of our times proclaims that no one theory, neither Marxism nor any other, has proved to be in itself an adequate "guide to action." In the hurricanes of the twentieth century those who have relied on one such unique guide have, as often as not, fared even worse than those who have trusted to empiricism, instinct, insight and sheer luck to see them through. Yet just because of all this, what is now, perhaps, chiefly needed is to strive to remember that empiricism also can become a dogma. In Britain and America we are only too ready to make a virtue out of our own intellectual laziness, and to plume ourselves, not only on freedom from enslavement to "a theory," which is prudent, but on sheer ignorance of political and economic *theory* in any shape or form. The sceptical and empirical tradition, pushed to this point, degenerates into mere illiteracy. The truth is that the more we reject any one all-sufficient theory, the greater is the obligation upon us to achieve a command over the whole range of political and economic thinking. Otherwise we shall inevitably repeat all the tedious re-discoveries of the autodidact. In a word, the complexities of social phenomena are a reason for viewing with scepticism any vast unifying hypothesis which is interpreted as giving all the answers, and giving them once and for all. But these complexities are no excuse for abandoning the task of interpretation as hopeless: that way lies despair, mysticism and the mutilation of the intellect.

Nor, of course, is such theoretical defeatism in the British intellectual tradition. On the contrary, and in particular in the field of political economy, with which this volume is concerned, the British theoretical tradition is the richest in the world. Generation by generation, for the last two hundred and fifty years, British thinkers, from Petty to Keynes, have striven to analyse the relationships into which men find themselves entering as a result of their efforts to gain their daily bread. Moreover, British public men, from the younger Pitt to Clement Attlee, far from being indifferent to the body of theory which has resulted, have again and again reshaped the British economy and the society which has rested on it, partly as a result of the current teachings of the political economists of their day—and partly even successfully. The fact is that a growing, living body of theory is an indispensable factor in successful social change. As Keynes wrote in a justly famous passage, a "know-nothing," contemptuous attitude to theory results merely in abject unconscious dependence upon some half-understood, vulgarised version of the dominant theory of the day before yesterday.

No one who has lived and worked in the British labour movement for over a quarter of a century can doubt the grave disadvantages of the anti-theoretical tradition when carried to excess. If the stock-in-trade of ideas, theories, plans and aspirations of a reforming movement does not grow at least in step with its practical activities, a painful hiatus may occur. The very success of such a movement in carrying out the main parts of its traditional programme may, as in the case of the British labour movement after the 1945-51 Government, produce a sense almost of bankruptcy. "Stout Cortez" in Keats' sonnet did not confront the Pacific Ocean with a greater air of "wild surmise" than that with which

some members of the British labour movement confronted
the new state of things which they had themselves brought
into being in Britain by the middle of the twentieth century.

WHAT IS NOT IN THE BOOK

It may be useful to say something as to what this volume
does not contain. It does not deal, except cursorily and in
passing, with moral objectives or social ideals. It expresses
few value judgments, that is to say, and those that it does
largely by implication. This is not because I fail to recognise
that the whole question of social purpose is more important than anything that is discussed herein. Nevertheless
the humbler matters in which these pages deal may not be
unworthy of the attention of those who feel the great moral
issues most keenly. We have a procedure in the British House
of Commons by which we go into what is called "a Committee of Ways and Means." When we do so we discuss,
for the time being exclusively, the means by which our objectives may be achieved. This study is written, as it were, in
Committee of Ways and Means.

Paradoxical in the extreme as it may seem, what has im-
pelled me to write this sort of book is, precisely, the conviction that issues of social morality are supreme. They are supreme, but for that very reason impossible, for me at least,
to deal with abstractly and except by the implication of concrete economic and political facts. For what has made men's
efforts at social improvement so partially successful at best,
and at worst so tragically abortive, has been insufficient
comprehension of the ways and means by which their objectives may be reached. I find it difficult to contemplate with
equanimity the amount of honest, selfless, and sometimes
heroic, social and political effort which, even in my own ex-

perience, I have seen run to waste and turn, first to futility, then to disillusionment and bitterness, so that in the end it becomes actively pernicious, for lack of such comprehension. That is why it seems to me that at this particular moment of history it is more useful to discover social interconnections than to exhort.

It is true that the economic and political questions with which this volume deals are not finally separable from those issues which turn upon a consideration of the deepest springs of human action. But I repeat that I cannot even approach those supreme moral issues except by means of the study of the labyrinth of contemporary social reality. I can only attempt to catch a glimpse of what ought to be by means of achieving some degree of insight into what is. Until I had made my best attempt at description, classification and analysis, I should have little to say about social ends which was not obvious and jejune. It is out of honest and diligent effort to describe, to analyse and to comprehend that there may emerge the light and glow of social purpose. Obviously no one who did not see that light and feel that glow would take the trouble either to write or to read such a book as this. The medieval clerks said that to work was to pray —*Laborare est orare.* If we strain every faculty we possess in the pursuit of social understanding, we may better serve the ideal than by talking about it in the abstract. That moral fervour which, undoubtedly, can alone move the mountain of social inertia will emerge, if, but only if, the work of description and analysis is sufficiently honest, objective, dry.

If, however, this volume is written "in Committee of Ways and Means," in the sense that it does not raise the great issue of what are the ends and objects of social life, neither, on the other hand, does it attempt to suggest specific policies and programmes. They are of the hour and the occasion. This is a descriptive, analytic and above all delimiting work, seeking to define the kind of things which in our period will lie within the ambit of the politically possible. It is an operational study seeking to elucidate the complex play of contemporary political and economic forces at their point of intersection. Of course I hope that it will be of practical use in shaping democratic socialist policies and programmes. But that is a task for its readers. Whether or not the study as a whole will in the end generate some suggestions as to lines of policy of a sufficiently long-term character to be worth while including in its text, I do not yet know.

PURPOSE OF THE STUDY

The purpose of this study is, then, to add a little to our slowly, painfully accumulating knowledge of how our contemporary societies actually work, and, consequently, of how they may be controlled and changed. It can offer no unified theory upon which dogmatic conclusions for action can be based. There is still, we have all discovered, no substitute for that patient political craftsmanship, reliance on which is the main tradition of British public life. Knowledge, however, can help slowly and painfully to raise the level of competence and coherence in the decisions which men and women of affairs must continually be making. To do no more, but no less, than that is the hope and purpose of this study.

1 ■ THE NEW STAGE OF CAPITALISM

AN ECONOMY OF LARGE AND FEW UNITS

You can change the very nature of a bowl of cream merely by stirring it. As you stir, it will begin to coagulate; lumps will appear in the once smooth and perfect liquid. At length you will transform the whole bowl into a solid: the cream will be butter.

For half a century now some such process has been at work within the economic system. The powerful hand which has solidified by stirring the once fluid medium of our economic relations is competition. And this is remarkable, for originally competition had an exactly opposite effect. Competition was once a mighty power to break up and break down the stiff, formalised economic relationships of the age before capitalism. It is a commonplace of economic history that it was this formidable force which pulverised every relationship built upon custom, status, sentiment—every relationship founded upon non-economic considerations, no matter what. The overriding tendency of competition was to put everything into the common crucible of a market of many sellers confronted by many buyers. It tended to make everything into a commodity, *i.e.*, into something exchangeable: to put up the sign "For Sale" upon everything in the world, to make the nexus of cash the sole remaining bond between individual "economic men" who had themselves been perfectly atomised by its pervading force.

And then, strangely, competition, prolonged and intensified beyond a certain degree, began to reverse its effects. From being a grinding power of social disintegration, it began to build up new relationships and new institutions: it became integrating, solidifying and constructive. In the smooth liquid of the perfectly competitive market the solid bodies of substantial new social and economic institutions began to form, modifying and in the end destroying the homogeneity of the medium.

To drop the simile, the competitive process, by its own ruthless strength, and in accordance with its own inner logic, continually creates bigger and fewer units with which to fight out the competitive battle. It does so because, on the whole and in the end, the larger units prove to have superior competitive power. It does so by carrying further an integrating process which had in fact been at work, underneath the destructive, atomising process, from almost the beginning of capitalism. Ever since the eighteenth century the individual craftsman, individual merchant, and later the individual industrialist, has been gradually outclassed; he has been outclassed by the partnership and the firm; then the firm and the partnership has in turn been defeated by the Joint Stock Company; next the small Private Joint Stock Company has itself been outclassed by the large Public Company; and finally there has emerged the giant Company or Corporation, typically a dozen or so of them to each industry, sometimes in the form of trusts, combines or cartels, occasionally, although not typically, as semi-monopolies or even monopolies. Such giant units are now the dominant, although by no means universal, economic institutions of our period. They have become the decisive *dramatis personae* of contemporary economic life.

EXTENT OF THE PROCESS

We may deal briefly with the question of the extent to which this process of the increase in size, and decrease in number, of firms has gone. For, on the one hand, the existence of the process is undisputed and, on the other, it is far from being part of our argument that it is complete. We must note, however, what has happened in each of the three major, highly industrialised capitalisms which will form the primary objects of our attention: namely, the United States of America, Britain and Western Germany.

We may begin with America, both because this is the predominant capitalist society of our times and also because information on the structure of the American economy is the best. We may follow Professor Galbraith's summary of the position. Professor Galbraith's brief but penetrating book, *American Capitalism* (Hamish Hamilton, 1952), is, in many respects, the most realistic picture of the contemporary American economy, and we shall use it on a number of occasions. Professor Galbraith writes that "the heads of the corporations that produce between a third and a half of the national product of the United States could be seated comfortably in almost any neighbourhood motion-picture theatre." * And, more particularly, that "a recent investigation by the Federal Trade Commission shows that, for the year 1946, the 113 largest manufacturing corporations owned forty-six per cent of the property, plant and equipment employed in manufacturing."

Or again (*op. cit.*, p. 42):

.. . Over an important sector of the American economy individual markets are shared by a small number of producers. In

* My American friends inform me that this means about 400-500 persons.

the production of motor vehicles, agricultural machinery, rubber tyres, cigarettes, aluminium, liquor, meat products, copper, tin containers and office machinery the largest three firms in 1947 did two-thirds or more of all business. In steel, glass, industrial chemicals, and dairy products the largest six accounted for two-thirds. There is a similar degree of concentration in a host of less important or derivative industries. And in a number more—gasoline, cement, mixed fertilizer and milk distribution —markets that are necessarily regional or local are typically divided between a similarly small number of sellers.

There are numerous industries where the number of firms serving the same market remains large and where no one or no small number have any considerable proportion of the total business. But for a large and important sector of the economy —indeed for the industries which are commonly supposed to typify American capitalism—this is clearly not the case. On the contrary, as one of the leading contemporary students of market organization has concluded, "The principal indications of studies of American market structure are (among others) that concentration of output among relatively few sellers is the dominant pattern." (Joe S. Bain in *A Survey of Contemporary Economics* [Blakiston, Philadelphia, 1948].)

There is an extensive literature devoted to the study of this process of centralisation, in this the most advanced unit of world capitalism. (See, for example, Berle and Means' great original study, *The Modern Corporation and Private Property*, New York Commerce Clearing House, Inc., and Macmillan, 1932; *The Structure of the American Economy*, Part I; *Basic Character*, National Resources Planning Board, U.S. Govt. Printing Office, 1939; *The Concentration of Productive Facilities*, U.S. Govt. Printing Office, 1947; *A Survey of Contemporary Economics*, 1948.)

In Britain the descriptive literature is less adequate. The work of Leak and Maizels in their analysis of the 1935 census of production is still usually taken as the last available indication. They concluded that in any given industry about a quarter of the total labour force worked in the three largest firms in that industry. (Professor P. Sargant Florence's recent book, *The Logic of British and American Industry* [Routledge and Kegan Paul, 1953] should be consulted. But it will be found that Professor Florence is interested in rather different aspects of the contemporary scene than those relevant to the purpose of this chapter.) We may make another approach to the matter if we note that there are in Britain under 12,000 "Public" Joint Stock Companies altogether, and that these 12,000 units are responsible for, it is estimated, about one half of the entire economic activity of the community. Thus these 12,000 firms do as much business as all the Private Joint Stock Companies (and there are more than a quarter of a million of these), the nationalised industries, direct State enterprises, the entire economic activity of Municipalities, the Co-operative movement, and all the innumerable firms, partnerships and one-man businesses of all kinds, put together.

Such figures indicate the steady, long-term drop in the number and increase in the size of the units of the British economy. But they give little idea of the extent to which the process has gone at the decisive points. In manufacturing industry, it has been calculated that as few as 2,800 firms now produce half the total product. But even this is not the heart of the matter. For within manufacturing industry itself the degree of concentration is most uneven. Some industries (cotton, for instance) are still conducted by a relatively large number of relatively small firms. But when we transfer our attention to the most important, expanding, highly developed and mechanised industries, we find that the drop in the number and increase in the size of firms have reached a point at which it has produced a new and easily recognised industrial pattern. This is the pattern of a handful of giant firms responsible for much the greater part of the industry's output, surrounded in most, but not all, cases by a fringe of remaining small "independents" producing, more or less precariously, the remainder. This, or some variant of this, is, to take the obvious examples, the pattern of the contemporary British chemical, oil, banking, motor-car manufacturing, steel, sugar-refining, newspaper-publishing and aircraft industries. The pattern is usually referred to as "oligopoly," or few sellers, by the economists. As we shall use it repeatedly, it will be worth while to define this term. By its use the economists mean that the number of the *dramatis personae* who produce and sell in any given industry has become so few as to cause certain highly significant changes in the workings of the economy.*

I am unfamiliar with the corresponding literature, if it yet exists, for the third major capitalist society of the contemporary world, namely, that of the Federal Republic of Western Germany. That economy has not yet settled into its post-World War II pattern; moreover the occupying powers made vigorous attempts to undo some of the most extreme examples of German concentration into few and large units, as in the case of the Ruhr heavy industries, by forcibly splitting up the few remaining highly concentrated and cartelised firms. For we shall find that German capitalism was in many respects the leader in the process of concentration which we are describing and that it reached, in the Third Reich, an unparalleled development. According to newspaper accounts, the process of re-integration was in full swing in Western Germany during the early nineteen-fifties.

* See Schumpeter's *History of Economic Analysis* (Allen & Unwin, 1955), p. 305, for an account of the *provenance* of the word oligopoly. Fascinatingly enough, he is able to trace it right back to Thomas More's *Utopia*. Moreover More, in the Latin original of his book, uses the term exactly in our modern sense. He notes that if sellers are few in number prices may stay high. For the few sellers, "if we cannot call them a monopoly are certainly an oligopoly."

CONSEQUENCES OF THE PROCESS: A SOCIAL MUTATION

I repeat that the existence of the above process of concentration is undisputed. What is often disputed is the assertion that this process has reached the point of creating *monopolies* in the major productive fields. But no such assertion is here in question. With one or two rare and perhaps transitory exceptions, none of the major industries of contemporary capitalism has come to be conducted exclusively by one all-embracing firm. (The production of aluminium in America is usually cited as the leading case in which this did actually happen.) What we are asserting is the different proposition that there exists a long-term tendency to fewer and larger units in the economic system.

We shall further assert that this tendency has now reached a point at which it has all-important consequences. But why should this be so? It is by no means self-evident that we should attach any special significance to this growth in the size, and shrinkage in the number, of the units which do the competing in our essentially (it is still assumed) competitive economic system. Is there any reason to suppose, it may be asked, that the mere growth in the size of the competitors will have changed the nature of the contest? True, the change in scale over the full historical range of development is very great. From the one-man enterprise of an eighteenth-century hand-loom weaver, through the typical nineteenth-century Lancashire cotton mill, to Courtaulds, Du Ponts, I.C.I., I.G. Farben, Unilevers, A.E.G., or United States Steel, is a long road. Nevertheless, are there any reasons which would make us expect that this mere increase in the size and decrease in the number of the units which produce, which buy, and which sell, will have changed the nature of the system?

There are such reasons. A whole literature analysing and discussing them already exists. Indeed, two whole literatures exist, each of which seeks to construct a different diagram or model for the study of the new stage of capitalism which has come into being. On the other hand, and in spite of the existence of these literatures, much of our political life is still lived on the basis of assumptions and preconceptions appropriate to the previous phases of capitalism alone. Many of the supporters and the opponents of capitalism today conduct a battle over the ghost of an economy which no longer inhabits the earth. Both, consequently, misunderstand or misinterpret the reality about them, by applying to it categories and concepts which have little relevance left in them. And finally, this new and culminating stage of capitalism has appeared in the world in very different forms, according to the political environment in which it has arisen.

In this chapter we shall seek to do no more than list the reasons which have caused an increase in the size, and a decrease in the number, of the competitors within the economic system, to change the nature of capitalism. They have changed its nature in the sense that the laws of development of the older stage of the system no longer fully apply to the new stage. Extreme theoretical confusion and ghastly practical mistakes, therefore, result from supposing that the new model will behave in the old way. The following list of reasons is conclusive, it will be submitted, in showing that a new and distinct stage of our extant economic system, namely, capitalism, now exists in the advanced industrial communities. But they do not show that the system as such, that capitalism itself, has been abolished, as it undoubtedly has been in Russia, for example. To use the biological analogy—imperfect but graphic—the extinction of the species and its supersession by another would be a change of a different order of magnitude. The species is still recognisably itself; but it has undergone a mutation.

In the process of enumerating the reasons which force us to conclude that a mutation has taken place, we shall give a brief initial statement of the main themes which will be elaborated in subsequent chapters of this volume. Finally, this list of reasons is in itself neutral as to the quality of the new stage of capitalism. The reader is earnestly entreated to suspend judgment till a much later stage in the argument, as to whether the new stage of capitalism is "worse" or "better" than the old. Such a suspension of judgment is much more difficult than is usually supposed. Not only will almost every reader have strong emotional reactions of a broadly pro- or anti-capitalist character. The writer also will inevitably use emotive words and phrases which will cause the reader to assume that he adopts either a positive or a negative attitude to the new stage. He does. No one is emotionally neutral over this central issue of our epoch. But he will endeavour to set out his own views in proper sequence, and to perform at least the work of description and classification as objectively as if the subject matter were planckton or fruit fly. That will not be easy, for what in fact we study is that net of social and economic relations in which our hopes and fears, our lives and deaths, are all enmeshed.

(I)   THE METAMORPHOSIS OF COMPETITION

The first and decisive reason why an economy of large and few units exhibits new characteristics is because at a certain point in the increase of their size and decrease of their number, the managers of the remaining units begin to be able to affect prices instead of being exclusively affected by them. It is impossible to exaggerate the importance of this transformation. Prices, from being objective data which move automatically in accordance with no man's will, become things which *may be moved, within certain limits*, by the conscious decisions of groups of men. Such a change nullifies some of the basic principles of capitalism.

Prices are the rates or ratios at which commodities exchange with one another. It is a major premise of the system, unquestioned equally by Marx and by Marshall, that these ratios must establish themselves by means of competition: by, that is to say, the higgle of the market when many sellers confront many buyers, none of whom commands a sufficient proportion of the total supply of the commodity being dealt in for his own actions appreciably to affect the price. Almost every "law" which it has ever been suggested that the capitalist system will obey, from the labour theory of value to the principle of marginal utility, takes this for granted. Nearly every chain of reasoning by means of which the economists have laboriously traced out, for example, how large profits will be, how the total national income will be distributed, what factors will determine the rate of interest, what will be the level of wages, etc., etc., has assumed that the buyers and sellers will be essentially the creatures, not the creators, of prices. It has been assumed that this will be so whether the buyers and sellers are the owners of firms selling industrial products, farmers selling the fruits of the soil, merchants dealing in them, shopkeepers distributing them, or wage earners selling their ability to labour. A major premise of economic thinking has been that prices—the ratios at which commodities will exchange—will be the determinate end result of the higgle-haggle of many buyers with many sellers, each indeed trying to sell as dear, and buy as cheap, as he can, but by the very uniformity of that attempt cancelling out each other's desires, and thus collectively establishing lists of prices which are settled by the will of no single buyer or seller.

It is no longer so. It is now a commonplace of the descriptive literatures of the contemporary economic system that in the case of all those industries which have reached the stage of large and few units, in which a handful of sellers controls the best part of the total supply, those sellers, acting in overt or tacit association, can, and do, consciously decide and determine, within certain limits, what the prices of their products and their supplies shall be.

It will hardly be necessary to give any lengthy account of how those who control a small number of firms which together are responsible for a high proportion of the available supply of any commodity can, within fairly wide limits, affect its price. For their procedure is obvious and familiar. It is important to note, however, that they do not necessarily, nor even typically, act by means of the organisation of a monopoly, in the proper sense of that word. In order to acquire a price-affecting power they need not, and often do not, organise themselves into a formal ring or cartel, with binding agreements between themselves as to prices. Still less need they amalgamate themselves into one single super-gigantic firm or trust. They may do no more, for example, than to begin to use the Trade Association, or Trade Agreement, one or other of which is quite sure to exist in their field, in order to move towards eliminating the decisive form of competition, namely, competition in price. A detailed examination of the actual workings of contemporary Trade Associations and Trade Agreements would probably show that they now play a significant part in the gradual atrophy of price competition, even in those fields in which the number of independent firms remains relatively high.

In those fields in which the number of firms has fallen to a figure low enough to produce the characteristic pattern of oligopoly, the atrophy of competition takes place in a still more natural way. All that need happen, and all that in the most typical cases does happen, is that the leading directors of the half dozen or so firms get to know one another. After that competition in the old, real, decisive sense of the word, namely, *price* competition, is not so much abolished as tacitly discarded. It simply fades out of existence like the Cheshire cat; and, like that famous animal, it leaves but a grin behind.

A typical way for the thing to happen is for one of the, say, half dozen remaining great firms to become the recognised leader of the industry. Such a leading firm becomes, like a British Prime Minister, first among equals. Its erstwhile rivals remain in every formal respect wholly independent and equal to it in status, above all in matters of pricing. But in practice they nevertheless invariably follow their "price-leader," as the outstanding firm in their industry comes to be called. (United States Steel is such a "price-leader" in the American steel industry, for example.) Moreover they follow its leadership not only in the prices which they charge for their products, but also in the prices which they pay for their raw materials and (above all) for their labour-power; they follow, that is to say, their price-leader in their wages policy.

The profound consequences of the development of a power to affect prices, when once the firms in any sphere of production have become large and few, will emerge throughout the remaining pages of this chapter. The reader will see immediately, however, that in principle, and in so far as this power exists,* it enables such firms *to affect the level of their own profits.* For their profits are determined by the margins between the prices which they charge for what

---

* In the transition stages at least all this is quite a subtle business. In a particular industry at a particular time competition, even over prices, may still be going on fiercely. And yet, if the number of competing firms has dropped to the critical point, it would be quite unreal to think that prices were *fixing themselves* in the old genuinely objective way. The price competition itself takes place by a series of conscious decisions to move prices. This is something different from prices moving themselves. I should guess that the British motor industry was in this transition stage at the moment (1955), for instance.

they sell and the prices which they give for what they buy. If they could set those margins wide enough, their profits could be, in principle, unlimited. In fact, there are always limiting factors which prevent those margins being widened beyond a certain point. But the limits within which they can, in the absence of outside, non-economic, pressures, be widened, and consequently profits be increased, are great enough to be highly significant. The vast consequences of all this for a system which has the making of profits as its direct aim and object can be readily envisaged. Thus a tacit understanding to abstain from the basic feature of competition, which *is* competitive pricing, is the essence of the metamorphosis which has taken place in our economy.

Moreover, in this form the metamorphosis is virtually impossible to prevent. A trust may be bust: a monopoly dissolved, a cartel forbidden: but how are the managers of half a dozen giant firms to be prevented from having dinner together? And, even if they could be, what would it avail, for all they need do is to follow their "price-leader" without any consultation of any kind being necessary? They can even put their hands upon their hearts and swear with the utmost sincerity that they are still actively competing with each other. So they often are, in every respect but one: they are often spending millions in mutually aggressive advertising campaigns: they may be making competitive offers of service, or making detailed improvements in their products: they may be competing actively in everything except the one thing needful to restore the old way in which capitalism worked, namely, competition in price.

(II) INTERNAL UNEVENNESS OF DEVELOPMENT

The second reason: the process of concentration into large and few units also changes the nature of the system because it proceeds unevenly. It proceeds unevenly in two respects, first, in respect of the different industries within each country, and second, in respect of one country in relation to other countries, and for that matter in respect of one continent in relation to other continents.

Let us take the internal aspect of uneven development first. We have seen that some industries achieve, or succumb to, the pattern of oligopoly or domination by a few large firms much sooner than others. For instance, concentration has gone much further in manufacturing proper as against what may be called the "service" industries, such as transport, commerce, the professions. On the other hand, the relative share of manufacturing proper in the economy as a whole appears to be declining in such far advanced economies as the American. For these reasons alone the progress of concentration must not be thought of as one steady, continuing flow going forward evenly in every sphere of the economy. On the contrary, it has gone and is going forward far more rapidly in one place than in another. Here it is subject to local and temporary retreats; there it makes sudden spurts. And this is why its effects are so disturbing.

Moreover we have not yet mentioned the two major spheres of the economy in which the process of concentration into large and few units went forward, until very recently, most tardily of all. In these two spheres of the economy the pattern of oligopoly was indeed so slow to appear that it was long thought that it would not appear at all. They are labour and agriculture. The sale of their ability to work by the wage earners and the sale of his product by the peasant or farmer long remained markedly competitive. We shall find that this particular instance of the unevenness of development must have had, if it had not been corrected, the most disastrous consequences. This is because an oligopoly of, say, half a dozen buyers confronting many thousands of sellers will be, to put it mildly, in the stronger position.

Hence, if labour and the farmers had been permanently unable to improve their competitive strength, by their own form of combination and concentration, they would have fared ill indeed. And in fact in the early decades of the process of concentration from, say, 1900 to 1930, this is just what did happen. The industrial employers got in first with the process of concentration and exploited the workers and farmers very gravely. We shall be much concerned with the consequences of this. Here we may merely note that in the last two decades both labour and farmers appear to have found their own forms of concentration. Labour has at length succeeded, for the present at least, in America, Britain and Germany, in building up its trade unions into effective combinations able to face the employers' combinations with some real bargaining strength.

Labour has done so by forming its own combinations, but also by using its political influence over the democratic state; for the democratic state has reinforced the power of the Trade Unions by means of legislation favourable to them, by providing the workers with sources of income independent of their employers, in the form of social services, and by full employment policies. The farmers have made less use of direct combination amongst themselves, and have relied mainly upon their political influence over the State. But so effective has this been that by the middle of the twentieth century they, too, have largely succeeded in getting out of the disastrously disadvantageous position in which they found themselves when, as a disunited and disorganised mob of sellers of the fruits of the earth, they faced the serried ranks of the oligopolists from whom they had to buy the products of industry. They have, for the present, largely succeeded in this major achievement by getting laws put upon the statute book, in both America and Britain, which prevent the prices of what they sell falling seriously in relation to the prices of what they buy. (It remains to be seen what their position will be in Western Germany.)

But the farmers and peasants who supply the fruits of the earth to the great industries of America, Britain, Germany and the other smaller metropolitan centres of the world do not by any means all live in those countries. On the contrary, food and raw materials flow in a ceaseless stream into these metropolises from every continent. And here, too, and more especially, the first effects of the concentration of economic power were to exploit, in the gravest possible manner, the almost helpless agriculturalists and primary producers of the undeveloped parts of the world. But this takes us to the second aspect of uneven development.

(III) EXTERNAL UNEVENNESS OF DEVELOPMENT

The third reason: unevenness of development in the process of concentration upsets the balance of bargaining power, not only between capital and labour, and not only between industry and agriculture, but also between country and country, and continent and continent. Just as the rise of oligopoly strengthened capital relatively to labour, and industry relatively to agriculture, so also it strengthened the industrial countries in relation to the undeveloped countries. Moreover, in this case the possibility that the oppressed interest would learn to combine for its own protection was much more difficult of realisation. The wage earners and the farmers of a highly developed country might learn to use their rights and their votes to redress the economic balance which had swung against them. It was, and sometimes still is, far harder for the farmers and peasants of the undeveloped continents to do so, for the simple reason that they had, and still have in some cases, neither rights nor votes to use. The undeveloped areas were, and to some extent still are, the colonies of the industrial metropolises. In these cases "their" governments did not belong to them, but to the metropolitan powers. That unevenness of development, which appeared within the industrialised states as an intensified maldistribution of income as between the owners of capital, on the one hand, and the wage earners and farmers, on the other, appeared, externally, as the exploitation of one country by another; as the exploitation of whole continents by the advanced countries. It appeared, in a word, as imperialism. This will be the subject matter of a later part of this study. There we shall discuss the extent to which all this has been mitigated by a process of what can only be called "dis-imperialism," above all in the last decade (1945-1955). For this latest process is in some respects the most significant single development which is going on in the world.

(IV)   ASSOCIATION WITH THE STATE

The fourth reason: whenever and wherever the process of concentration into large and few units reaches a certain point, the State itself becomes closely associated with the productive process. In order to appreciate the magnitude of this change we have only to recollect that one of the essential features of the previous stage of capitalism was that the State should scrupulously avoid such association. The State's function was that of umpire, or arbitrator, of the competitive process; it was to be the enforcer of those contracts which were to be the only connections between essentially independent competitors. If, therefore, the State was to step down from the umpire's stand and itself take a hand in the game of production, the very nature of the economy would be transformed. Yet, as and when the competitors have be-

come few and large, this is just what the State has been
forced to do.

One of the reasons why the State has been forced into
participation in the process of production has been because
it was discovered by painful experience that if things were
left to themselves the economy showed an increasingly disastrous tendency to instability.* It gradually became clear
that an economy of large and few units tends to lose the
rough-and-ready, painful but in the end effective, self-
regulating mechanism of the truly competitive stage of capitalism. Accordingly, the State has come, in the advanced
industrial nations, to feel that it must, and can, control
such basic things as the pattern of the distribution of income
between social classes and individual citizens, instead of
leaving that pattern to the consequences of the play of the
market. Again, the State now concerns itself with maintaining the total demand, in terms of money, for the whole national product at the right figure, so as to avoid, if it can, a
tendency for prices persistently to rise or fall, with all the
fearful consequences of inflation or slump which that en-
tails. Again, the State attempts to watch over and to influence
the proportion of the country's productive resources which
it will devote to current consumption, on the one hand,
and the production of new capital assets, on the other—over,
that is to say, the rate of accumulation. Or, yet again, the
contemporary State attempts to pull or push resources from
one sphere of production to another: from the internal
market to exports: from peace production to rearmament, or
vice versa, etc., etc. For these and other purposes the contemporary State sometimes actually fixes prices, profit margins, and rations supplies, either of raw materials to producers or of each product to individual citizens. Or, again,

---

* This was the economic reason for state participation: we shall discuss the
political reason, namely, democratic pressure, itself generated by the social
agonies of instability, in Chapter 8 below.

it may have to take special care to regulate and control the foreign transactions of its citizens, if these are tending to upset its balance of payments with other States.

Finally the State is sometimes forced to undertake direct production itself. It "nationalises" industries for a variety of reasons. It may do so because the process of concentration has reached its logical end, and a clear-cut private monopoly has been created in the form of an omnipotent single firm. Or, on the contrary, it may do so because concentration has lagged, as in the case of the British coal industry, and a backward industry, with weak bargaining power, is endangering a vital point in the economy.

(V)   TECHNICAL PROGRESS AND ACCUMULATION

The fifth reason: the large and few units of the new stage accumulate the fresh capital necessary for technical progress in a new way. In the previous stage of capitalism, savings were supposed to be made by individuals. Nothing in the whole *lore* of the system was more cherished than the description of the thrifty individual, abstaining from spending his available resources, putting them aside, either to use himself as capital, or to lend to someone else, and so providing the indispensable sinews of economic progress. Whatever the truth may once have been, this is no longer how new capital is provided for the decisive part of industry. The giant firms largely do their own saving. They often find the new capital for their technical progress by the simple process of withholding from their shareholders an important part of their annual surpluses and using it for capital development. Of course they sometimes still "go to the market" to get outside capital for very large schemes of development. But even such outside capital is now largely provided by other giant financial institutions rather than by private, individual savers.

This, then, is a *new form of accumulation,* since it depends upon different methods, and different motives, from that of the individual saver. The giant firms have become real "persons" on their own account and as distinct from their shareholding owners. They have become persons who can accumulate for themselves, through the action of their managers, without the new capital ever effectively becoming the individual property of any particular capitalist. This amounts, in a certain measure, to the transformation of accumulation, perhaps the key function of the whole system, from an individual to a semi-collective basis. To be sure that transformation is partial and accumulation remains a function of a narrow section of the population. Nevertheless the new method of accumulation makes nonsense of a substantial part of the precepts for the management of the system which many politicians are still accustomed to use. For example, it alters the alleged dis-incentive effects of taxation. Moreover, it must not be supposed that the new methods of accumulation are ineffective. On the contrary, given a favourable environment, such as existed in Britain after 1945, these methods have provided the new capital required for a more rapid rate of technical progress than had been previously achieved in Britain. And in America they have largely provided the capital resources for a continuous technical revolution, the thunder of whose power has filled the whole earth.

(VI) THE SEPARATION OF OWNERSHIP AND MANAGEMENT

The sixth reason: the management of the decisive units of the economy has become separated from their ownership.

This process also has been going on throughout the history of capitalism, but now it has reached a new stage. The hand-loom weaver owned the tools of his trade and ran his own business. So, for that matter, did the Lancashire mill owner —the representative figure of the capitalism of, say, a hundred years ago. He differed from the hand-loom weaver only in that he did not himself work directly at the productive process. Instead he bought the power or ability to work of operatives or, as they were aptly called, "hands." But in the year 1862, in Britain, a further change began. The Joint Stock Company with limited liability came into existence. The modern class or category of shareholders was born. (It is worth remembering that shareholders, as a decisive social category, have not yet been in existence a hundred years.) And this new race of beings had, and have, the distinguishing characteristic that they own, but do not conduct, the main body of the economic activity of the country. Another new race of men, the managers or directors, who conduct but do not own, had consequently to be born. (The two categories interpenetrate, of course. Some shareholders also manage. Some managers own; but the tendency is for them to become more and more differentiated.) Gradually but persistently for the past ninety years ownership and management have come apart. In so doing they have begun to remove a feature of the system which its early theorists had always considered basic to it. Adam Smith, for example, has a famous passage in which he denounces the principle of joint stock precisely because it involves one man managing another man's property. And indeed, although we are now so used to it that we can scarcely imagine our economy without it, it is clear, when we think of it, that the separation of ownership and management, carried to the lengths that it has now reached, dilutes what was to Smith and his contemporaries the very essence of the system. Smith's doctrine—and this is still the current doctrine, conscious or unconscious, of the truly orthodox economists today—is that every man, by which he means every *owner*, will strive so to manage his affairs as to maximise his returns, and so will be led by the hidden hand of competition to maximise the general wealth. But what if the owner no longer has any real say in the management of his affairs? Unless the managers whom he appoints conduct the enterprise exactly as he would have done himself—an assumption which Smith said it was impossible to make—an essential link in the basic mechanism of capitalism will have been severed.

In fact, as we shall see, the appointed managers did, for a long time, and by and large, and on the average, conduct the new large enterprises very much *as if* they had been their owners. Thus it may have seemed pedantic to go back to the Companies Act of 1862 and the principle of joint stock, in order to illuminate this aspect of the change in the nature of capitalism. For, in fact, the separation of ownership and management, or at least its sociological consequences, did not become apparent till much later. It was not until the new joint stock enterprises became really large; it was not until, above all, they became really *few*, in each sphere of the economy, that the fact that ownership and management had been put asunder began to obtrude itself upon our always tardy social consciousness. But then it did. For it became apparent that the managers were not conducting those large and few enterprises in the same manner, or wholly with the same objects, as were conducted the individual enterprises of the former managing-owners.

They could not have done so, even if they had wished to. Or, rather, if they had attempted to conduct the giant enterprises of today in the strict tradition of the individual capitalist, seeking, with singleness of mind, to maximise his profit, they would have disrupted the whole social fabric in a few years. For their very largeness and fewness had, partially, removed from them that hand, invisible but guiding and restraining, that hand of competition, which had been the indispensable regulator and governor of the system.

The above paragraphs can do no more than note the existence of this important new development of the system. We shall return to it in greater detail at a much later point in the study.

(VII)   CONTROLLABILITY

The seventh reason: loosely, but yet, I think, undoubtedly, associated with the concentration of production into relatively large and few units, there has been a remarkable development, partly in the field of theory and partly in the field of practice. The economy has become much more susceptible to statistical measurement, and so to control, than before. It has become possible to measure and assess its total output, both gross and net. A statistical picture of the economy as a whole begins to appear. And whatever is measurable is on the way at least to becoming controllable. The importance of this factor should not be minimised. Professor Galbraith (*op. cit.*) has a striking passage on the subject—a passage which puts the claims of economic measurement at their highest.

> At the outbreak of World War II the new system of national accounting, now generally familiar through its summary figure of the Gross National Product, had just come into use in the United States, the United Kingdom and Canada. It proved indispensable for the guidance of a modern mobilization policy. It had not yet fully penetrated Germany. Partly because they were less clear than the democracies about what they were producing, how they were dividing it between military and civilian use, how they were allocating resources between immediate use and investment and how the corresponding income was being divided—all information that was displayed

by the new accounts—the Germans mobilized their economic
resources with considerably less skill and boldness than did
England or the United States. Because they are modest men,
economists never advertised the power of the weapon they had
placed in the hands of their governments although its bearing
on victory was considerably greater than that of atomic energy.
Perhaps they were wise. Had their wartime significance been
fully appreciated, some aggressive patriot would almost certainly have demanded that national income, gross national
product, their components and the manner of their calculation
all be made subject to strict security.

This passage vividly proclaims the practical consequences
of the new characteristic of the system. For it has been a
change in the nature of the system, rather than any sudden
stroke of genius on the part of the economists, that has made
all this possible. Nevertheless it will emerge from these pages
that something of great significance occurred when during
the first half of the century the economists began to try actually to measure economic quantities. (In Britain Professor
Bowley, the original pioneer, and Mr. Colin Clark in 1930,
were the decisive pathfinders.)

In the immediately following chapters we shall see that the
theoretical consequences of the new method of national accounting are equally momentous. We shall see that our new-
found ability to add up the national product, and consequently to see how it is being divided among different
classes, and for different purposes, has gone far towards settling the basic problems which have baffled and divided the
best intellects which have devoted themselves to economics.
The great controversies which have riven economic science
have had to do with this question of whether you can add up
the product of society into a meaningful total: of what the
units of such a total would be (the units of value), and,
inextricably bound up with this, what will be, and what
ought to be, the distribution of the product: *e.g.*, does labour

produce all and should labour have all? Or does capital, and so the capitalist, contribute to "the heap of values" and so be entitled to a share of it?

In my opinion, the new accounting has not indeed solved the problem of value: but it may be that it has circumvented it. For the fact is that these totals—these summations which we now make of what we have all produced each year, however rough and ready they still are—have proved in practice to be meaningful. They have worked. They have worked in the sense that, with a given distribution of the national income, they enable us, roughly, to see how the material welfare of the community varies with the gross national product, and, *vice versa,* how, with a given gross national product, welfare depends upon the distribution of income.* (Naturally conservatively minded economists tend to stress the importance of increasing the gross national product and radically minded economists tend to stress the importance of improving its distribution.) Thus the new accounting has made possible a new approach to the two basic and interlocking problems, namely, what is the product of economic activity and how is it distributed amongst the producers? These were the problems which, we shall find, were tackled by the founding fathers of economics, but were then abandoned as insoluble.

Finally—and politically this is crucial—the new accounting has enabled governments, as Professor Galbraith points out, to effect their purposes, peaceful or warlike, much more completely than ever before. And this in turn has had profound consequences. For no sooner does it become possible to measure, to comprehend, and so to open up the possibility of controlling, the economy, than the question will be put —*in whose interests* is it to be controlled?

---

* At the outset the reader should note that the gross national income and the gross national product are two names for the same thing. They are an aggregate, a summation, a total of everything the community produces.

THE ESSENCE OF THE MUTATION

We are now in a position to see that it is the first of our seven "reasons" that has been decisive. It is the ability of the producers in some, but not in all, of the spheres of production to affect prices, instead of merely being affected by them, that is the root of the matter. It is this which has caused that double unevenness of development which we noted as the second and third characteristics of the new stage. The social consequences of this have helped to draw the State—usually against its will—into the productive process. The State in this more active role may itself be used by the oligopolies to enhance their price-fixing policies. On the other hand, if the oligopolists do not control the State, the rest of the community—the wage earners and the farmers in particular—will certainly try to use its power to protect themselves against the otherwise overweening power of the oligopolists.

Thus the ability to influence prices will inevitably sap the automatic, self-regulating character of the economy. It will consequently provoke and require more and more State intervention, and will lead to an intensified struggle for the now all-important levers of economic power which will be in the hands of the State. At the same time the conduct and the ownership of the main enterprises of the economy are becoming separated, and, largely consequentially, the key function of accumulation is taking on a new and semi-collective character. Finally, the growing integration of society has enabled its theoreticians to measure it, and so, potentially at least, to comprehend and to control it.

Thus the characteristics of the latest stage of capitalism both make possible a much higher degree of social control and at the same time make such control imperative. We here catch a glimpse of the concept that the new stage may be either far worse than the old, if it is uncontrolled, or if it is controlled solely in the interests of the oligopolists; but that, on the other hand, it may be superior, both in stability and equity, to the old stage, if it is controlled adequately and in the interests of the population as a whole.

A NAME FOR THE NEW PHASE

Many names, favourable and unfavourable, have been suggested for the new stage which capitalism has entered. These names have often better expressed the desires, the prejudices and the passions of those who have coined them than the character of the thing described. Thus Marxists, when the symptoms of oligopoly first appeared, called the new stage "Monopoly Capitalism" or "Imperialism." On the other hand, liberal, conservative and social democratic writers have now begun to use such terms as the Mixed Economy, the Managerial State, Statism, the Welfare State, Progressive Capitalism, Fair Dealism, State Capitalism, the First Stage of Socialism, and so on and so forth. The one thing common to these terms is that they pick out the particular characteristic of our present economy which the writer desires to emphasize. For example, one social analyst sees that the State now plays a far more active role than formerly, and calls the new stage statism; another emphasizes the decay of competition and refers to monopoly; a third sees chiefly the vast outward, expansive drive of the system and calls it Imperialism; a fourth considers the much greater attention given to the human needs of the population at home to be its main feature, and calls it the Welfare State; while a fifth, concentrating attention upon the growing divorce between the ownership and the control of productive resources, calls it the Managerial State.

It may be that it is not possible adequately to subsume under one name the various important respects in which mid-twentieth-century capitalism differs from the previous version of the system. It may, therefore, be better to call it simply "the latest stage of capitalism."

The system has shown itself to be much more protean than was once supposed. May it not suffer, or achieve, another mutation, as marked as that of the last fifty years, and survive in some still newer form? This seems improbable. After all, some third of the world's population already live in communist societies, which, whatever mutations they also may experience (and it is greatly to be hoped that they experience many), are not likely to return to anything which could be correctly called capitalism.* True, the larger part of the rest of the world's population live in under-developed societies which are only approaching the capitalist stage. They are approaching it, however, in a way which suggests that they do not mean to stay long in it, even if they traverse it.

All this is by no means to prejudge the question of how long the present stage will endure or the respects in which it will continue to evolve until the point is reached at which it can no longer usefully be called capitalism.

---

* As this study develops there will be several occasions for attempts to compare and contrast contemporary communist societies with the latest-stage capitalisms. Their outstanding difference is in the political rather than the economic field: the difference between dictatorship and democracy. In fact, certain similarities are appearing between some of the strictly economic aspects of these two major extant forms of human societies. But this does not mean that the communist societies are in the least likely to evolve into anything which could correctly be called capitalism. It is much too early to enter into all this here.

2. ▪ THE ECONOMISTS OF VALUE

The immediately following chapters are much concerned with the development of economic theory. This may seem a digression from the direct description of contemporary capitalism attempted in the preceding chapter. In fact it is a short cut. Economic theory, at each stage, has been the best account available of the economic relations in which men have found themselves enmeshed. By considering these successive summaries, accounts, diagrams, models—call them what you will—these mental constructions of the by no means inconsiderable intellects which have devoted themselves to economics—we may hope to understand what is happening in our own day.

In particular, in order to appreciate the extent of the mutation which capitalism has undergone, we must recollect not only what the system was, but also what it was supposed to be. We must recall its theory as well as its practice; we must see what men thought they were establishing when in fact they established capitalism. For the theory of capitalism contrasts even more with mid-twentieth-century reality than does its previous practice.

THE VISION OF PERFECT COMPETITION

Modern economics began with a vision and a demand. The vision was of a world of perfect competition. The demand was that the vision should be made flesh. Every let, hindrance and restraint which prevented the development of competition must be removed—*laissez faire, laissez aller.** Moreover this vision of perfect competition was not intended to be a description of then existing reality. On the contrary, it was a revolutionary demand for the destruction of what was and the rebuilding of the world according to a new ideal.

The vision which inspired alike the French *philosophes* and the English founding fathers of the science implied the division of labour; it was a vision of a world in which each man was to have, in the words of Doctor Johnson, "his single talent well employed." Each man was to produce exclusively what he best could and then bring it to market in order to satisfy his wants by competitive exchange. The weaver was to sell cloth to buy food, boots, shelter, fuel and the rest: the baker to sell bread, the doctor medicine, the smith horseshoes, the cobbler boots—each to satisfy his manifold wants. It was to be a society based on the division of labour, and yet a society of perfectly free, equal and independent producers, buyers and sellers. There could be waggoners to sell the commodity "transport," and so fetch and carry to market, and merchants to sell the act of mediat-

---

* *"Laissez faire, morbleu! Laissez faire!"* wrote the impassioned Marquis d'Argenson in 1751. But he in turn, it is thought, was echoing the answer of Legendre, the seventeenth-century merchant, to Colbert's question, *"Que faut-il faire pour vous aider?"*—*"Nous laissez faire."* (See Keynes' pamphlet, *The End of Laissez Faire,* for a delightful account of the provenance of the phrase.)

ing the buying and selling. But that, in principle, was about all the complications allowed for.

True, in the real world there were landlords who had no need to sell anything in order to buy: for they received money for nothing in the form of rent. But the more radical at least of the prophets of what was to become capitalism regarded them as painful anachronisms, to be got rid of sooner rather than later. The landlord was the one man who enjoyed "unearned income," as we should call it. The early theorists had not really distinguished between the wage earner and the capitalist: they lay together, undifferentiated, in the form of independent producers, neither employed nor employing—the peasant, the yeoman farmer, the hand-loom weaver, and the other independent artisans. None could doubt *their* contribution to the national wealth. Their fission into wage earner and capitalist, although it had in fact begun, was still largely unnoticed. They could still combine against the one parasitic class who lived by owning. And they did so under the banner of freedom of exchange in perfect competition, for that alone would ensure to each man the enjoyment of the full fruits of his labour.

The new dispensation was to be an essentially two-dimensional economy: a flat land in which no buyer or seller was to be taller than any other—so that none could overreach his neighbour. The exchanges were envisaged as horizontal, as it were. They were to be exchanges between free and equal producers, between, in a word, men who all belonged to one category or class of society. No one had even whispered the idea that there might be another kind of exchange; that there might be *vertical* exchanges, as it were—exchanges which took place actually within, and in the course of, the process of production, instead of between independent possessors of the finished product. No one had whispered that there might be exchanges between men belonging to different social classes, between men who were so differently situated in society that even apparently free exchanges between them bred, not a mutual freedom and equality, but the reverse. There was no hint in the original vision that the produce-sellers might be themselves employers of other men who could not, for some reason, independently produce for themselves. There was to be no third economic dimension, no economic depth, as it were, to a society founded upon the original vision of perfect competition.

This was the vision which inspired the stormy political forces which sought and achieved revolution in France and America, and reform in Britain. Men passionately believed that if only the stale feudal restrictions, the overgrowths of landlordism, monarchic arbitrariness and mediaeval superstition could be cast down, a classless Utopia founded upon free exchange in perfect competition must be the result. This was the mighty aspiration of which the demand to *laissez faire, laissez aller* was merely the sober economic aspect.

No doubt many of the early economists—the ever-cautious Smith himself, for example—by no means shared the more Utopian dreams of the "left wing" theorists—such as Godwin. Nevertheless I think that it is true to say that the semiconscious major premise of the economists' own theory, till the end of the eighteenth century at least, was a society of free and equal independent producers—largely classless if the landlord interests were overcome—rather than a society of employers and wage earners. Moreover we shall find that to a remarkable degree what is still, in Britain at least, the main body of economic thought has, in one sense, retained this character right down to the present day. Nor can the inability of the genuinely die-hard section of present-day economists to bring their theory into contact with mid-twentieth-century reality be understood, unless we realise that they are under the continuing spell of the original vision of perfect competition.

We must also recollect, however, that in fact the vision
of perfect competition was never made flesh; perhaps that
is the very reason why it still haunts us in frustration. That
was not indeed because feudal and monarchical restraints
were not in the end effectively destroyed. It was because,
before the vast process of clearing the ground for competition had been completed, the new qualifications, restraints,
and in the end actual negations, of competition which we
described in the last chapter had grown up. They are indeed
only the final consequences of tendencies which appeared
at the very birth of the system. For the truth is that the earliest development of capitalism proper: namely, the appearance of dependent wage earners in factories, marked the
divergence of reality from the noble vision. For then already
the true *dramatis personae* of the economic process had
ceased to be individual producers, buyers and sellers, and
had become employers of hired labourers.

We shall attempt to trace the vicissitudes of economic
theory as it strove, turning and twisting, and then splitting in
two in the great schism of Marxism, to keep contact with
this untoward development.

THE LABOUR THEORY OF VALUE

In doing so we must at once attack the problem of value.
For the concept of value lies, both historically and theoretically, across the threshold of economic thinking. We cannot
make a beginning without settling our accounts with it in
one way or another.

The problem of value arose in this way. No sooner had an
economy of free exchange in perfect competition begun to
come into existence than the economists found themselves
confronted with the need to explain the rates or ratios at

which commodities would, and should, exchange. Now that the producers of corn, or of boots, or of soap, or of nails, or of chairs, and of everything else, were becoming perfectly free to exchange their products with one another, the question of the day became: *how much* corn would, and should, exchange for a bag of nails? How many pairs of shoes for a table, and so on? Not only would, but *should,* for the economists wished not only to explain, but also to *justify;* to show that in their world of freedom of exchange each man would automatically get what was due to him, no more and no less. They felt that they had to show that a society consisting of perfect competitors would give to each man, if not what he had actually produced, yet its true equivalent in value. That it should do so was the essential justification of the system of which they were the prophets.

For this purpose they evolved the labour theory of value. For all of them, for Smith and Ricardo, as for Marx, the ratio at which commodities will exchange will both tend to be, and ought to be, proportionate to the amount of labour which it has been necessary to put into them. The labour theory of value in its most generalised form was the common ground upon which they all stood. It is difficult for us to realise this fact, for, ironically enough, the labour theory of value is today chiefly remembered as the foundation of Marx's system. Yet in fact it was the coping-stone of the system of the enthusiastic prophets of capitalism. This was the law by means of which they explained why and *how* the new order would bring freedom and justice to mankind.

This historical fact is one of the two reasons why it is still indispensable to understand the labour theory of value. But it must not be supposed that our interest in it is merely historical or pious. True, almost every contemporary economist regards the labour theory of value as a disused eighteenth-century cart-track, when compared to the great metalled high-road of "equilibrium economics" and the rest of the apparatus of modern analysis. True, we ourselves shall see that the labour theory of value cannot deal with some of the decisive characteristics of our contemporary economics. True, we shall find that in consequence blind reliance upon it produces disastrous misappreciations of the contemporary scene. Nevertheless we shall also find that this old cart-track leads us, before it finally peters out, to the very heart of our contemporary economic and social problems. For instance, it raises, both by its insights and its limitations, the whole question of which matters most, the *share* of the total national product obtained by the different classes, or, *per contra,* the overall size of that product. Moreover we shall find that the high-road of "equilibrium analysis," in spite, or perhaps because, of the refinement and complications of its construction, may lead us, if we follow blindly, to nowhere in particular. Compared to *that,* the labour theory of value is still a fruitful hypothesis. We shall eventually conclude that it is now time to discard it. But that will be only because economics in the past twenty-five years has begun to open up a third road, which, while it also is anything but free from obstacles and difficulties, does, in my view, at last provide us with a less defective guide to action than the labour theory of value, and a less barren theoretical basis than equilibrium analysis.

And then there is a third reason for the continuing importance of the labour theory of value; it is simply that, like Marxism as a whole, it is today taught as dogma to some one-third of the entire living generation of mankind. And we shall find that, sure enough, blind reliance upon a basic theory which has become inadequate to the facts accounts for some of the most sweeping of the misconceptions from which the contemporary communists so evidently suffer. For all these reasons it is impossible to proceed without getting to the bottom of this matter.

ORIGINS OF THE THEORY

A century and a half ago, in the epoch of the founding fathers of the science, the labour theory of value had long passed current, in one form or another. Locke had foreshadowed it (p. 231); Petty had stated it crisply: it permeates the text of *The Wealth of Nations;* but it had not, till the nineteenth century, received a precise formulation. Even when economics in the late eighteenth century definitely emerged as a science* this was still so. The capacious, ruminative, canny mind of Smith may never have even wished to make certain quite what he meant by it. In particular, he never made clear whether he meant that commodities exchanged in proportion to the *quantity* of labour which had been necessary to make them,† or that, as he often wrote, they exchanged in proportion to the *value* of the labour which had made them.

The distinction did not matter very much if you were still mainly thinking of independent craftsmen: of "one-man-businesses," as we should call them. You have not got to distinguish between the quantity and the value of the labour of such indifferentiated producers, because they do not pay themselves wages. The payment of wages, as we shall find (p. 95 below), is itself an act of exchange. Therefore the characteristic of the one-man-business world is that there is in principle no act of exchange in the course of the produc-

---

* If it is a science. The reader will find that if I call it so I mean no more than that it has been, and is, the object of systematic study.
† With this word "necessary" labour the old economists guarded themselves against the naïve objection that it could not be true that the more labour you chose to put into a thing the more valuable it became. Moreover they took into account varying skills by saying that one hour of skilled labour counted, for example, as two hours unskilled labour.

tive process. Accordingly, for such producers, when you talk about either the value of their labour, or the quantity of their labour, you mean, broadly, the same thing: you mean the work they have had to do, the trouble they have had to take, the "dis-utility," to use the word of a much later generation of economists, which they have had to undergo. If this was the sort of world which occupied your mind, and to which you were sure the real world should and would approximate, then the labour theory of value in its Smithian form served well enough. In a pre-capitalist, or at most very early capitalist, world, the representative units of which were particular, individual producer-manager-owner-sellers; in which such individuals did much of the work of actual production themselves with their own means of production; in a world of which the yeoman farmer and the hand-loom weaver were the representative figures; in which there were few wage earners; in the world of what Marx was to call "small commodity production"—it was held as axiomatic that, if all interferences with perfect competition could be removed, each of the useful commodities brought to market would tend, "in equilibrium," * to exchange in accordance with the amount of labour which had had, directly or indirectly, to be put into making it. This was the very basis of the economic thought of the period.†

---

* "In equilibrium" is an economist's term meaning, first of all, a state of things in which the opposite forces of supply and demand are just balanced, and, more generally, the theoretical balancing point towards which the manifold opposite, self-correcting oscillations of price are tending to average out, so that, once reached, there will be no further tendency to change.

† Mrs. Joan Robinson in her contribution to *Science and Society*, Spring 1954, pp. 145-6, writes that this was a strange view. She is easily able to show how extreme an abstraction from any society which ever existed is this vision of small commodity producers exchanging in equilibrium their products according to the man hours of socially necessary labour time used in producing them. All societies which have even approximated to the model of small commodity production have in fact been custom ridden to a degree. Moreover, as she also shows, the reduction of skilled labour to a larger num-

RICARDO'S "LAW OF PRICE"

Even before the end of the eighteenth century, however, the real world had ceased, in Britain, to approximate to this ideal of a world of one-man-producer-owner-managers. No sooner was this realised than it was seen that the labour theory of value in its original imprecise form would no longer serve. This was a first instance of something which has happened again and again in the development of economic thought. In this field men repeatedly believe that they have made a major intellectual discovery; that they have at length laid down firm foundations for the science of political economy; that they have corrected the unaccountable errors of the thinkers of the last generation. But what has in fact happened is that the underlying economic reality which they are trying to describe has itself changed. The system has passed through one of its mutations. When that happens the theories by means of which men described and explained the previous stage (more or less adequately) are seen to be no longer applicable. They are duly overthrown. But it is not an intellectual error which is being corrected. It is theory limping painfully after new practice.

It was so in the first decades of the nineteenth century. It was not, indeed, that the semi-feudal restraints on free and perfect competition did not continue, one by one, to be struck off. It was rather that simultaneously another, and for the future far more significant, process began to assert itself.

---

ber of hours of unskilled labour is a highly abstract proceeding in such a society. Nevertheless in historical fact men *did* explain the ratios at which commodities both would and should exchange upon a free market in a society of small commodity producers, by assuming that they would do so in equilibrium according to the amount or value (they were not clear which) of socially necessary labour which it had taken to make them.

The one-man-owner-producers began, more and more rapidly, to be pushed aside; the representative, dominant form of production began more and more to be carried on by two relatively new classes of persons—by employers or capitalists and by wage earners. At that point a new version of the labour theory of value became indispensable. There was still no need to give the theory up. But there was a necessity to re-state it in a much more rigorous form, and it was so re-stated (in 1817) by the genius of David Ricardo.

It had become indispensable to re-define the theory because the splitting up of society into employers and wage earners had given "the value of labour" an actual, concrete form, as it were. "The value of labour" had now become something which could be seen in practice every day. It was the level of wages. So it was clear for all to see that if you said that prices—the exchange ratios of commodities—depended upon "the value of labour," you were saying that what determined prices was the level of wages. But this would not do. For if the level of wages went up, for example, it would clearly send up *all* prices. But if it sent up *all* prices it might—if it sent them up equally—leave the *ratios* at which things exchanged, which were the reality of prices, unchanged. If, say, wages doubled from 1s. a day to 2s. a day, the price of both bread and boots must, if "the value of labour" (*i.e.*, wages) were the sole determinant of prices, double too. But in that case a pair of boots would still exchange for the same number of loaves of bread. Only "the value of money" or "the general price level," as we should now say, would have changed. It was clear that you could not explain real prices—the ratios at which one thing exchanged with another—in this way. And it was, precisely, to the purpose of discovering what determined *prices* that Ricardo bent the formidable powers of his intellect.

In 1816 Ricardo was writing to the elder Mill that "I have been beyond measure puzzled to find out the law of price." * Observe the turn of the phrase. It is the *law* of price that he must find out. There must be one unique determinant of price. There must be something about commodities, something *in* them, something common to them all, in the way weight, for example, is common to material objects, something which will render them comparable to each other and in terms of the units of which they will exchange with each other.

By the time that he published his *Principles* (1817) Ricardo believed that he had found this unique determinant of price. He had found it by making a more precise and rigorous re-statement of the labour theory of value. Commodities, he taught, did not exchange in proportion to the *value* of the labour which it had been necessary to put into them. At bottom that was a meaningless phrase. For labour *was* value. Therefore, if you tried to talk of the value of labour, you were trying to talk of the value of value. No, commodities exchanged in proportion to the *quantity* of labour that had had to be put into them; they exchanged, in equilibrium, in proportion to the actual number of man-hours of socially necessary labour time which it had taken to make them. This was the Ricardian "law of price" and law of value alike. Hours of socially necessary work were the true measure of all things.

THE AGE OF CERTAINTY: ABSOLUTE VALUE

It is impossible to overestimate the impact of Ricardo's theory upon his contemporaries. They were convinced that he had discovered the basic, unifying law of economics, comparable, for example, to the Newtonian principles in the

* Letter to Mill, Oct. 14, 1816, p. 82, Vol. VII of Mr. Piero Sraffa's superb edition of Ricardo's works.

physical sciences. In man-hours of necessary labour, they were convinced, value itself had been discovered. If you have found the unit in terms of which commodities establish their exchange ratios, then you have also found the very stuff or substance of value; you have found "absolute value"; you have found a constant against which you can measure the endless fluctuations of exchanging commodities. You have found something which will do for economics what the standard yard or gramme will do for physical measuring and weighing. And if you have done that you will have laid the foundations of economics as an exact science. If you have really done that, you should be able *both* to add up the national product in terms of the units of your absolute value and then to measure off what share goes to each class of the community. You will have made yourself able to measure, and potentially therefore to control, society.

We have now largely forgotten how completely this Ricardian vision dazzled the eyes of the intellectuals of the first half of the nineteenth century, including, fatefully, those of two young German students of the 'thirties and 'forties, Karl Marx and Frederick Engels. But we may judge of the sledge-hammer impact of Ricardo's book from its effect upon a contemporary *litterateur*. When in 1817 Ricardo published his *Principles*, Thomas de Quincey lay in his opium dreams and it seemed that nothing could rouse him. But one of his dreams, he writes in *An English Opium Eater*, had always been that a new law and a new "transcendant legislator" must appear in the field of political economy. Then he receives the labour theory of value in its Ricardian form.

Suddenly, in 1818, a friend in Edinburgh sent me down Mr. Ricardo's book; and, recurring to my own prophetic anticipation of some coming legislator for this science, I said, before I had finished the first chapter, "Thou art the man!" Wonder and curiosity were emotions that had long been dead in me. Yet

I wondered once more—wondered at myself that could once
again be stimulated to the effort of reading; and much more I
wondered at the book. Had this profound work been really
written during the tumultuous hurry of the nineteenth century?
Could it be that an Englishman, and he not in academic bow-
ers, but oppressed by mercantile and senatorial cares, had accomplished what all the universities of Europe, and a century
of thought, had failed even to advance by one hair's-breadth?
Previous writers had been crushed and overlaid by the enormous weight of facts, details, and exceptions; Mr. Ricardo had
deduced, *a priori*, from the understanding itself, laws which
first shot arrowy light into the dark chaos of materials, and had
thus constructed what hitherto was but a collection of tentative
discussions into a science of regular proportions, now first
standing upon an eternal basis." *

IS THERE A FOOTRULE?

Such were the high and passionate claims of the Ricardians.
They had the talisman. They knew what absolute value was.
With this measuring rod they would rule off the economic
magnitudes of society. The comparison with seventeenth-,
eighteenth- or early nineteenth-century physics is obvious.
There is the same conviction that "laws" have been discovered which provide "an eternal basis" for "a science of
regular proportions." There is also the same conviction that
anything which does not rest upon clear-cut laws, which
deal in simple, determinate quantities of some real thing, is
unscientific. There is a straightforward materialism about it.

* How historically apt it is that while the contemporary intelligentsia, who
were in sympathy with the development of capitalist social relations, felt
like that about Ricardo, Cobbett, the spokesman of the dying yeomen and
artisans—of the small commodity producers—wrote that he was "a stupid,
bothering stockbroker, with a head full of discounts, percentages, omnium,
scrip, prices and shades."

Quantities are quantities which can be given numerical values. This is the Newtonian epoch of economics. How satisfactory it would have been if it had worked. If developing reality could have been accounted for on these lines, sufficiently adequately at least to provide a practicable guide to action, the economic problem would have been solved long before this. It was not to be. The pursuit of absolute value was to prove a wild-goose chase; then the abandonment of even the attempt to find absolute value led down what proved to be an enormous blind alley. And it is only recently that a glimpse of a way forward has been caught.

It is, in my opinion, the greatest claim of Ricardo to genius that he himself was never wholly satisfied with his discovery. We now know, thanks to the researches of Mr. Sraffa, that literally on his death-bed Ricardo was still searching for a more satisfactory re-statement of his theory of value. We now possess the draft of the posthumous essay on which Ricardo was at work in August and September, 1823, until within two or three days of his death. It is entitled "Absolute Value and Exchangeable Value," and it begins with the words, "All measures of length are measures of absolute as well as relative length." The dying economist sets out from this point to seek for a measure of absolute value which will determine the relative values, and so the exchange ratios, of commodities in the way that "a footrule which was itself neither liable to contract or expand" will determine their lengths.

He makes it clear that in this search for absolute or intrinsic value he was doing something more even than seeking to determine the "law of price." He was seeking for something in terms of the units of which we may not only equate commodities in exchange one with another, but also *add* them together to form meaningful totals. For if there is no such thing as absolute value, in terms of what units are we to express the total national product or its division between the social classes?

Ricardo's last essay comes to the conclusion that man-hours of socially necessary labour must be, and are, the units of absolute value. But he comes to this conclusion reluctantly. For in what form, he writes, are these units of socially necessary labour in practice applied to the computation, or measuring, of economic quantities? In practice, he acknowledges, they are, and can be, applied only in the form of money. At bottom it is an ounce of gold which becomes the measure of all things, for in this ounce of gold is contained, as it were, a standard number of man-hours of socially necessary labour, against which the number of such man-hours in all other commodities will be measured off.

But Ricardo sees that this is a most rough and ready, a most unsatisfactory, footrule of value. It *is* "liable to contract or expand" when, for example, new gold-fields are discovered or with the introduction of new mining techniques. It is by no means a reliable measure of value in the same way that the standard yard is an absolute measure of length. Thus Ricardo in his search for absolute value was partially dissatisfied to the end. Nevertheless he concludes that man-hours of labour as expressed, however imperfectly, in the monetary commodity, gold, are the indispensable units of economic calculation. And he reaches this conclusion essentially because in his own work he had found them apt for the purposes which he had had in mind.*

---

* There is something startlingly apt about this breaking off of Ricardo's life-long search for absolute value upon his death-bed. It is as if the thread of the science snapped at this point. For it is hardly too much to say that after that no one else was "puzzled beyond measure to find out the law of price," or to discover the measure of absolute value, for a hundred years: no one at least amongst the economists and prophets of the system. One man alone, Marx, sought to take up the search for that "footrule" of value which would, he believed, enable him to comprehend, and so ultimately to control, the system as a whole.

THE DIVISION OF THE PRODUCT

We shall not understand the sway which the labour theory of value in its Ricardian form exercised unless we understand the purpose for which it was used. That purpose was simply to elucidate the division of the national product between the different social classes. And for this particular purpose the Ricardian theory was exceedingly apt. Ricardo sets out this purpose with characteristic precision in the first words of the Preface to his *Principles:*

> The produce of the earth—all that is derived from its surface by the united application of labour, machinery and capital is divided among three classes of the community: namely, the proprietor of the land, the owner of the stock or capital necessary for its cultivation, and the labourers by whose industry it is cultivated. . . . To determine the laws which regulate this distribution is the principal problem of political economy.*

For this purpose of discovering how a capitalist society will tend, if left to itself, to divide up the national product, units of socially necessary labour time (man-hours) appeared to be an apt unit calculation. Accordingly, Ricardo and the Ricardians strode confidently forward, their footrule in their hands, to measure off a diagram of the capitalism of their day. They showed how the workings of perfect competition must distribute the national product between the three social classes. They developed a theory of rent, a theory of profit, and a theory of wages.

---

* Note the fact that still in 1817 agriculture is in Ricardo's mind so overwhelmingly the most important sphere of production that he does not, in this opening passage, mention any other. (Mr. Sraffa thinks that these words were actually written by the elder Mill, who did a lot of work on Ricardo's MSS., though he did not, Mr. Sraffa considers, supply any of the basic ideas.)

And what a diagram it was! Ricardo drove his passionate, un-English logic clean through the original, optimistic vision of eighteenth-century political economy. Commodities would exchange, he agreed, in ratio to the man-hours of labour necessary to produce them. But the result would not be a society of free and equal one-man businesses, exchanging like with like, without mutual exploitation, in freedom and fraternity. For Ricardo had applied his theory of value to the determination of the price of labour. He wrote: "The natural price of labour is that price which is necessary to enable the labourers, one with another, to subsist and to perpetuate their race, without either increase or diminution." (*Principles*, Chapter V, "On Wages," p. 93 of Volume I of Sraffa's edition.) In a word, Ricardo had developed a subsistence theory of wages. True he did not work out the relationship between his theory of value and his subsistence theory of wages in the full and systematic way in which Marx was to do. Therefore we shall await our consideration of Marx before following out the argument that the value, not of labour, but of the thing which the worker has to sell, namely, his power or ability to labour, can be nothing but subsistence. Briefly, however, under the labour theory of value it must be so, for the commodity which the worker has to sell must be sold at its value like every other commodity. Its value is the number of man-hours necessary to produce it. And the number of man-hours necessary to produce the commodity labour-power is the number necessary to produce the goods which will just sustain the labourer, and his family, *i.e.*, subsistence. Therefore the value of labour-power, in our terminology the rate of wages, must be in the long run subsistence. If wages rise permanently or substantially above that rate, the commodity labour-power will not even tend to sell at its value and the labour theory of value will be deeply impaired. All this, however, is Marx's version of the theory rather than Ricardo's. Suffice it here to say that Ricardo, as the whole of his chapter on wages shows, held a subsistence theory of wages, based partly upon his theory of value and partly upon the Malthusian theory of population.

This subsistence theory of wages, which is thus partly an application or special case of his version of the labour theory of value, is in some respects the very basis of Ricardo's system. It is this subsistence theory which governs his views of how the national product will be bound to divide itself up between the three great classes of wage earners, capitalists and landlords. It is this subsistence theory of wages which forces him to display the harsh diagram of a class-divided society in which the laws of economics condemn the mass of the population, now become wage earners, to a perpetual subsistence level, unless by some unlikely means they may encroach upon the rent or profit of their masters.*

THE MALTHUSIAN TRAGI-COMEDY

At the same time, this suddenly pessimistic prognosis of what was to be the character of the new society received powerful reinforcement from what was in effect an early attempt at sociological theory. This was Malthus' theory of pop-

---

* Ricardo once told McCulloch that the division of the national product had little to do with his theory of value. "After all," he wrote, "the great question of Rent, Wages and Profits must be explained by the proportions in which the whole produce is divided between landlords, capitalists and labourers, and which are not essentially connected with the doctrine of value." (Letter of June 13, 1820.) But, as Mr. Sraffa points out in his introduction, this was written in a moment of discouragement. Ricardo did connect his theory of value with his theory of wages, but never as clearly or completely as did Marx. His letter to McCulloch was, however, a glimpse of something which has now become a practical possibility, namely, a theory of distribution which is independent of the labour theory of value, or indeed of any theory of value. We supply the indispensable thing, namely, a unit of calculation in

ulation. Malthus was the son of one of those who had shared the dazzling illusions of the end of the eighteenth century. His father was a "perfectabilian," as they were called—that is to say, a man who, like Godwin and the rest of the "left wing" of the period, believed in the early perfection of human nature, as soon as feudal tyrannies were struck down, a man who shared those illusions of which the doctrine of *laissez faire* was, in a sense, merely the sober, economic aspect. (Rousseau himself had come to stay with the Malthuses.)

It was no doubt extremely irritating to have a perfectabilian as a father—especially if you possessed a solid intellectual equipment, as the younger Malthus certainly did. A reaction was inevitable. But how far Malthus reacted! The message of his theory of population was, in his own words, that "the principle of population" was "conclusive against the perfectability of the mass of mankind." This was because "population when unchecked, increases in a geometrical ratio. Subsistence increases only in an arithmetical ratio. A slight acquaintance with numbers will show the immensity of the first power in comparison with the second." The political, as opposed to the mathematical, "point" of Malthus' theory was that, unfortunately, all measures to improve the lot of the mass of the population were consequently futile. Every easement would merely increase numbers instead of improving conditions. Did a philanthropically inclined landlord want to build better cottages? It was useless! The improvement would merely enable more babies to survive, and soon the new cottages would be worse slums than the old. Far from Utopia being round the corner, the exact opposite was true. In the very nature of things

---

terms of which we can add up all sorts of commodities, in the form of an index number. We shall discuss this issue in Chapter 6. We shall find that the index number solution is by no means satisfactory. Nevertheless it is the least defective available.

there was nothing whatever to be done for the labouring classes. The upper classes must merely continue, however mournfully, to spend their unearned incomes.

It is easy to trace in all this not only the parental refutation, but also how well it fitted into the Ricardian analysis, in spite of the disputes of the two men on specific economic issues. Malthus' mind was also dominated by the idea of an economy in which agricultural production was almost everything; in which production per acre of land could be increased only to a very limited degree, and in which a rising population really would, therefore, quickly come up against a lack of means of subsistence. Such economies have, of course, existed and, to some extent, still exist. All the great stagnant empires of the Orient have been of this character and their populations have duly pressed against the subsistence barrier. (And are in many cases still so pressing, so that control of their rate of population increase would be, if it could be achieved, a most important matter for them.) But once industrialisation, mechanisation—the, in principle, unlimited growth in production per head—has begun; once, in particular, the problem of increasing the food supply almost indefinitely by the application of larger quantities of capital and labour, without necessarily using more land, has been solved—as, in principle at least, it has probably been solved already, and as it obviously will be solved by further scientific advance—the Malthusian theory has little remaining relevance. Moreover, long before scientific development had reached its present stage, it had made possible the opening up of the New World, which, for a century, removed the threat of a land shortage even for rapidly rising populations. In such conditions every new mouth is also a new pair of hands—and the hands can more than feed the mouth.

Mrs. Joan Robinson has an acute analysis of the matter in Chapter XXXII of her important book, *The Accumulation* *of Capital** (Macmillan, 1956). She shows in which types of economies a rising population is likely to slow down, or reverse, a rising standard of life and in which types it will actually promote it. What an irony it was that the Malthusian theory should have been produced just at the moment when, for the first time in human history, an economy was passing into the new, dynamic phase of industrialisation and geographical expansion in which the theory lost nearly all its relevance. Nevertheless the popularity of the Malthusian theory in the upper-class circles of the time and the corresponding hatred of it on "the left" are easy to understand. What a relief to the upper classes it must have been to be able to answer, not only the harmless "perfectabilians," but also the pernicious Jacobins, and only less dangerous radicals, with the lofty argument that it had now been "scientifically proved" that all their hopes of human improvement were impossible of fulfilment.

Perhaps the textbooks of the future will give the Malthusian theory as an example of the tragi-comedy of the early attempts at sociological theory in a class-divided society. In such cases some powerful mind is suddenly seized, in all sincerity, with some simple idea, as in this case the idea that *if* productive resources are limited the growth of population must tend to reduce the standard of life. He is so impressed by it that he soon sees little else. He is soon ignoring all the other equally important factors in the real situation, which are all variables also, and the actual variations of which are making his own idea true here, false there, false now, true then.

Then, if his idea suits the dominant interest of the time, it is made dogma and stands, often for a hundred years, as a

---

* By the kindness of the author the text of this new work has been made available to me in typescript before publication. It is discussed in Chapter 8 below.

barrier to further progress. Nor is the harm over and done with when at length the idea is overthrown. For, as in this case, the new social interest which the theory did not suit, and which has always opposed it, when it comes to power proceeds to make the old theory anathema. Because Malthus thought that he had proved that all human improvement was impossible he drew down upon himself the full torrent of Marx's denunciation. Because Marx denounced Malthus it has become an article of faith in all present-day communist societies that any proposal to control or limit the size of the population is a vile capitalist heresy. Thus the governments of hundreds of millions of the present generation of mankind are vowed to oppose any attempt to control the growth of population in any economic circumstances. Because it is absurd to suppose that no improvement is ever possible without the limitation of population, communist dogma now proclaims the extreme *non sequitur* that any increase in population, however rapid, in any economic circumstances, however adverse, is always to be welcomed. Thus the communists join hands, on this one matter, with their bitterest opponents, the Roman Catholic Church. Truly sociology has a long, hard road before it.

THE LABOUR THEORY OF VALUE UNDER ATTACK

The rigour of the Ricardian diagram dominated and daunted the imaginations of men during the whole of the first half of the nineteenth century. Combined with the Malthusian jeremiad, it earned for economics the title of "the dismal science." But there is a splendid candour about it. "This is how things are," Ricardo writes in effect. "I did not make them so. I cannot change them. I can only elucidate them. This is the system which you have in fact established when in the name of liberty, equality and fraternity you stormed the bastilles of privilege. It is a system which will hold down the standard of life of the wage-earning mass of the population to a subsistence minimum and in which the capitalists and the landlords will struggle fiercely with each other over their respective shares of the whole surplus of society."

Such supreme social frankness could not last. Such a description of their handiwork could hardly appeal to the new masters of English society, the new men of capital. If any flaw could be found in the reasoning which supported it, such a flaw would be quickly pointed out and made the most of. And in fact a flaw was discovered. Once again it became apparent that the nature of the economy was changing.

Hardly had Ricardo drawn his stark diagram than an undeniable new fact began to be apparent. And this fact seemed to strike at the labour theory of value. Whatever may once have been the case, whatever Smith, or Ricardo, or anyone else had said, commodities were palpably not now even tending to exchange at ratios exclusively determined by the man-hours of labour which had been necessary to make them. Soon the thing could no longer be denied. The trouble was not, of course, that prices often fluctuated widely from values as determined by hours of labour. The old doctors had fully allowed for that. Values were the ratios of exchange *round which* prices fluctuated. The pull and push of supply and demand were, it had been supposed, forever adjusting the economy by means of the fluctuations of prices round and about the normal or average ratios of exchange which alone expressed values. All that was necessary for the preservation of the Ricardian hypothesis was that prices should *tend* in the long run to average out at ratios of exchange proportionate to the man-hours of labour which it had taken to produce each commodity. But that was just what they were more and more ceasing to do. In the early days of the factory system, before any large masses of capital were used, the thing was evidently not very noticeable. But as industry developed, as, above all, different industries developed differently, some using more capital in proportion to labour and some less, as large-scale industry in our modern sense of the term, as distinct from *manufacture*, became dominant, it became apparent that commodities were no longer even tending to exchange in exact proportion to the amount of labour which it had taken to make them.

The trouble was not that their costs of production, and so their prices in equilibrium, depended also upon the amount of capital *used up* in making them. There was nothing damaging to the theory in that. The prices which commodities actually fetched could reflect the amount of capital in the form of raw material, as well as in the form of subsistence for the labourers, which had had to be *used up* in making them, without impairing the theory. In the same way, prices could reflect the amount of wear and tear to the fixed capital—machinery, buildings, etc.—which their production had occasioned. For all these kinds of capital were themselves products of labour. Therefore the portions of them which had had to be used up in making a commodity merely represented man-hours of labour used indirectly instead of directly in its production.

The real difficulty was more obstinate. Nothing was more apparent than that in practice prices in equilibrium fixed themselves so as to tend to provide a standard or average rate of *profit* on capital throughout the system. But how could values, determined *exclusively* by man-hours of socially necessary labour time, be the points round which prices fluctuated, if prices tended in fact to settle themselves so as to give an average rate of profit? For it was becoming more and more obvious that much more capital as compared to labour was being used in some branches of production than in others. Therefore the points round which prices tended to fluctuate were not being determined by socially necessary man-hours of labour alone. In real life the points round which prices fluctuated were being affected by the need to provide the standard amount of profit as well. The averages of prices were being deflected, as it were, to allow for a standard rate of profit for the capital used. It was only too apparent that social reality was again ceasing to correspond to the current elucidation of it. It had escaped again.

What was now left of the labour theory of value? What was left of it as an explanation of the real-life prices at which commodities would tend to exchange in perfect competition on a free market? What was vital to the theory was that the long-run averages of prices should be determined by the number of man-hours of socially necessary labour which had had to be used to produce each commodity. Now it seemed that this was not so: that the averages round which prices fluctuated—their equilibrium points—were deflected, much as the compass is deflected from the true to the magnetic north, by the fact that competition was bound to tend to equalise the rates of profit between industries which were unequally capitalised. *In other words, in real life not only man-hours of socially necessary labour but also a reward of some sort for capital entered into the determination of the points round which prices fluctuated.*

Ricardo himself had been aware of all this. But in the end he came to the conclusion that it was not a fatal objection to the use of the theory for what, in his (and in Marx's) mind was its real purpose, namely, the elucidation of how the national product would be divided up between the three great social classes, of wage earners, capitalists and landlords. For what really mattered for that purpose was the special case of the theory afforded by the subsistence view of wages. Moreover, it could be said (as it was said by Marx in the third volume of *Capital*) that a sort of average as between all the different industries could be struck: that the deviation introduced by the varying capital structures of industries made no difference to the overall division of the product between classes. Man-hours of socially necessary labour could thus still be held to be the right measuring rod for the division of the social product between classes.

But what are we to say of the theory in respect of its original function of explaining the ratios, or prices, at which commodities will exchange? We must now acknowledge that man-hours of socially necessary labour time will not determine the averages round which demand and supply will make prices fluctuate, but only *the average of those averages,* as between the different spheres of production. At first sight it seems that only the most remote and tenuous connection with real-life prices is preserved.

Whole generations of economists have triumphantly concluded that by these means they have got rid of the telltale labour theory of value, and got rid of it once and for all. For they profoundly objected to a theory the *political* implication of which was that labour was alone truly productive: that the remunerations of capital and of land (profit and rent) were simply deductions from, or tolls upon, the national product. This, and no scruples about its inadequacies, real or imagined, as an explanation of how prices were determined, was the reason why they all fell upon the theory with such glee.

For, after all, and contrary to all this weight of received opinion, are the deficiencies of the theory as a general guide to the determination of prices, in the long run, anything like so grave as they have been alleged to be? After all, the deflection of "prices of production" (as Marx called these points which allow for average profits in costs) from values as determined by man-hours of socially necessary labour time is not very wide. It remains true that "in equilibrium" the number of man-hours of socially necessary labour time which have had to be used to produce commodities is the *predominant* determinant of the ratios at which they will in the long run tend to exchange with each other. If this were not so: if, say, jet air-liners, on which an enormous number of man-hours had been directly and indirectly expended, as often as not sold for less than bicycles; or if electric kettles habitually fetched more than turbo-generators, then we should have to say that the labour theory of value had no contact with reality. But they do not. On the contrary, and in the long run, things which have a lot of work in them habitually do sell for more than things which have only a little work in them.

Moreover, changes in the number of man-hours needed to produce one broad type of commodity as compared to that needed to produce another type really are the main determinants in changing the ratios at which the first type of commodity will exchange with the second. For example, if the number of man-hours needed to produce primary agricultural products, such as corn, decreased (as it did in the nineteenth century, for example, owing to the opening up of the virgin prairies) as compared with the man-hours needed to produce manufactures, a given amount of agricultural produce did exchange for less manufactures. (And we are experiencing the opposite tendency today.) Over these broad, long-term, historical trends the labour theory of value does retain its essential contact with reality. In these cases labour time *is* the main explanation of the movement of real-life prices.

THE REAL OBJECTIONS

As the argument proceeds we shall find that the real objections to the use of the labour theory of value are not that it will only give a first rough approximation to the elucidation of prices. The first real difficulty is that, if we take man-hours of socially necessary labour time as our unit of value, we shall have no way of expressing changes in the productivity of labour. For if we use these units to add up the national product we shall get, of course, a total of man-hours. Therefore, with a given working population and given hours of work, that total must always be the same. If we reckon in these terms it is clearly impossible for a community ever, for example, to get any richer except by more of its inhabitants working, or by working longer hours. But this is to fly in the face of experience. Over the past 100 years many communities have got much richer and, though the proportion of their populations doing productive work has risen, their hours of work have greatly fallen. Notoriously we have got richer mainly because our productivity per hour of work has risen vastly, by means of the application of new techniques. But this all-important development cannot be displayed if we reckon exclusively in terms of man-hours. *Reckoning in terms of man-hours of socially necessary labour, the total national product is a given figure: all that can really be considered is its division between the social classes.*

As we proceed we shall find that this is no academic objection to an outworn theory. On the contrary, this defect, this one-sidedness, in the labour theory of value conditions the whole outlook of every communist upon basic economic problems to this very day. All that they do and say (see footnote p. 126, for example) shows that at heart they take little or no account of the rising total national product to be distributed; for them, as for the elder Mill, for Ricardo, and for Marx, its distribution between the classes is everything. Of course this is not mere intellectual error on their part; it fits in with their whole political and emotional outlook. But so does the labour theory of value. In the same way we shall see that some contemporary defenders of capitalism fall into the converse error. All they take account of is the increase in the total to be distributed; let the distribution look after itself. An equally convenient doctrine from their point of view.

The second real objection to the labour theory of value has already been mentioned. We noted (p. 60 above) that a subsistence theory of wages must be part of the wider theory of value. For the commodity which the labourer had to sell (his labour power, as Marx was to call it) must also sell at its value, *i.e.*, in proportion to the number of man-hours of necessary labour taken to produce it. And that number must be the minimum needed to produce "the wage goods" (as we should call them now) necessary to sustain the labourer and his family, *i.e.*, subsistence. Therefore a subsistence theory of wages has always been, implicitly for Ricardo, explicitly for Marx, an essential part of the labour theory of value. But wages have not remained at subsistence. Therefore one vitally important commodity, namely, labour power, has not even tended to sell at its value. This formidable fact has driven a great hole not only in the labour theory of value, but also in the associated Ricardian-Marxian diagram of what the distribution of the national product will be among the classes. It is the fact of rising real wages which has above all done the damage to the whole schema. Nevertheless we shall find that it has by no means destroyed its importance as an elucidation of what would happen unless tireless and drastic steps were taken to prevent it. That, I repeat, is one of the reasons why it is still indispensable to master the labour theory of value.

We shall find that it is these two deficiencies, and not the so-called "great contradiction" about the differing amounts of capital used in different industries, which have impaired the utility of the labour theory of value. All this, however, is to anticipate. The labour theory of value was not rejected by the economists of the second half of the nineteenth century because it proved unable to measure the gross national product or because of rising real wages. All they did was to find a fairly good excuse for rejecting it in the fact that it provided no complete explanation of the movement of relative prices. And then they concentrated their attention upon this one aspect of economic enquiry. For nearly a hundred years the fluctuations of price became the subject matter of economics.

3 ■ VALUE AND THE ECONOMISTS

During the nineteenth century there occurred one of those shifts of attention which are the true landmarks in the development of economics. It is not so much that new answers were found to the old questions; it is rather that, by common consent, the old questions were dropped and new ones asked.

This shift of interest began, as we have seen, over a hundred years ago. With the failure of Ricardo satisfactorily to solve the problem of value, the economists began to turn their backs upon this whole question. At first they simply said, in effect, that value was determined not only by man-hours of socially necessary labour time, but also by the current level of return on capital. For capital could, and should, secure, they said, a remuneration for the abstinence which its possessors had shown in not spending it. (This was Senior's way of putting it.) At first it was not apparent how vast a change in the nature of economics was being made when they said that. But in fact, when once the return on capital, which was simply a sum of money, was admitted as a constituent of value, as well as man-hours of socially necessary labour, the theory ceased to be a theory of value in the original sense and became merely a theory of how costs were determined. The economists were trying to add together two entirely different kinds of things, a sum of money (whatever that was) and man-hours of socially necessary labour. The search for *one* thing in the units of which economic quantities could be measured had been abandoned. All that the economists were now saying was that in equilibrium commodities would exchange in accordance with their costs of production. And if you asked what their costs were, why, then you were told that they were the sums of money paid out in the course of production. In a word, a commodity's costs of production were what it had cost to produce it. The very need for an objective "footrule" with which to measure economic quantities was no longer realised.

MARGINAL UTILITY

From one point of view this was the essential break in tradition. Once, however, the search for a theory of value in the old sense, the search for "absolute value," for "the footrule not liable to contract or expand," had been abandoned, things had to go much further. And around 1870 this duly happened. The theory of marginal utility was evolved.

As every undergraduate reading the now dominant studies at our universities knows, this theory holds that prices are determined, *in perfect competition* (this was the not always adequately articulate premise of the whole proposition), according to a subtle calculus, analogous to the differential calculus in mathematics, which shows how much each buyer will give (in order to satiate his wants) and how much each seller will *take* (in order to cover his costs), for *one more*, of the commodities which they are exchanging. It is the cost of producing from the least productive mine the last ton of coal which needs to be raised to satisfy the last ton demanded, which will determine the price. As more and more units of the commodity are produced, the consumers will begin to need the extra supplies less and less, and at the same time (it was assumed) it will become more and more costly to produce them. At some point a balancing price will be struck at which it just pays someone to produce one more unit and at which it is just worth the while of some consumer or other to buy it. That will be the going price. We are in a world of *gently* rising and falling curves upon the economists' charts, expressing at their points of intersection the price which will equate supply with demand "at the margin."

This development of marginalism in the eighteen-seventies, rather than the defeat of the Ricardians in the nineteen-thirties, is usually considered the main break in tradition. For once this had happened it had become almost undeniable that what was now in question—for good or ill—was no longer a theory of value in the old sense, but a theory of prices. It was at most a theory of average prices: of prices in equilibrium. For marginalism does no more than account for the fluctuations of relative prices. In essence it does so by an enormously refined and developed version of common or garden demand and supply reasoning.

Moreover the economists' attention tended to shift more and more towards the demand side, and away from the question of supply and costs. True, Alfred Marshall, ever anxious to preserve tradition, endeavoured to hold the balance even with his famous simile of the scissors. He declared that it would be as meaningless to say whether it was supply or demand at the margin, which determined prices, and values in his limited sense of the equilibrium points towards which prices will gravitate, as to say that either the upper or the nether blade of a pair of scissors cuts the paper. But both Jevons and the great Austrian marginalists from Menger onwards went further. They derived prices and value from the demand side, from utility at the margin, and applied their basic concept of marginalism only secondarily to supply and costs of production. In any case, once the attempt to find a standard of absolute value had broken down, it made only a secondary difference whether you explained prices by a cost of production theory, such as Senior's or Mill's, a marginalist theory with an equal emphasis on supply and demand, such as Marshall's, or a marginalist theory with all the emphasis on demand, such as the Austrians'. The essence of the matter was that economics could now concern itself only with the exchange ratios of commodities: with relative prices and their fluctuations; with the equilibrium points towards which prices would, in conditions of perfect competition, tend to gravitate. Prices were now just prices. They did not express anything in particular. As Mrs. Robinson puts it: "Marshall turned the meaning of value into a little question: Why does an egg cost more than a cup of tea?" (*On Re-reading Marx,* p. 22).

But marginalism, equilibrium analysis even in its more complete, its Austrian, form, was not the end of this story. In the concluding years of the last century the final steps were taken away from the whole kind of economics, based on the attempt to establish absolute value, which we described in the preceding chapter. What is called "equilibrium analysis" was developed out of marginalism, originally by the French economist Walras and his successors, such as Pareto and Wicksell. Indeed it is apparent that if we concentrate upon the essential point of marginalism, we shall become more and more concerned with the equilibrium points at which commodities will exchange, if there are no interferences with perfect competition. In this way we shall come into sight of the project of elaborating a set of interlocking equations which will express the whole gamut of the exchange relationships of a perfectly competitive society. And that is just what the economists did. Economics became more and more mathematical. It was less and less concerned with aggregates, with totals, with measurement, or with the division of those totals between persons or classes of persons. It simply contemplated the immense web of interlocking relationships of exchange. Ratios were all: aggregates nothing; everything could be depicted by a set of simultaneous equations. When this third step had been taken the science had become something which would have been unrecognisable to its founding fathers. What was it all worth?

The best account of this whole development is to be found in Part IV of Joseph Schumpeter's great posthumous work, *The History of Economic Analysis* (George Allen and Unwin, 1955). Just because Schumpeter was himself both a most distinguished professor of the equilibrium analysis school, and yet stood to some extent outside and beyond it—with his profound historical sense, his command of Marxism, and his passionate desire to relate his analysis to the facts of real life—just because of his double rôle, he was by far the most persuasive advocate of equilibrium analysis. Yet his claims for it are in the end modest. True he undoubtedly believed that equilibrium theory, in the form of elaborate series of simultaneous equations, set out a sort of basic logic of economics. Moreover, quite unlike most of its practitioners, Schumpeter, anxious to preserve the honour of economics as a genuinely objective and impartial science, was determined to show that this logic could be used to demonstrate not only the theoretical perfection of a fully competitive capitalism, but also the possibility of a rational socialist system. No doubt it can be so used. But then, has anyone, except the ignorant and foolish, or conversely the highly intelligent but uncontrollably prejudiced (Von Mises and Von Hayek), really ever doubted that both competitive capitalism and centrally planned socialism can be rational ways of running an economy, and not mere nonsense? Schumpeter writes, "But at the same time this is all. We must not forget that, just like the pure theory of the competitive economy, the pure theory of Socialism moves on a very high level of abstraction and proves much less for the 'workability' of the system than laymen (and sometimes theorists also) think." (*op. cit.* p. 989).

There is something engaging about Schumpeter's illusion that laymen will attach *too much* practical importance to the fact that certain sets of simultaneous equations are soluble. It is far more likely that laymen will see little significance in the complex algebra of equilibrium analysis, either for its main purpose of expounding and justifying the workings of perfectly competitive capitalism, or for sustaining the possibility of a rationally planned socialism.

The question is, will the layman be wrong in such scepticism? Well, of course he will be wrong in the sense that it is wrong to ignore the wonderfully complex mathematical structure of equilibrium analysis. But, with all due deference to such elegant formulations, I cannot for the life of me believe that this whole theoretical structure has proved anything but conspicuously barren of predictive power and consequently an extraordinarily feeble guide to action. (Indeed at one level its basic assumptions rule all that out. But at another level it certainly does attempt to be "a guide to action," or rather perhaps to the inaction of *laissez faire*.) Just as Ricardian economics was an attempt to apply a basically Newtonian science to social and productive relations, so the nineteenth-century development, culminating around 1900 in equilibrium analysis and another period of supreme self-assurance, was an attempt to apply more developed mathematical thinking—above all algebraic thinking—to those same relations. What it produced was an incomparably more refined method of analysing the fluctuations of relative prices under the pull and push of supply and demand, in perfectly competitive conditions. That was by no means useless. But it told us little about the large simple questions which had occupied the minds of the founding fathers. Moreover, as the twentieth century wore on those same crude considerations began to occupy men's minds again. For equilibrium analysis told them little about what, in particular, was the total national product, what increased or diminished it, and how it was to be divided up.

Moreover equilibrium analysis assumed a degree of "perfection" in the competitiveness of capitalism which was becoming more and more at variance with reality. In so far as mature late nineteenth-century capitalism really did establish a freely competitive economy, carrying through all its transactions without exception by means of freely negotiated exchanges, equilibrium analysis was a highly sophisticated attempt to express and reflect those transactions in mathematical formulae. (But even in this it was a mirror rather than a *critique*. It did not attempt to establish standards of comparison by which the true performance of the system could be either measured or judged.) Moreover capitalism, even at its moment of greatest "purity"—some time towards the end of the nineteenth century—was never anything like perfectly competitive. That would not have mattered if the trend had remained towards greater and greater competitiveness. Equilibrium analysis would in that case have at any rate established a model towards which reality was approximating. But in the event just the opposite occurred. While the economists were developing with incomparable subtlety and complexity the theory of perfect competition, in the algebraic form of equilibrium analysis, the economy itself was becoming less and less perfectly competitive. The development, which, as we saw in Chapter 1, has amounted, in the end, to a new stage of capitalism, was taking place. And for the new stage which capitalism has now entered equilibrium analysis is less and less appropriate.

Marginalism and equilibrium analysis became less and less faithful mirrors, even for the economies which they purported to elucidate. They reflected, rather, what the now triumphant middle class dreamed those economies to be. Professor Tawney has a famous passage in his *Religion and the Rise of Capitalism* (Murray, 1936) in which he writes:

> There is a magic mirror into which each order and organ of Society, as the consciousness of its character and destiny dawns upon it, looks for a moment, before the dust of conflict or the glamour of success obscures its vision. In that enchanted glass, it sees its own lineaments reflected with ravishing allurements; for what it sees is not what is, but what in the eyes of mankind and its own heart it would be. (p. 210.)

The mature middle class of the late nineteenth century— though certainly not lacking either the dust of conflict or the glamour of success—sought a mirror for the economic world which it had created. True the glass contained only the glacial image of a set of simultaneous equations. But that image was intended to guarantee nothing less than the perfection of the system. The fact that those equations were soluble gave an assurance, the professors implied, that satisfactions for all were being maximised, or at any rate that they would be if the remaining interferences with the system were but eliminated. For, though the best of the economists of the period all protested their qualifications and their exceptions, that was the real impact of their teaching. The algebraic remoteness of equilibrium analysis had not made the main body of economic thought politically indifferent or neutral. On the contrary, the claim was, I repeat, that this was the image of an at any rate potentially perfect system. The workings of the price mechanism, it was confidently taught, *must* automatically maximise satisfactions for all; such questions as how big the total national product was or how it should be divided up among the classes need not even arise.

In the end it was the divergence of the economy from the algebraic model of equilibrium analysis, founded upon the assumption of perfect competition and automatic adjustment, that drove the economists out of this blind alley. Capitalism was steadily developing into its latest stage. Competition was becoming less and less perfect. The hypothesis of automatic adjustments, leading to a universal maximising of satisfactions, was becoming more and more untenable. For the maladjustments (*i.e.*, mass unemployment, extreme maldistribution of income, manifest inability to use all the available productive resources, grave instability) were now enormous. It was in this situation that, in the nineteen-thirties, several new tendencies in orthodox economic thought developed.

A MAN OF THE TRANSITION

From the loins of the most orthodox tradition, out of Cambridge itself, there sprang, as a child of that tradition's old age, a genius, eccentric in the strictest sense of that term, who began to shift his attention away from the passive contemplation of prices. As we shall see (Chapters 10 and 11 below), the main life work of John Maynard Keynes was to evolve one whole aspect of the theory of that new, latest stage of capitalism in which we now live. But in his earlier work he was already shifting his attention from the fluctuations of prices back to those central issues of the total social product—what made it grow and what inhibited its growth —and, closely linked with that, its division between the different sections of those who produced it. Keynes was quintessentially a figure of the transition. On the one hand, he stands at the end of the whole two hundred years of development of British economic thought, commanding it absolutely, with every element of it at his fingers' ends. But he was by no means merely its culmination. He was in many respects rather its disintegration. It was his destiny to transcend many of its possible limits, to see things in a way that they must not be seen from the angle of vision of the economists of the system. Contrast, for example, the whole spirit and emphasis of the following famous passage from Keynes' first major work, *The Economic Consequences of the Peace,* with the work of any other orthodox economist of the period. Keynes is painting the picture of Western society in the epoch which ended in 1914. His first sentence reads: "Europe was so organized socially and economically as to secure the maximum accumulation of capital."

Immediately we are in another world. The economist's promised Arcadia of harmonious commodity exchange—of which equilibrium analysis is in a sense only the final monument—has disappeared at one stroke. Moreover the passage proceeds immediately to define the means by which the maximum accumulation of capital was secured.

> While there was some continuous improvement in the daily conditions of life of the mass of the population, Society was so framed as to throw a great part of the increased income into the control of the class least likely to consume it. The new rich of the nineteenth century were not brought up to large expenditures, and preferred the power which investment gave them to the pleasures of immediate consumption. In fact, it was precisely the *inequality* of the distribution of wealth which made possible those vast accumulations of fixed wealth and of capital improvements which distinguished that age from all others. Herein lay, in fact, the main justification of the capitalist system. If the rich had spent their new wealth on their own enjoyments, the world would long ago have found such a regime intolerable. But like bees they saved and accumulated not less to the advantage of the whole community because they themselves held narrower ends in prospect.

Accumulation was effected by extreme inequality of income. Nor was this inequality a law of nature: society was deliberately "so framed" as to produce it. But accumulation depended not only upon inequality, but also upon the decisions of the rich. Since society's surplus became their absolute private property, it could only be used for investment if "like bees they saved and accumulated." Keynes suggests that they did so out of an innate Puritan strain in their psychology. Perhaps this was important in the early days. But the main factor soon became the pushing of inequality to such a point that the incomes of the rich were virtually too big to be spent at all. Almost any standard of the life which the rich could think of was compatible with accumulation. Keynes goes on to emphasize remorselessly the point that the only real "abstinence" which made accumulation possible was the enforced abstinence of the wage earners.

> The immense accumulations of fixed capital which, to the great benefit of mankind, were built up during the half century before the war, could never have come about in a society where wealth was divided equitably. The railways of the world, which that age built as a monument to posterity, were, not less than the pyramids of Egypt, the work of labour which was not free to consume in immediate enjoyment the full equivalent of its efforts.

After another passage in which the alleged puritanism of the rich and the enforced abstinence of the poor are shown to work together blindly for a maximum rate of accumulation which is in the immediate, personal, interests of neither, Keynes gives his justification of the arrangement.

> In writing thus I do not necessarily disparage the practices of that generation. In the unconscious recesses of its being Society knew what it was about. The cake was really very small in proportion to the appetites of consumption, and no one, if it were shared all round, would be much the better off by the cutting of it. Society was working not for the small

pleasures of today but for the future security and improvement of the race—in fact for "progress." If only the cake were not cut but was allowed to grow in the geometrical proportion predicted by Malthus of population, but not less true of compound interest, perhaps a day might come when there would at last be enough to go round, and when posterity could enter into the enjoyment of *our* labours. In that day overwork, overcrowding, and underfeeding would come to an end, and men, secure of the comforts and necessities of the body, could proceed to the nobler exercises of their faculties. One geometrical ratio might cancel another, and the nineteenth century was able to forget the fertility of the species in a contemplation of the dizzy virtues of compound interest.

There were two pitfalls in this prospect: lest, population still outstripping accumulation, our self-denials promote not happiness but numbers; and lest the cake be after all consumed, prematurely, in war, the consumer of all such hopes.

This is a vision, unique so far as I know, in the vast corpus of orthodox economics, of the historical task—and in its day justification—of capitalism. Here is a recognition that the nature of unmodified capitalism was not to produce welfare, or to "maximise satisfactions." Least of all did it produce a harmonious society of free and equal producers, each exchanging like value with like value to their mutual benefit. Its historical function was to build new means of production at the maximum rate, to accumulate capital by means of holding down the incomes of the wage earners to the minimum practicable level, and to do so no matter what the cost to human beings.

Partly by means of, and because of, this vision of Keynes, one part of the orthodox economic tradition is in our day finding its way back to a realistic appraisal of capitalism. The first essential thing that Keynes did was to stand, to some extent at least, outside the system and so to look at it as a whole. For the first time for a hundred years orthodox economics became concerned again with the whole, with *to-tals*, with the social product as a sum. In this way alone could such concepts as the gross national product and its division between the social classes re-enter the picture. And this meant, as we shall find, that Keynes' doctrine gradually became linked with the other major development of the nineteen-thirties, namely, the use of statistics by a new school of economists. This is the second of those developments out of which there has emerged a new phase in orthodox economics: a phase as different again from the phase of equilibrium analysis as that was different from the economics of the founding fathers.

Nor was it more than superficially a paradox that we find Keynes in the passages just quoted *defending* extreme inequality of the distribution of income as necessary in order to maximise accumulation. True, his life work was to be to show that this inequality had been carried to a point where it became self-defeating and actually frustrated accumulation. The essential thing, however, was that from the outset he turned his attention to these issues: to these issues which had been obscured by a Victorian suppression of attention no less rigorous than that which had been applied to the natural functions. It is, therefore, possible to see what Schumpeter meant by his at first sight startling verdict that the whole essence of Keynes' vision is contained in *The Economic Consequences of the Peace*, and that the rest of his life work was an attempt to work out the implications of that vision. Schumpeter believed that this is indeed how all fruitful work in economics has to be done. First there must be something in the nature of an inspired guess. Then there must be anything up to a life time of labour testing and trying that guess against the facts. The passage reads:

The process stands out in this case with such insurpassable clearness because we can read a formulation of the vision, as yet analytically unarmed, in a few brilliant pages of Keynes' *The Economic Consequences of the Peace* (1919). So far as this line of endeavour of a man of many interests was concerned, the whole period between 1919 and 1936 was, then, spent in attempts, first unsuccessful, then increasingly successful, at implementing the particular vision of the economic process of our time that was fixed in Keynes' mind by 1919 at latest. (p. 42, *op. cit.*)

Schumpeter simply ignores the fact that in the 1919 vision Keynes was deeply concerned *lest* capitalism should no longer accumulate fast enough, while the essential message of his main work, *The General Theory of Employment, Interest and Money* (Macmillan, 1936), is just the opposite, namely, a concern that it will attempt to accumulate so fast as to become self-defeating. But the contradiction is only superficial. Schumpeter is right in pointing to the fact that what really mattered was that Keynes had shifted his attention back to those original questions of the total product, the rate and method of accumulation which will maximise its growth, and how it is to be divided among the different classes of producers.

Keynes, as we shall see (p. 267 below) would not have wasted his time if he had studied the antithetical diagram of the system drawn by Marx. That he could not bring himself to do. His contribution was to shake off—though with what difficulty!—the vast, encumbering web of inhibitions and obfuscations which orthodox economics had largely become. He describes the mental travail he underwent in so doing in the Preface to *The General Theory:*—

The composition of this book has been for the author a long struggle of escape . . . a struggle of escape from habitual modes of thought and expression. The ideas that are here expressed are extremely simple and should be obvious. The difficulty lies, not in the new ideas, but in escaping from the old ones, which ramify, for those brought up as most of us have been, into every corner of our minds.

This Houdini-like feat of intellectual evasive action was indispensable to Keynes' achievement. His mind was all of quick-silver: he slipped out of the prison-house that economics had become before the professors could stop him.

For when the economists abandoned the pursuit of value they abandoned the most vital aspects of their science; they abandoned "the desire and pursuit of the whole." Yet it may be that we are now in sight of the ability to distinguish which of the old problems are really soluble and which are merely defective statements of the issue. The essential thing, however, is that we have returned to that consideration of *the whole social product,* and consequently of its division between the social classes, which the science cravenly abandoned a century ago. True, the intervening work was not wasted. Someone, no doubt, had to work out all those equations. Marginal utility and equilibrium analysis are a genuinely illuminating conception for some purposes. But if we ask the blunt question, what was the value of the economists after they abandoned the search for value, we shall be bound to answer: something, but not very much.*

---

* When the economists concentrated their attention on the short-term fluctuations of prices, they abandoned the attempt to predict, and so to make history. But it might have been supposed that they would at least have evolved, in compensation, a technique for making money. Yet in fact their methods yielded no even short-term predictive power, or they would have become richer men than they were. Indeed it is an ironical fact that the two major economists who really did make money were Ricardo and Keynes. And Ricardo was the last respectable economist to concern himself with the economy as a whole and the division of the whole product among the social classes, and Keynes was the first to do so again.

THE MARXIAN SCHISM

The Keynesian break through was only one of the roads by means of which the economists regained contact with a reality which was always tending to escape them. As we noted in Chapter 1, others of them began to study intensively the phenomena of an economy of ever larger and fewer units and to elucidate the profound effects of this development upon the basic assumptions of their science. And again, another school began to use statistical methods in an attempt to deal quantitatively with those aggregates, the national product and its division, that had been neglected for a hundred years. And this third development also was, as we noted in Chapter 1, associated with the entry of the economy into its new phase.

We shall be much concerned with the character and consequences of the new economics which these three developments of the last twenty-five years have at length produced. But before attempting to deal with them we must consider the other great school of economic thought, namely, Marxism, the emergence of which split the nineteenth-century tradition in two. For we shall find that Marxist economics, although following a completely different path, also reached the point at which it had to deal with the latest stage of capitalism. In fact it reached that point some two decades earlier than did orthodox economics. Hence it seems possible that a good deal may be learned from a comparison of the two quite separate methods which are currently being used to attempt the elucidation of contemporary capitalism.

In order to do so we must go back to the point at which the Ricardian attempt to find, in man-hours of socially necessary labour time, an absolute standard of value broke down. We have just seen what happened when the economists attempted to carry on the science without any such standard. It would be wrong to deny that great developments in analytic technique were achieved, but they were achieved at an ever mounting, and at length prohibitive, cost in terms of abstraction from reality. But another reaction was possible. It was possible to stick at all costs to man-hours of socially necessary labour time as the standard of value, and to see what kind of a diagram or model of the economy could be built on this hypothesis. And this is what Marx did. He did it, no doubt, because Ricardo's hypothesis exactly suited his underlying purposes. The labour theory of value, as we saw, could display one, but not the other, of the two great simple issues of economics. It, and the subsistence theory of wages associated with it, could deal effectively with the division of the total product between different categories or classes of producers, but it could not deal with the question of what tended to increase or diminish that total. But this was not even a disadvantage from Marx's point of view. He was convinced that what mattered was precisely the division—just as was Ricardo (see p. 58). And he developed the labour theory of value to display, even more effectively than had Ricardo, the view that what that division must in fact be under capitalism was subsistence for the wage earners and the accumulation of ever more mountainous wealth for the owners of capital. It was upon this issue that Marx directed the battering ram of his attention.

ACCUMULATION

In a sense all this could be regarded as the question of accumulation. Whence came the great masses of new capital which were visibly pouring into the system year after year? It was on this issue of accumulation that the attempt of the nineteenth-century economists to depict the whole economy in terms of an immense web of free exchanges at fluctuating prices met with its main difficulties. True, it was just possible to describe every part of the vast and intricate mechanism of competitive capitalism in terms of fluctuating prices—in terms of self-adjusting, self-compensating ratios of exchange: of exchanges entered into by the uncoerced free will of wholly free and independent citizens. But at two points at least in the immense diagram such a treatment was always strained. On the one hand, could it really be said that there was nothing special or peculiar about that price which determined the reward for labour—about that price at which what was becoming the great majority of the working population sold what turned out to be the one commodity they had to offer, namely, their ability to labour? Was it really true that if only no one interfered with the virgin purity of the automatic mechanism, the wage earners would always get what it was right and proper—indeed inevitably foreordained—that they should get, no more and no less? Was it really true that the very different magnitudes which were being received by the owners of capital were also an exactly proportionate reward for their services—their indispensable, if curiously passive, services of, in Marshall's phrase, "waiting"?

And then there was another price which it was not always easy to regard as just the same as any other. And that was the price paid for the new capital which was constantly being poured into the ever-expanding system. This price was called the rate of interest in one aspect and the rate of profit in another. It was the price, the economists said, which had to be paid to induce people to accumulate their money instead of spending it. This led them to express a remarkable view of how capital was accumulated. And this in turn involved in the last resort a theory of where capital came from. What, in effect, they all said was that accumulation took place by means of individual savings. People—any people, from peers to paupers—they said, abstained from spending all of their incomes, saved up, and then used their savings to start some new enterprise. The profits or interest they received for so doing were a reward for this self-denying abstinence.

In the very early days of the system such things could and did happen. It was possible for a prosperous peasant to, say, start a flour mill out of his savings. It might even have been possible for a wage earner to have done something of the sort. The minimum sum necessary to start a new enterprise— the minimum sum necessary to constitute a sum of *capital*— was, at that simple technical level, very small. Nevertheless, from the very outset there were other and important sources for this process of "primary accumulation." This was not, for example, a convincing account either of how the British landlords carried through the enclosures, or of how the British nabobs accumulated in the East or West Indies. Still, the economist's theory of the origins of capital did bear some resemblance to *early* capitalist reality and to the origins of the capitalist system.*

But, once the process of capitalism had got going, this story that capital was formed by the individual savings of any citizen who was thrifty and upright enough to abstain from riotous living became a mere fairy tale. Once capitalism was a going concern, it was, or it should have been, obvious that the source of further capital was overwhelmingly the profits (plus the rent and the interest) of existing capital. The

---

* Schumpeter in his *Capitalism, Socialism and Democracy* considers that Marx, in emptying the full vials of his wrath, scorn and irony on this conception overstates his case and reveals an uneasy consciousness that, after all, individual savings, made by abstinence, did play a significant part in primary accumulation. I agree. But that does not prevent the theory from being any less inadequate as an explanation of the continuing process of accumulation. But see Schumpeter (*op. cit.*) for a comparison of Marx's and the economist's diagrams of accumulation.

only people who were really in a position to save substantially were those who already possessed capital and so received profits. Profits themselves were the source of accumulation. But, if it were once admitted that new accumulations of capital came from old accumulations, the question of where the accumulations had come from in the first place would have to be faced.

We shall see in the next chapter what is the only rational or candid answer to this question. And that will reveal that these two difficulties of the late nineteenth-century economists' diagram were really one and the same difficulty, looked at from the opposite angle of vision. It was precisely because they saw nothing special about the price which the wage earners got for their ability to labour that they failed to give an even remotely realistic account of the accumulation of capital, and so of the source and origin of profit. It was because they averted their eyes from the dependence of the wage earners that they had to invent their fairy tale about the source of accumulation. For it was from, because of, and out of the dependent position of the wage earners that capitalist accumulation took place. No rate of interest could have induced the necessary saving had the wage earners been free to consume the full equivalent of their product.

In substance, as we have just seen, this was recognised by Keynes in his original, 1919, vision of the system. But seventy years before that Marx had made it the centrepiece of his diagram or model of capitalism. He, too, may have arrived at his conclusion more by means of an inspired vision of the nature of social reality about him than by means of the conscious use of the technique of economic analysis that was available to him. But, just as Keynes attempted to "arm his vision" with all the twentieth-century instruments of economic analysis, so Marx used the analytic technique available to him: and that was Ricardo's system, with all its Newtonian rigidities. We shall see that the fact that the Marxian schism broke out of economic tradition at this point in the latter's development has had consequences the importance of which it would be hard to exaggerate.

4. ■ MARX

The very title of Marx's main work is premonitory: "Capital." Marx's main subject is to be, not the universal benefits which will arise if only men are left free to exchange their products. No, the theme has changed. Now we are to study how capital has been accumulated *out* of that process of free exchanges, how a great pile of wealth has appeared at one end of society, and an equal and opposite morass of destitution at the other. His task is to explain how and why the accumulation of capital in private hands is at the same time a process by which all but a handful of the independent producers lose their means of production and become dependent wage earners. This polarisation of society, as he called it, is Marx's essential subject matter. For Marx was the first economist to be emotionally hostile to the system. The unexpected and terrible fission of the promised society of free and equal producers into wage earners and owners of capital had made the economists after Ricardo shy away from the attempt to elucidate the division of the national product. He had no such inhibitions.

Marx also begins the construction of his diagram by a consideration of the exchange of commodities. He accepts the labour theory of value: commodities will, he agrees, exchange at ratios determined by the number of man-hours of labour which have had to be used in producing them. Apparently, then, the exchanges will be fair and just. How, therefore, out of this harmonious exchange of like value with like value, in which each man takes out of the market what he brought to it, changed indeed in physical form—a bushel of wheat for a bag of nails—but constant in value: how out of such a process, can *profit*, a surplus, an accumulation, a fund for new investment, arise? And how upon the basis of that surplus does the fatal polarisation of society develop?

In order to provide an answer he rivets our attention on that ever-growing army of wage earners, more or less overlooked by the earliest economists of the system, who go indeed to market, but go with empty hands, since they have no product to sell. They have no product to sell because, unlike the farmers, peasants, craftsmen and handicraft workers, who were the *dramatis personae* of the vanished world of small-commodity production, they have no land or other means of production *with which* to produce. What, then, do they sell? They sell their ability to work, their "labour power," as Marx called it. They sell it by the hour, the day or the week. The payment and receipt of wages are the purchase and sale of labour power. They are a process of exchange which takes place within the productive process itself; they are a process of exchange upon the terms of which everything else hangs. The capitalist system comes into existence when, and not before, labour power comes on to the market as a commodity. This is the point at which the system of "small-commodity production," which was the pattern and ideal of the early economists, splits in two and is swallowed up in capitalism proper. And this can happen only as and when the small independent producers lose their means of production, their land by enclosures, their hand looms by the competition of the power looms, etc., etc.

Marx then proceeds to work out what will be the terms upon which this fateful act of exchange, going on within the productive process, the exchange of the workman's ability to work for the means of subsistence owned and controlled by the employer, will take place. And in so doing he derives his subsistence theory of wages much more directly and clearly than had Ricardo from the labour theory of value. "In equilibrium" (not that Marx uses such words) this new commodity, labour power which has come upon the market, will be sold, like every thing else, at its value. What, then, will determine the value of labour power? Marx's answer to this question is the kernel of his economic thought. For the value of labour power will, clearly, determine the level of wages and so will be the essential element in deciding the division of the total national product among the different classes.

Marx has no doubt about the answer. He concludes that the value of labour power will, like the value of every other commodity, be determined by the number of man-hours of labour necessary to produce it. But this is to say that the value of labour power—the level of wages—will be determined by how many hours of labour have had to be devoted to sustaining the life, the strength, and the reproductive power, of the worker. In other words, the size of the weekly wage will be determined by the number of man-hours of labour necessary to produce a heap of commodities made up of the food, shelter, clothing, etc. (what modern economists call "the wage-goods") needed to sustain the worker and his family for the week in which he is paid his wages. That is the value of the wage. It will be no more than that. This is all-important. For, if it is true, it proves that the real wages of the worker will never substantially rise above what is necessary to sustain him and his family, *i.e.*, subsistence. For that is the value of what the worker has to sell, *i.e.*, his ability to work.

To put the point in different words, it means that the level of wages will be determined by what it takes to "produce" (and reproduce) the worker and will have nothing to do with how much the worker produces. Moreover—and here is the second essential point—the worker will in fact produce much more than it takes to "produce" (*i.e.*, sustain) him. The difference is the source of rent, interest and profit: of "surplus value," as Marx called all three lumped together.

This is the foundation stone of Marx's economics. Marx taught that this particular commodity, labour power, had a unique characteristic; that it was, as it were, a living commodity. It produced more than it cost to produce. The wage earner produced more value than he was paid. This, then, was where profit, where surplus, where accumulation, came from. Profit was unpaid labour. Of course Marx did not suppose that the capitalists spent all the surplus value that resulted from this process on riotous living. On the contrary, he emphasized that they accumulated most of it. This was the fount and origin of all those incomparable works of the capitalist age: those works, greater than pyramids, dwarfing the achievements of antiquity, changing the face of the earth.

MARX'S THEORY OF VALUE

Well, it was a marvellously ingenious way of putting it. Marx succeeded in demonstrating, on the basis of the economists' own theories, why the free exchange of commodities had, by, say, 1840, undeniably produced not social harmony, but ever-growing inequality and social polarisation. How much insight, however, into contemporary, twentieth century reality does it give us? This is the labour theory of value, in its Marxist form, in which it has become the theory of *Surplus* value: the theory of where profit comes from: the theory of accumulation: the theory of capital. What Marx is saying, in his Ricardian terminology, is that the only creators of wealth are those who work by hand or brain: that any sums spent by the capitalists are a *deduction* from the national product, not some share in it proportionate to a contribution made by "waitings." That is the practical political meaning of saying that man-hours of labour are the sole source of value. The question is, how much more insight does this way of putting it give us, for example, than Keynes' terse statement that society was "so framed" as to throw a great part of its ever-increasing income into the control of the class least likely to consume it?

As we shall see in succeeding chapters, we can now (we suppose) add up the total "gross national product" to a meaningful statistical total and, consequently, show in more or less precise figures how it is divided up among the various classes. This, we noted in Chapter 1, was one of the changes in the nature of the system associated with its major twentieth-century mutation. As a result we shall find that the fact of a division among the classes on the line, though not in the proportions, which Ricardo and Marx had to struggle to demonstrate, is becoming undeniable. Before, however, we conclude that Marx went a long way round to make his point, we should remember several things. First, Marx's way of putting it was inevitable in an age which both lacked statistical equipment and which assumed the labour theory of value as unquestioned. For until Marx found his consummately ingenious way of turning their own weapons against them, the early economists' theory of value seemed to exclude the very possibility of the exploitation of the wage earners. They had satisfied both themselves and their readers that all exchanges, including the exchange between wage earners and their employers, would tend to take place at their value, *i.e.*, in proportion to the man-hours of necessary labour which it had taken to produce the respective commodities bought and sold. How, then, could the slightest wrong be done to the wage earner, since, like everyone else, he was paid the full value of what he had to sell? His position,

the economists implied, was really no different from that of
the peasant or artisan who sold a material product. Appear-
ances might, to put it mildly, be against it in the Britain of
the hungry 'forties, but the fact was, they considered, that
the wage earner was just as well placed as everyone else and
got the full value of what he had to sell.

Marx found a way of reconciling their theory of value,
which he enthusiastically accepted, with the facts of life as
he saw them all about him. He showed, by means of the above
argument of the special character of the unique commodity,
labour power, that the very fact that the wage earner was
paid the value of his labour power must mean that he was
paid no more than a subsistence wage: that this in turn
meant that he was "exploited" by the whole difference between this and the value of what he produced. For Marx
meant something clear-cut by exploitation. He did not simply
mean that some people were richer than others. He meant
that some people, the employers as well as the landlords,
were living off other people's labour: that they gave no
equivalent in exchange for the commodities they received:
that they could buy without selling—or, to put the point in
the cold and colourless language of H. M. Treasury, that they
lived off "unearned income." It is always important to remember that for present-day Marxists, as it was for Marx,
it is the *source*, not the size, of incomes that matters. They,
and he, are and were perfectly prepared to tolerate large
inequalities of incomes if they are all derived from work—if
they are all earned incomes in the Treasury sense of the
term. But they are not, and he was not, in principle, willing to tolerate the existence of any property-derived, *unearned*, income, however small. This scale of values is often
confusing to non-Marxists, but it stems directly from Marx's
original and basic economic analysis.

Marx cut his way through to the essential tendency of
capitalism, which, however you express the point, is to chan-

nel the whole of its ever-growing *surplus* towards the owners of the means of production to spend or invest, and thus to deprive the mass of the wage-earning population of any part of it. It matters little whether we think that the intellectual tools which he used are of an antique shape: they did the job for him. For, as we shall see, unless we keep this conclusion in view, there is no hope of our understanding the world in which we live.

Nevertheless, and as the argument of this study proceeds, the reader will notice that it is in fact based upon contemporary statistical concepts such as the gross national product and its division between the major social classes. It does not in fact seek to use Ricardo's foot-rule or to found its contentions on the Marxian categories, such as surplus value, constant and variable capital, and the like. He will further see that by so doing we by no means avoid all difficulties. On the contrary, the contemporary methods for measuring the economy are extremely rough and approximate. Moreover, they rest upon a decidedly shaky logical basis. They employ money, pounds or dollars or what you will, as their unit of value, correcting, of course, by means of index numbers for changes in the value of money. But to do this is to use a foot-rule which is "liable to contract or expand" with a vengeance, a foot-rule the vagaries of which can be corrected only by the elaborate and logically doubtful process of comparing it in turn to the *average* vagaries of everything else! We shall discuss this issue in Chapter 6 below. Here we must merely say in advance that we shall conclude that, in spite of all these difficulties, the contemporary statistical method does appear, in the light of experience, to produce *less* gross errors than has the use of categories founded on the labour theory of value. (The intervening economics, which used neither method, did not produce errors, but then they did not produce very much else either—except such a *reductio ad absurdum* as that unemployment could not exist.)

Moreover, the contemporary statistical method is well adapted to exhibiting such great blunt truths as that the whole wealth of society, past, present and future, derives from the blood, sweat and toil—mental and physical—of its inhabitants: that, while a vital contribution to that wealth may be made by enterprise, managerial skill and technical know-how, no contribution to it is made by persons in respect of ownership which they may have in this or that part of society's capital equipment: that the division of the total annual product of wealth both among social classes, and for that matter among different purposes, such as consumption or the acquisition of new means of production, or, for example, defence, is not something governed by immutable "laws," but can be regulated by the conscious will of society.

What remains, then, of the labour theory of value? On that subject, as on many others, Frederick Engels had something sensible to say. In a letter to a young German Social Democrat named Schmidt (March 12, 1895), at the very end of Engels' long life, he wrote that the labour theory of value was a *concept*, like any other concept—say, feudalism—and as such could not correspond exactly to reality. It is true that he added that, on the other hand, this did not mean that it was a mere fiction, to which position he accuses Schmidt of having tended to regulate it. ("You degrade the law of value to a fiction, a necessary fiction, rather as Kant makes the existence of God a postulate of the practical reason.") But, if it is agreed that the labour theory of value, though not a fiction, is simply a *concept:* an attempt, that is to say, to sum up the baffling, changing, horribly complex characteristics of economic reality, it must stand or fall by its *utility.* It is a tool, a working hypothesis, like any other of the mental tools fashioned by the economists. Both for the early economists and, in its revised form, for Marx, it was an indispensable tool—even though its use led him towards his chief error. But if we ask today how much additional insight the use of this particular tool will give us, can our answer be anything except—"Not much"? Hence, if the reader, noticing the absence of the actual employment of the labour theory of value in these pages, asks how this can be, I must make the same answer as Laplace made to Napoleon when the latter taxed him with the absence of an even more fundamental concept (that of the Deity) from his cosmology. *"Je n'avais pas besoin de cette hypothèse."*

THE CENTRAL MESSAGE

Marx, I repeat, fixed squarely in the foreground of his diagram the above "law," strictly derived from the labour theory of value, that the level of wages would be determined by what it took to "produce" the worker, and not at all by what the worker could produce. It is hardly too much to say that every other part of the huge Marxian diagram follows from this. This is the statement that wages will in all capitalist societies tend towards what is for that time and phase a subsistence level. But society, once it has become truly capitalist, is becoming year by year more and more productive. Therefore, since the workers will get only a constant amount per head (as we shall see, Marx thought that they would in practice get even less), an *ever-growing* surplus must be going to the capitalists.

Marx supports this assertion in the central chapters of Volume I of *Capital* with some elaborate economic reasoning, and equally elaborate historical evidence, designed to show that there will in fact be no tendency for the competitive forces of the market to bid up the price of labour power and so give the wage earners a share in the ever-growing product of society. For, as Marx clearly anticipated they would, his critics have often asked why should not this happen as capitalism developed. Why should not the sheer extension of the system cause a shortage of labour and so, by the workings of the free competitive market itself, raise the level of wages? * It would not happen, Marx wrote, because of two factors. First, natural fertility would be continually increasing the number of workers competing for jobs. (To this extent, in spite of his violent dislike of Malthus and all his theories, Marx agreed that *under capitalism* a rapidly rising population would help to depress the standard of life of the wage earners.) Moreover, Marx held, the number of jobs offered would not increase by any means in proportion to the growth in the size of the system. The sheer piling up of capital would not increase the demand for labour in direct ratio: for less and less labour would be employed per pound of capital used. What Marx called the "composition of capital" would change. In the productive process, in other words, more and more capital in proportion to labour would be used. Therefore the system would grow in size indefinitely without any tendency to produce a labour shortage and so bid up the price of labour power. We may feel that this, too, is a rather elaborate way of stating the familiar proposition that mechanisation tends, other things being equal, to produce unemployment. But again there is no doubt about the reality of the tendency. In spite of the gigantic growth of the system since Marx's day, its besetting characteristic has been unemployment, not labour shortage.

The essential message of *Capital* is, in effect, this: Do what the economists demand: establish perfect competition upon the market as the universal principle of human intercourse upon the economic plane: let all do and all go to your heart's content; you will found no Arcadia of free, equal and fraternal producers exchanging their products, like value for like value, in simple peace and justice. On the contrary, a profound process of social polarisation will set in, by which the

* See p. 178 for a further discussion of this view.

whole of the ever-growing surplus of society will be concentrated in fewer and fewer hands; and by the same process the mass of the population, who once owned small, scattered means of production of their own, will be reduced to dependent wage earners, earning no more than a bare subsistence.

To put the same point diagrammatically, it was as if Marx had drawn a chart of the workings of capitalism, and the result looked like this: The level of wages, or, more broadly, the standard of life of the mass of the population, however derived, is represented by a straight line across the bottom of the paper, at subsistence level. It never rises; indeed, as we shall see, Marx believed that it would actually fall below subsistence. The total national product, on the other hand, is represented by a curve which rises steadily towards the top right-hand corner of the paper as the unparalleled productive power of capitalist society is unfolded. It grows with the rise in the productivity of labour at, in favourable conditions, something like 1½% to 2% per year cumulative. Thus there is an ever-widening and at last immense gap between the two curves. And the width of that gap measures the ever-growing, the at length immense, surplus of society available, either for accumulation or for spending upon luxuries, over and above the subsistence incomes of the mass of the population. It measures what Marx believed to be the finally intolerable and impossible degree of inequality which capitalism would produce.

MARX'S THEORY OF SLUMPS

On the basis of this diagram Marx can account for the salient characteristics of the system. It enabled him, for example, to point towards the final and basic cause of its cyclical crises. Here, he concludes, is the basis for the ten-yearly slumps which interrupt capitalist progress. How could you expect anything else from a system of this character? For if you pile up wealth at one end of the social scale, in the hands of a tiny minority, while holding down the consumption of the rest to a subsistence level, you will continually tend to destroy the market for your final products. The rich will not need, and the workers will not be able to buy, the ever-growing stream of commodities which will emerge upon the market. They will remain unsold and slump will ensue. For a time this can be staved off by the rich accumulating and investing the whole of their surplus, *i.e.,* spending it upon new capital equipment. But in the end you cannot go on making machines to make machines to make machines forever. You are bound to increase your end product of ultimate consumers' goods, and then you will have a slump. For by holding down the workers to subsistence level you will have prevented the possibility of the growth of your own market.

This "crisis theory" of Marx was elaborated with great subtlety and penetration, especially in Vols. II and III of *Capital,* and was an extraordinary technical achievement. It was made long before the economists had any comprehension of these phenomena: while they were still denying the very possibility of such crises of under-consumption. It is true that Marx the politician, the revolutionary, the exile, as opposed to Marx the economist, made the most extreme errors of *timing* in his assessment of the social consequences of capitalist crises. He was convinced that each decennial spasm was the last, the final, the apocalyptic convulsion which would provoke universal revolution. But this was an expression of Marx's human fallibility of judgment when his own passions were engaged. It had little to do with his economic theory. His insight into the cyclical crises of the system will always remain a monument to his economic genius. We shall find that it has not been until the past twenty-five years that orthodox economic science has rediscovered these truths.

MARX'S ACHIEVEMENTS AS AN ECONOMIST

The next chapter is devoted to tracing out the far-reaching consequences of the falsification by events of one of Marx's major predictions. But let us not allow this indispensable task to obscure our recognition of the immense advance which Marx's diagram of capitalist society represented over that of the economists. It will be worth while to attempt to repeat, in summary form, what that achievement was. It is hardly too much to say that, while neither they, nor he, nor perhaps anyone else, has yet succeeded in giving the *answers* to the economic and social problem, Marx alone even asked the right questions. He alone saw that, by the middle of the last century, the task of economic analysis had ceased to be the description of the exchange relations of independent and equal producers upon a competitive market, and the demand that they should be freed from restrictions. He alone saw that henceforward the task of economics was to describe and elucidate the process by which, out of those very exchanges, capital would accumulate at one end of society, and dependent wage earners, who had not the means for independent production, at the other: that what was to matter henceforward was the exchange relationships of the, say, 10% of capital owners, *not with each other, but with the 90% of wage earners.*

There is a graphic passage in the first volume of *Capital* in which Marx describes how the economists had hitherto always stopped at the factory gates, daunted by the notice "No

Admittance Except on Business." * The economists had studied, in a word, the relationship between each independent
capitalist producer. But Marx penetrates within the factory
and studies the hidden process of exchange going on within
its walls. This is the process of the exchange of the workers'
power to labour for the means of subsistence controlled by
the owner. It is Marx's supreme achievement that he focuses
our attention upon his particular act of exchange. By doing
so he is able to give us the first description of the process of
accumulation which is not manifestly a fairy story. He shows
us that the new wealth of the world does not come pouring
in because a few hundred thousand capitalists "wait" or "abstain" from ordering a second Rolls-Bentley or another dozen
of champagne; the new wealth and capital of the world accumulates because the vast mass of the population, now become wage earners, produce much more than they consume.
It is true that this demonstration also has now become, in
one sense, a mere commonplace. Keynes evoked no denials
when he wrote, thirty years ago, that the capitalist world had
been "so framed" that "Labour was not free to consume in
immediate enjoyment the full equivalent of its efforts." But
to become a commonplace without ever being recognised as
a valid discovery is a fate which has overtaken much of
Marx's work.

. . . AND HIS ORIGINAL ERROR

When, however, Marx penetrated the iron curtain of the
factory walls and showed how the process of the accumula-

* "We will follow the owner of money and the owner of labour power into
the hidden foci of production, crossing the threshold of the portal above
which is written: 'No admittance except on business.' Here we shall discover
not only how capital produces, but also how it is itself produced." (Conclusion of Part II, Vol. I, of *Capital*.)

tion of new capital arose out of the process of exchange between the workers and their employers, he concluded that he could lay down a "law" as to the exact terms on which that exchange would take place. And then he fell into what the experience of a hundred years makes it possible to say definitely has turned out to be a crucial error. Or rather, it would be fairer to say, his "law" has turned out to be an account of a *tendency* which truly exists in the system, but which may assert itself or be overridden. It may be overridden, experience indicates, by men themselves taking a hand in the matter and, more or less consciously, using the political institutions which they have established to modify the tendency of the system.

Marx concluded (to restate more precisely the proposition of p. 96 above) that the terms of the exchange between worker and employer would inevitably be such that the wage earner would never get more than enough to sustain his power to work with the required strength and skill (and breed a replacement), however much he produced. He would get no more than a subsistence wage. Marx believed, I repeat, that in a sense he *could*, in capitalist society, get no more than this. For precisely this was the value of his labour power. And prices—in this case the price of labour power—could not widely or for long deviate from value. If they did so, the labour theory of value would be gravely impaired, and that he could not admit.

Or rather—and here we return to those basic issues of value which had so plagued Ricardo—this is what Marx seems to me to have thought with one half of his mind. With one half of his mind he simply applied, perfectly logically, the theory that all things exchange in proportion to the number of hours of socially necessary labour which they contain, to the problem of the determination of wages. On the assumption that this theory is true, there can be no doubt that wages can never substantially depart from a subsistence level.

For the commodity labour power requires the number of man-hours necessary to sustain the labourer and his family, and no more, to produce it. In that case, as we have seen, the whole of the rest of his vast diagram of capitalism follows. But so far we have no proof—only an assumption—that commodities do exchange in proportion to the number of man-hours of socially necessary labour contained in them. Well, do they? If they do so, always and as a law, and without possibility of substantial variation, then the subsistence theory of wages is established without any further need of proof: it is a mere special case of the general theory. In fact, however, as we saw in Chapter 2, all that can really be said is that commodities do tend in the long run and as a rough first approximation to exchange in accordance with the number of man-hours of socially necessary labour contained in them. Far from this being an invariable and fixed law, they neither do so in the short run (because of variation in supply and demand) nor even tend to do so exactly (because of the varying amounts of capital used in their production) in the long run. It seems clear enough that we are concerned with a broad general tendency and not with a fixed law. If this is so, however, it will be necessary to look factually into the question of whether the particular commodity labour power does always, and will always, in fact exchange in proportion to the number of man hours of labour contained in it, or will merely tend to do so if no other influence is brought to bear on it. And with the other half of his mind this is what Marx did. As we have just seen, he devoted a whole series of chapters of *Capital* to the question of whether the real, historical, market forces will hold labour power down to subsistence, and he concludes that they will. But this whole discussion ought to be unnecessary, if, as he has done, he has already assumed that *all* commodities, including labour power, must exchange in proportion to the socially necessary labour time contained in them.

Is not this the basic point at which Marx's thought divides into an inductive, historical, verifiable, scientific element and a deductive, in essence metaphysical, element which makes one major and insufficiently verified assumption and works out everything else upon that basis? For the assumption that all commodities exchange in proportion to the socially necessary labour time contained in them contains in it the conclusion that wages will be at subsistence. And this conclusion is in fact the real basis of Marx's system. Therefore in this sense Marx assumed his basic conclusion from the outset—which is always a help.

When, however, Marx used the other side of his mind and sets out to show that in historical, empirical fact real wages *will* never rise above subsistence, he fares no better than the rest of us when we try to predict. He predicts that population will always grow too fast for there to be a shortage of labour such as will cause what we should call its supply price to be bid up. And he shows that the demand for labour will not rise anything like in proportion to the growth of production, because of mechanisation. These are powerful arguments and we shall be much concerned with them. But they are empirical, historically verifiable issues of fact. And we shall find that, while it is perfectly true that both these factors have exerted, and still exert, a powerful downward pressure on wages, tending to hold them to subsistence, yet they may, at certain times and places, and under certain conditions, be overcome. In particular they have, quite incontrovertibly, been overcome in those advanced latest-stage capitalisms, *operating in a democratic political environment,* with which we are primarily concerned in this volume. On the other hand, at other times, and other places, in other political environments, they have proved decisive and have kept wages at subsistence.

We reach the conclusion that, whether you take the general labour theory of value—the proposition that all com-

modities exchange in proportion to the labour time
contained in them—or the special case (all-important for the
division of the product between classes), that labour-power
exchanges in proportion to the labour time contained in it,
what you obtain is a *tendency,* not a *law.* What you find is
that if nothing else intervenes to override it this tendency
will in fact operate to its logical conclusion: but that in historical fact it can be, and has been at certain times and certain places, overridden.

Naturally this does not make the elucidation of the tendency useless. *In the political and social conditions with which
Marx was alone familiar,* the tendency of wages to a subsistence level was overriding. While they persisted, and in those
parts of the capitalist world in which they still persist (and
they are considerable), these do indeed tend to be the terms
of the exchange between employers and wage earners. But
in the major advanced capitalist societies these political
and social conditions did not in fact persist. And in this new
social and political environment the terms of the exchange
between employers and wage earners have been significantly
modified. They have been modified enough to necessitate a
drastic revision of those all-important economic and political predictions which Marx made upon the assumption that
the standard of life of the wage earners of capitalist societies
could not rise, and must indeed fall.

Marx, then, when he predicted that real wages *could*
never rise above subsistence so long as capitalist relations of
production continued, made an error of the very mechanistic
type against which he was always warning us. He was betrayed by the deductive, anti-empirical strain in his thinking.
He underrated the element of liberty and overrated the element of necessity in man's condition, even within a given social and economic system. His categories were altogether too
hard and fast. Accordingly, what might have been, and indeed still are, if taken critically, marvellously illuminating

elucidations of the tendencies of the system, became errors which have cast gigantic shadows over the world.

APPLICATION TO THE LATEST STAGE

It is now time to link up all this with our initial description of the latest stage of capitalism. By this time it should be apparent that men trained in Marx's analysis of the earlier, competitive stage of capitalism would be likely to "spot," well before anyone else, the salient characteristics of the mutation of the system which we described in Chapter 1. And this is what in fact happened. It was not until the nineteen-thirties that orthodox economic thinking noticed that anything particular was happening to capitalism. And then it was only a small advance-guard, who were decidedly *libres penseurs,* who pointed out the fact that competition itself, the mainspring and regulator of the whole system, was suffering a sea change. The decisive book was probably (at least for Britain) Mrs. Joan Robinson's *The Economics of Imperfect Competition,* published in 1932.* This was a pioneering, severely technical work. Its immense merit was that it proved that the thing had happened and was happening. But it did not attempt to deal with the vast social and political consequences of the mutation.

On the other hand, the Marxists had seen what was happening nearly twenty years earlier. The second generation of Marxist economists—Hilferding, Bukharin, Luxemburg, Bauer, Lenin—began to describe the emergence of what they called either "monopoly capitalism" or "imperialism" at the time of the First World War. They seized on the character of the *particular* distortion which was bound, they were con-

---

* In America, I believe, the corresponding book was Professor Chamberlin's *Theory of Monopolistic Competition* (1932).

vinced, to result from the progressive weakening of competition. They seized on the fact that the immensely increased bargaining power acquired by the oligopolists would, unless something drastic was done about it, worsen still further the relative position of the wage earners and independent producers, such as the farmers. At heart they saw the whole process as merely an intensification of the drive of capitalism as a whole to a more and more "capitalistic" structure. They saw the draining away of purchasing power, and every other kind of power, into fewer and fewer hands so that the exchanges going on in society became less and less exchanges between free and equal independent producers, and more and more exchanges between all-powerful oligopolists, on the one hand, and helpless wage earners and farmers, on the other. They saw the emergence of the oligopolists as, above all, the fulfilment of Marx's forecast of an ever-growing centralisation and concentration of capital in fewer and fewer hands—of that "progressive diminution in the number of the capitalist magnates who usurp and monopolise all the advantages of the transformation process," of whom Marx had written in the thunderous peroration to the first volume of *Capital*. They saw the metamorphosis of competition, and the consequential reinforcement of the bargaining power of the employers, as the collapse of all barriers to the unlimited exploitation of the wage earners, the peasants and, above all, the colonial peoples.

Lenin and his contemporaries were sure that now there would be nothing to prevent the oligopolists, or, as Lenin called them, the monopolists, from driving up their rate of profit indefinitely, and grinding down the workers and peasants both at home and abroad to any degree. And he proceeded from this diagnosis to pursue his well-known argument that this process of ever-increasing exploitation was in the last analysis self-contradictory. For it cut off its own markets by the very act of screwing down the standard of life of the overwhelming majority of the population. Thus it could survive only by means of a process of limitless geographical extension into the underdeveloped world.

We shall devote a later section of this study to this theory, which describes the economic basis of imperialism. Here it is only necessary to notice that such, quite unmodified, is still orthodox communist theory. In 1952, Stalin, in what proved to be his political testament, gave the following characterisation of "monopoly capitalism," or, in our terminology, of the latest stage of capitalism, a characterisation stemming directly from Marx's "law" of subsistence wages:

> Modern capitalism demands not any sort of profit but precisely the maximum profit. That will be the basic economic law of modern capitalism. The main features and requirements of the basic economic law of modern capitalism might be formulated roughly in this way: the securing of the maximum capitalist profit through the exploitation, ruin and impoverishment of the majority of the population of the given country, through the enslavement and systematic robbery of the peoples of other countries, especially backward countries, and, lastly, through wars and militarisation of the national economy, which are utilised for the obtaining of the highest profits.
>
> It is said that the average profit might nevertheless be regarded as quite sufficient for capitalist development under modern conditions. That is not true. The average profit is the lowest point of profitableness below which capitalist production becomes impossible. But it would be absurd to think that in seizing colonies, in subjugating peoples and engineering wars, the magnates of modern monopoly capitalism are striving to secure only the average profit. No, it is not the average profit, nor yet super profit—which as a rule represents only a slight addition to the average profit—but precisely the maximum profit that is the motor of modern monopoly capitalism. (*Economic Problems of Socialism in the U.S.S.R.*, J. Stalin, pp. 43-44. Foreign Languages Publishing House, Moscow, 1952)

All the emphasis in this passage is on the concept of "maximum profit," *i.e.*, on the concept that such barriers as existed in the older, competitive, type of capitalism to unlimited profit making, are now down. Consequently unlimited exploitation can now take place; and this involves the ever-growing impoverishment and ruin of the peoples of both the capitalist states themselves and of their undeveloped colonies.

How extraordinary it is to find that Stalin, in the year 1952, was still assuming that this was what had in fact happened. For, of course, as a description, not of an underlying tendency which must produce disastrous results unless it is counterbalanced, but as a description of what has actually happened in the capitalist world, Stalin's account is grotesque. There is, indeed, a very real measure of truth in saying that "monopoly capitalism" has indulged in "the enslavement and systematic robbery" of the peoples of other countries, although even this is a misstatement of present-day tendencies on balance. But to say that in addition contemporary "monopoly capitalism" secures "the maximum profit . . . through the exploitation, ruin and impoverishment of the majority of the population of the given [*i.e.*, its own] country" is simply flying in the face of the most undeniable facts. In 1952 American "monopoly capitalism," for example, had unquestionably provided the majority of the American people with the highest standard of life ever reached by the human race at any time or in any place (see a later section of this study for an attempt to evaluate this standard.)

How can we hope for sanity in a world in which one of the ablest, and perhaps the most powerful, statesmen then alive flatly asserted that the highest standard of life ever reached by the human race was one of "ruin and impoverishment"? If that had been even remotely true, American "monopoly capitalism" would have been a feeble thing indeed, totally incapable of holding the loyalties of the American people. Moreover, the standard of life achieved in Britain, and even in Western Europe, cannot possibly be called one of "ruin and impoverishment," for, if so, what are we to call the Russian standard which, though rapidly rising,* is still much lower?

One simple explanation of such a statement as Stalin's is, of course, that he did not believe a word of it, but was merely repeating a formula for propaganda purposes. It is to be hoped that this was so, for then, at any rate, his successors will not base their actions on completely false premises. But an unpleasant suspicion remains that Stalin, in this his considered political testament, in which he wrote with evident insight about Russia's own economic problems, really thought that the outside world corresponded to his unbelievably distorted picture of it.† So drastic a breach with reality as that exhibited by this Stalinist description of contemporary capitalism must have a long history behind it. And in fact Stalin's disastrous present-day error, which led him into extreme miscalculations of capitalist strength, undoubtedly arose out of Marx's original error, namely, the prediction that the standard of life of the wage earners could not rise even under the earlier form of capitalism.

Marx's error was in turn consequential upon his acceptance of the labour theory of value, as interpreted by him. Thus the labour theory of value at one and the same time did him great services and grave damage. On the one hand,

---

* Mr. Colin Clark (in a letter to the writer) computes the increase in the Russian real product per man-hour, including agriculture, to have been going on at the rate of some 2% per annum, which, if it proves correct, is quite fast but not sensational.

† It is extremely significant that while these words were being printed, in February, 1956, Mikoyan repudiated Stalin's assessment of contemporary capitalism in this political testament. This was one of the most hopeful things that has ever been said by a leader of the Soviet Union.

it enabled him to avoid the *cul de sac* into which nineteenth-century economics wandered. He had a footrule of some sort, even if a most defective one, with which to attempt the measurement of the different parts of the economy and to assess the division of the social product between classes. But he had no way of measuring the growth of the social product as a whole. And, though his footrule was capable of telling him something approximate about the division of the product, he attempted to get far more clear-cut results from it than it was capable of giving. In this way he came to base a large part of his system on a prediction which has been falsified by events. Before we take up the further study of the latest stage of capitalism it will be necessary to trace out the history of this prediction and of its falsification. For the consequences were immense.

5. ■ THE DOCTRINE OF EVER-

INCREASING MISERY

Marx in fact taught that not only was it impossible for the wage earners to raise their standard of life under capitalism; he went further and announced that their standard must steadily decline. This was the famous "doctrine of ever-increasing misery," or "immiseration," as it is sometimes called. The crucial passages leave no doubt that Marx took this view. It may be sufficient to quote two of them, the one from the great pronouncement of his youth, *The Communist Manifesto*, the second from the work of his maturity, Vol. I of *Capital*.

The Manifesto reads: "The modern labourer . . . instead of rising with the progress of industry, sinks deeper and deeper below the conditions of existence of his own class. He becomes a pauper and pauperism develops more rapidly than population and wealth."

Here an ever-falling standard of life for the wage earners is alone asserted. The peroration of the first volume of *Capital* states both sides of the process of social polarisation which, Marx believed, must be the fundamental effect of a capitalist economic system.

"While there is thus a progressive diminution in the number of the capitalist magnates (who usurp and monopolise all the advantages of this transformative process) there occurs a corresponding increase in the mass of poverty, oppression, enslavement, degeneration and exploitation. . . ."

Thus, not only would there be no improvement in the conditions of the wage earners as total production increased, but capitalism would, as it were, overstep its own normal laws and actually force down the standard of life of the workers below its true value, which was subsistence level; even below the level, that is to say, which would produce "hands" of a really adequate strength, and "brains" of an adequate intelligence to do the work which was then and there required of them. For Marx this, and not any question of cyclical crises or imperialist development, was the heart of the matter. It was the ever-increasing, ever more intolerable, *misery* of the mass of the population which, he was convinced, must and would produce the revolutionary overthrow of capitalism. He says so in the immediately following words of the peroration of Vol. I of *Capital*. ". . . but at the same time there is a steady intensification of the wrath of the working class, unified and organised by the very mechanism of the capitalist method of production."

NATURAL CHARACTER OF MARX'S PREDICTION

This prediction of ever-increasing misery for the wage earners of the major capitalist societies has been falsified. But let us not suppose that in Marx's day it was far-fetched, perverse or contrary to the observable facts. In the London, and still more the Manchester, of the eighteen-forties things must have looked as if they would certainly go this way. We have only to read the contemporary novels, of Disraeli, of Dickens, of George Eliot, or the contemporary Blue Books of the early factory inspectors—and the evidence of these is nowhere better assembled and presented than in the first volume of *Capital*—to see before our eyes the immense, and apparently* ever-increasing horror of the conditions of the wage earners in the early stages of a capitalist society. Nor can there have seemed to be any substantial prospect, short of the overturn of the system, of the wage earners improving their lot. They had no political power. Very few of them in Britain had a vote. The parliamentary system was strictly and admittedly a method by means of which the British capitalists, and the middle class generally, were asserting *their* political power against that of the landlords. Trade unions were few, weak, unsuccessful and persecuted.† Such was the situation in what was then incomparably the most advanced capitalist nation in the world. The conditions of Marx's native Germany, which was both capitalist and backward, were worse still, as he pointed out in the Preface to the first German edition of *Capital*. It is then foolish to blame, in the light of our hindsight, the young Marx for drawing what no doubt seemed obvious conclusions from what he saw about him—and from what, let it not be forgotten, he experienced in his own person.

It would be more reasonable to criticise him for failing to take account of the way in which the situation developed in Britain in the latter part of his life. After all, well before his death in 1883, certain changes, which we can now see to have been decisive, had taken place. The franchise had been extended to wage earners. A steadily growing trade-union movement had been established; consumers' co-operation had become a factor. And in fact the impact of these events can

---

* It may be, as many historians now calculate, that the standard of life of the masses did not really fall, even in the period of early industrialism, from that of the pre-industrial peasants and agricultural workers, which was very low. But as the peasants and craftsmen lost their land and their hand-looms, and so their *independence,* and became helpless wage earners, herded into the slum cities, the impression of ever-growing misery was evidently overwhelming.

† No doubt the growth of population, as well as the political powerlessness of the workers to get a share of what net product there was, was also important.

be traced as an undercurrent in Volumes II and III of *Capital,* and still more in Engels' later pronouncements. But Marx's basic ideas, like most people's, had become fixed in the early part of his life. He was under an inner emotional compulsion to fit the new facts as they arose into his old arraignment of capitalism: for his hatred of the system was consuming. This he did with consummate ingenuity in the two posthumous volumes of *Capital.* But he could not, and would not, revise his system as a whole. For, in addition to his intense emotional resistance to admitting that any improvement in the lot of the workers could possibly be taking place under capitalism, he had "proved," as we have seen, by his application to the labour theory of value to the commodity labour-power, that it would be "unscientific" to suppose that any such improvement, except in the short run and by way of exception, was possible. Marx could not be anything but a nineteenth-century scientist, trying to apply the apparent certainties of nineteenth-century physical science to society. His generation had not learned to be as cautious, as content with approximation, as we have—or at least should have—learned to be. For if such caution is necessary even in the physical sciences, it is a hundred times more necessary still in the social sciences. It may be that the real reason why he was unable to finish *Capital,* his life work, to which, as he wrote, he had sacrificed "his health, his family and his happiness in life," and had to leave it to Engels to put two-thirds of it into anything approaching a finished form, was because of the unresolved conflict which the unexpected development of capitalism in the second half of the nineteenth century produced in him.

Be that as it may, let us not doubt for a moment that, *if* the economy had developed as Marx thought it must, that if the standard of life of the wage earners as a whole *had* steadily dropped below the level of the eighteen-forties, instead of having steadily risen, as it did, then his political predictions must have proved correct. There must have been a revolutionary explosion, above all in Britain, well before the end of the nineteenth century. There must have been such an explosion not only because of the ever-growing horror which would have resulted from the workers' conditions worsening from those of the eighteen-forties, but also because the system would in that case have become unworkable for lack of even the minimum necessary consuming power. If Marx had been right in his prediction of an ever-dropping standard of life for the immense majority of the population, no practicable degree of outward, geographical expansion could have saved it from breakdown for lack of anything like an adequate market for its products. The depressions of the late nineteenth century would have known no periods of recovery; mass unemployment (which did periodically appear) would have grown uninterruptedly; the system could not have continued to function. On his own hypothesis, then, Marx was perfectly justified in his prediction of approaching breakdown. Moreover, as we shall see, he was right in his diagnosis of the basic tendency of a system which concentrates the ownership of almost all society's means of production in the hands of some 10% of the population. Such a system does undoubtedly *tend* to reserve for these owners the whole of its increase in wealth. What was it, then, which in the event overrode this tendency and so disproved Marx's essential prediction of ever-increasing misery?

THE IRON LAW OF WAGES AND TWENTIETH-CENTURY COMMUNIST TACTICS

Before answering that question, we should first notice, however, one important political corollary of Marx's fundamental position, a corollary which at once became apparent. If wages, and the general standard of life of the mass of the population, can in no circumstances be pushed up under capitalism, but must, on the contrary, decline into ever-increasing misery, what is the use of trade unions and of the labour movement generally? Marx had said unequivocally that there was a "law" which decreed that while capitalism existed the wage earner must, inevitably, "sink deeper and deeper below the conditions of existence of his own class"; that there must inevitably be an *increase* in the "mass of poverty, enslavement, degeneration and exploitation." And he defined "the natural laws of capitalist production" as "tendencies which work out with iron necessity towards an inevitable goal." (Preface to the first German edition of *Capital*.)

What good was it, then, to organise trade unions or political labour movements in order to attempt the inherently impossible task of pushing up the standard of life of the wage earners? No sooner had Marx made it clear, in *The Communist Manifesto*, that this was his basic view than the most brilliant of those who were influenced by him, Ferdinand Lassalle, asked this question. Moreover, Lassalle answered it by announcing his "iron law of wages," and led a large section of the German labour movement on a policy which had the impossibility of improving working-class standards of life under capitalism as its principal tenet.

Much to his astonishment, Lassalle drew down upon himself the thunder of Marx's denunciation for drawing this, after all, very natural conclusion. In spite of the doctrine of increasing misery, it was utterly wrong, Marx pronounced, to belittle trade unionism or the demand for "partial" political reforms such as factory acts, limitation of hours and the like. On the contrary, said Marx, the young labour movement must largely concentrate on such demands. How did Marx reconcile this eminently sensible view with the doctrine of ever-increasing misery?

He did so on two levels, as it were. At the more super-
ficial level he made exceptions. While, he said, it remained
true that the overriding "law" of capitalism was that the
workers must sink deeper and deeper into ever-increasing
misery, that did not mean that well-organised workers might
not win particular battles over particular wage claims or particular political demands at a given time and place. Nor was
there anything illogical in such an admission of exceptions to,
and possible arrests in, the operations of an overriding law.
Only this by itself was not a very encouraging doctrine for
the workers! They were told, in effect, that by the most
heroic endeavours at organisation they might here or there
check, or even momentarily reverse, the operation of the main
laws of capitalist development, which were inexorably thrust-
ing them deeper and deeper into misery and starvation. If
this was all that Marx had had to say, it would have been
rather as if a general had told his troops to fight and die, for
they might win a battle or two here and there, but of course
nothing they could do could possibly prevent them from
losing the war.

But this was by no means all that he had to say. He had a
justification of his position at a much deeper level. The real
reason why both trade-union and political organisation of
the working class were vitally important was not that they
might make small gains here and there, and temporarily,
within the capitalist system. Their real importance was that
such organisations prepared the workers for their true task,
which was the revolutionary overthrow of capitalism. The
passage which immediately follows the words from the peroration of Volume I of *Capital* which have just been quoted
makes this clear. The working class, Marx goes on, is to be
"unified and organised" for the purpose of overthrowing the
system.

Thus for Marx it was quite logical to hold that the workers
would inevitably be thrust lower and lower into ever-in-

creasing misery and yet passionately to support their every effort at organisation. For, in spite of the fact that these efforts could not, on the whole, win immediate advantages, they were anything but futile. They were the great school in which the workers developed their power to overturn the system itself. The workers, he taught in effect, could not as a class gain anything without gaining everything; but they *would* gain everything in the end, and so even their "partial struggles" were supremely worth while, if not to them, then to their successors. It was a perfectly logical view on the basis of its major premise that the workers could not make substantial gains until capitalism was overthrown. But in fact that premise has proved to be the most important error in Marx's whole system of thought and prediction. And, as its premise has proved to be an error, his theory of trade unionism has had, and still has, disastrous consequences for all those who have accepted the Marxist tradition.

Here is a second instance (in addition to Stalin's profound misappreciation of contemporary capitalism) of this apparently obscure theoretical controversy of the nineteenth century having profound practical consequences in our own times. All those who have accepted Marx's system of thought as a whole, and that means essentially today the communists, have naturally accepted his approval of the trade-union and political organisation of the workers also. They vehemently support the principle of trade-union and political organisation. But they do not do so from the same point of view as that of the ordinary working men and women who create and maintain these organisations. The wage earners of the major capitalist societies, Britain, America and Germany, have built powerful trade unions and have, by one means or another, exerted an ever-growing political influence. But they have done so simply and directly in order to get better wages, shorter hours, social services, etc., etc., in order precisely to improve their here-and-now standard of life. And, never having heard of the doctrine of ever-increasing misery, they have had the temerity actually and substantially to improve it. It has never crossed their minds that what they were really doing was merely to school and steel themselves for the revolution. They have cared passionately about the concrete, financial outcome of each partial struggle, each strike, each political agitation, and have only been willing to engage in them when they considered that they had substantial prospects of success.

The communists, on the other hand (reproducing faithfully Marx's exact attitude), while pouring their enthusiasm into all such struggles, have had what was at bottom a very different approach. They have never believed in the possibility of substantial or permanent gains within capitalism;* they have always felt that what really mattered was not the exact outcome of the particular strike, but its educative effect on the workers. This basically different attitude has often led, and still leads, the communists, in spite of their extraordinary enthusiasm, ardour and self-sacrifice, to prove them-

* If the reader supposes that this is an exaggeration, he should turn to the report of the Congress of the communist-dominated French trade unions, the C.G.T., in the summer of 1955, where the doctrine of ever-increasing misery is solemnly reaffirmed and the non-communist delegates who expressed doubts of it are as solemnly condemned. The London *Times'* report refers to "a sudden public disagreement between communist and non-communist union leaders as to whether the working classes must be considered (in accordance with strict communist doctrine) to be condemned to 'progressive pauperisation' so long as the capitalist system survives, or whether by energetic trade-union action they can improve their lot."

The *Times* correspondent points out that, while it is "almost certainly" not the case that immiseration has taken place, yet this is by no means so obvious in France as in Britain or America. This, however, "was not in fact the question at issue."

"The point on which discussion has been raging in the various newspapers for ten weeks past is how the working class can be expected to take an interest in strike movements or social agitation if so much insistence is placed on the fact that it is condemned to 'inevitable pauperisation' whatever happens." (Report of the Thirtieth Annual Congress of Confederation Générale du Travail. *Times*, June 13, 1955.)

selves disastrously incompetent leaders for the trade unions. At its worst their attitude leads to a criminal frivolity in calling strikes, demonstrations, political agitations, etc., in the conviction that every strike, no matter what its outcome, will always do good. And, even at its best, the communist attitude leads to a failure to look single-mindedly at the actual interests of the workers concerned, to a concentration upon long-term political objectives to which the strikers themselves may be indifferent, and to which they are often sacrificed. In my experience it is this flaw in the basic attitude of the communists to the contemporary struggle of working-class organisations which has alone prevented them from acquiring dominating positions in the trade-union movement. This is a remarkable example of how a theoretical error in the evaluation of historical development may affect the course of social struggles over a long period.

WHAT HAS IN FACT HAPPENED?

Let us now return to a consideration of the extent to which Marx's prediction of ever-increasing misery has been falsified, and of the reasons for its falsification. The fact is that the standard of life of the wage earners of the advanced capitalist societies has risen, not fallen. It is very difficult to measure the amount of the rise; different explanations can be given as to its cause, but the *fact* of the rise is a matter of common observation.

That is one side of the picture. And, of course, all the supporters of capitalism have no difficulty in seeing *it!* On the contrary, they dismiss, on the strength of it, not only this, but all the rest of Marx's predictions as not worth the paper they were written on. They proceed gaily upon the assumption that there is no tendency, even, in capitalism towards holding wages to a minimum and reserving the whole of the ever-growing surplus for the owners, to spend or to accumulate. Marxists, on the other hand, have either, by a prodigy of inattention, averted their gaze from the whole matter, or have excelled themselves in special pleading to explain away this scandalous deviation of reality from Marx's theory. Neither party has been willing to look directly at what the real development has been. And so the Marxists and their bitterest critics alike have both failed to be wise, even after the event.

The real development, however, has been by no means simple. It may be useful to summarise in advance the main features of what our examination will show it to have been. First, then, the standard of life of the wage earners has risen considerably in the advanced capitalist societies. But these societies, even taken together, comprise only a small part of the capitalist world. They exhibit certain special features, not found elsewhere, or found to a much smaller degree. Shift your attention from them to the capitalist and pre-capitalist world as a whole and the picture is different. It becomes a matter of argument whether the standard of life of the people (they are not most of them wage earners) has or has not risen. Moreover, even within the advanced capitalist societies closer examination reveals some highly significant phenomena. It is not really that the standard of life of the wage earners "has risen"—such a phrase seems to imply some automatic process, built into the system itself. What has really happened is, on the contrary, that the wage earners, by political and trade-unionist efforts, sustained over a century, have *forced up* their standards of life in the teeth of the economic tendencies of the system. Anything less automatic than the real process cannot be imagined.* Far from the rise

* The apparent exception is America in the second half of the nineteenth century. There the wage earners' standard of life undoubtedly rose while trade unionism remained weak. But is not this accounted for, first, by the

being due to the automatic operation of capitalism, it has
been imposed upon the system by sheer political and trade-
union power, in the face of the most determined opposition,
both practical and theoretical. Moreover, when you examine
the matter you find that measures, which everybody thought
would drastically increase the wage earners' share in the
national income, have done little more than enable them to
hold their own, and so rise about in step with the general rise
in wealth. The more you look into the matter, the clearer it
becomes that there does exist such a tendency as Marx described. His predictions would have been justified, instead of
falsified, by the event if only he had been content to diag-
nose a tendency instead of an irreversible "law." Capitalism,
if it had functioned automatically according to the orthodox
economists' text books, instead of being faced with the
"countervailing power" of a labour movement, would indeed
have tended to reserve the whole increase in wealth to a
small class of owners. *But this tendency has been overruled,
in the advanced capitalist societies, but not elsewhere, by essentially non-economic forces, the existence of which Marx
overlooked.*

---

existence of free land? By taking up free land an American wage earner
could at any time escape right out of the capitalist system, as it were, back
into the world of "small commodity production." And, second, the *political*
pressure exercised by the American wage earners, and more especially by the
American farmers, during the whole period was far from negligible. After
all, America, and America alone, possessed fairly effectively functioning
democratic institutions (in the twentieth-century sense—see Chapter 8 below) during the whole period.

6 ∎ MEASUREMENT, VALUE AND THE LIMITS OF ECONOMICS

Of the list of assertions made at the end of the last chapter, the basic one is that the standard of life of the wage earners in the advanced capitalisms has risen, instead of fallen. It might be thought that this was a simple and straightforward assertion which could be easily demonstrated by unchallenged facts and figures. In fact, however, it opens up a difficult and controversial question—namely, the measurement of economic magnitudes: a question that raises not only baffling economic but also sociological, and indeed philosophical, issues.

A brief inspection of these issues will enable us to do two things. We shall contrast the hypothesis that value can and must be measured in man-hours of socially necessary labour with the methods used by those contemporary economic statisticians who, with the Keynesians, and the elucidators of imperfect competition, form the three schools of thought which are building up (rather tardily) an economics of latest-stage capitalism. Second, a discussion of these issues will force us to consider the scope and limits of economics itself—in both its Marxian and its orthodox form.

STANDARDS OF LIFE

Economic statisticians are accustomed to estimate that the standard of life of the British wage earners has more than doubled since Marx's day. (Mr. Colin Clark says about three-fold since 1850.) The more we examine this estimate, however, the more approximate we shall conclude that it must be. Perhaps it would be safest to say that the rise has been somewhere between two and four times—all according to the way you look at things. And when this degree of approximation is admitted even in regard to his own country, it may be best for a British writer to say no more about other countries than that some such rise has evidently also taken place in the two other really advanced capitalist societies, in America a greater rise (Clark estimates three-and-one-half-fold): and in Germany, a similar rise (Clark estimates three-fold). But why, it will be asked immediately, need we be so vague?

It is in this connection that we must complete our discussion of the labour theory of value. For it is when we face the problems of measuring or comparing such economic magnitudes as standards of life or gross national products that we shall, above all, miss that "footrule liable neither to expand nor to contract" for which the dying Ricardo sought in vain. For if only we possessed such a footrule of absolute value we could, of course, confidently measure off our economic quantities with it. But the only units of absolute value which have ever been suggested, namely, man-hours of socially necessary labour time, are quite inapplicable for these purposes. Whatever else you can do with them, you cannot measure the total gross national product or the current standard of life in terms of man-hours of socially necessary labour-time. (For, if you try to do so, you will have no way of expressing the rise in the productivity of labour: and this is a *reductio ad absurdum.* For rising productivity is perhaps the biggest single factor in the whole calculation.) Accordingly, we shall be driven back onto the use of those statistical methods for the estimation of such magnitudes which, as we saw, are now being used increasingly. Nevertheless, we must not underestimate the difficulty of the problem which faces the contemporary economic statisticians, nor the partial nature of their success in solving it.

CAN WE MEASURE SATISFACTIONS? *

At first sight there is no great difficulty. A wage earner used to be paid, say, £2 a week. Now he is paid £8 a week. He is four times as well off? But the value of money may in the meanwhile have been halved. Still only the simplest arithmetic seems to be required to see that he is, on balance, twice as well off as before. It is by no means so simple. The catch is in that phrase "the value of money," for here is value turning up again. And we have formed no clear idea of what value is. Obviously, what we have got to compare is not the amounts of money which the wage earners get, for money may change drastically in value, or even become valueless; what we have to compare is "what the money will buy." Now what the wage earner's money will buy each week is at first sight a heap of commodities. You can envisage the heap, sitting on the kitchen table. The pictorial statisticians will draw the heap for you in one of their pretty coloured charts showing so many loaves, so many potatoes, so many vegetables, so much meat, butter or margarine, such and

* The reader who is interested in the basic theoretical issue as it appears to orthodox economists is referred to Professor Robertson's graceful essay, *Utility and All That.* (Allen & Unwin, 1952.)

such a supply of clothes, such and such an entry in the rent book, so much fuel—the regular family budget.

Well, then, is what we mean by a doubling of the wage earner's standard of life that this heap shall get twice as big? Two loaves for one, four lbs. of margarine instead of two, twice as much meat, twice as much fuel? At the very lowest standard of life of all, at real subsistence level, no doubt that is approximately what we do mean. Give the very poorest of the poor more money and they will, on the whole, simply buy more of the bare necessities of life. But at even a slightly higher standard of life than that the first complications begin to appear. A poor family gets better off. They will spend the extra money for the most part on food. But not on the *same* foods as before. They will buy more meat and, say, butter instead of margarine. At a certain not very high level, experience shows, they will begin to buy *less* potatoes; a little further up the scale they will begin to buy less bread. They will now be getting their nourishment in the better, more attractive, more expensive form of eggs, butter, meat, milk, etc. Clearly comparisons are beginning to get a little more complicated. The heap of commodities has begun to change not only in size but in kind, to change in quality as well as in quantity. We are not quite comparing like with like any more.

However, the statisticians and economists can easily cope with this degree of complication. If this was all there was to worry about, it would be the merest pedantry to suggest that there was any real difficulty in measuring and comparing people's standards of life at different times and places. But this is only the very beginning of the complications. Raise the level some more. Now the extra money is by no means all spent on more food, drink, clothing, shelter, heat, light, power. At a very modest standard of life, at a standard well below the actual present-day (1956) standard of most of the

British wage earners, there appear in the heap of commodities such things as amusements, entertainment, travel, education, "hair do's," and all the endless (but endless) rest of it; there appear, in a word, the almost innumerable "objects of expenditure," as the economists call them, which quite ordinary people do in fact buy.

At this level the two heaps of commodities which we have got to compare really begin to look complicated. In fact, our whole concept of a "heap" of material objects is getting strained. Take, for example, one of the most important elements in the increase in the standard of life of the British wage earners since Marx's day: the provision of educational facilities. Remember that up to and beyond the publications of the first volume of *Capital* the British state provided no educational facilities at all for the children of British wage earners, who were consequently for the most part illiterate. And compare that with, first, the universal free elementary education effectively provided by the end of the nineteenth century, and, second, with the elaborate, complex, by no means wholly satisfactory, but extensive range of opportunities for primary, secondary and higher education available to the children of British wage earners today. Compare them, I repeat; but how? In order to compare two magnitudes it is usually supposed that you must be able to measure them. How are we to measure one "heap" of educational facilities and say it is larger than another? A heap of educational facilities is not a very convincing image. At this level we begin to see that the difficulties of measuring relative standards of life are real enough.

We have got to face the awkward fact that commodities consist not only in material objects, but in what the economists call "satisfactions," namely, anything which satisfies a human want. As Marx says in the very first paragraph of the first volume of *Capital,* a commodity is something which satisfies a want, whether that want "arises in the stomach or in the imagination." (Thus the sillier amongst Marx's critics, who continue to allege that he was a crude or naïve kind of materialist, would confound themselves if they read even his first page: which may be why they never do.) So what we have really got to compare is the "heap," or total, of "satisfactions," material and non-material, obtainable by one man in one period of time, say, 100 years ago, with that obtainable by another man in another period, say, today. Or, alternatively, we have to compare the total of satisfactions obtained by one man in a given country today with another man in another country today. Now we begin to see the full extent of the complications. What we really have to compare are "satisfactions"; but satisfactions are subjective things; they are states of mind. How, then, can one possibly compare one man's subjective satisfactions with another's? For one man's drink is proverbially another man's poison. Are people really happier for having hair-do's or learning quadratic equations? Or, again, what is the answer to the old Oxford "Greats" question: "Could a man be happy on the rack?" It will be recalled that the hopeful examinee's reply was that a man *could* be happy on the rack, but that it would have to be "a very good man on a very bad rack." Such an answer nicely illustrates the fact that both subjective states and objective commodities have qualitative as well as quantitative differences and the consequent difficulties of measuring them.

Some of those present-day economists who maintain the theoretical position described in Chapter 3 say flatly, but perfectly logically from their point of view, that it *is* impossible to compare one man's satisfactions with another's, because it is impossible to measure either of them. And they face—as a matter of fact, they are eager to face—the full consequences of this declaration of impotence. It is impossible, they claim, to say that one man in one period is "better off" than another man in another period. In the same way they hold that it is impossible to say that one man in one

country is better off than another man in another country at
the same period. It is impossible, they claim, to compare
the standards of life of different persons over either time or
space. And, they continue, if it is impossible to compare the
standards of life of individuals, it is *a fortiori* impossible to
compare the standards of life of groups or classes, again
either over time or space. Therefore it is quite impossible to
say that the people of any country, say, America, are richer
or poorer than the people of any other country, say, India,
at the same time; or that the people of a given country, say,
Britain, are richer or poorer than they were at some earlier
period. On this recently fashionable view, both Marx's prediction of ever-increasing misery and the assertion that, on
the contrary, the standard of life of the wage earners of the
main capitalist states has risen over the past 100 years are, of
course, meaningless statements. (For a full dissection of this
view see Chapters II and III of *The Socialist Case* by the Rt.
Hon. Douglas Jay, Faber and Faber.)

The thing to notice about the above view is its remarkable
convenience for those who do not *want* to make such comparisons. If you find that your economic system is under attack because it gives people such extremely unequal standards of life, according to whether they are wage earners or
employers, or according to what country they live in, what a
wonderful discovery it is to be able to say that, "really" no
one can be said to be any better off than anyone else, that
no country is richer or poorer than any other, because, after
all, you cannot measure standards of life at all. What a
triumph! Such a majestic denial of the possibility of making
comparisons is obviously far more effective than arguing
that the inequality is not so great after all or than justifying
it by saying that it promotes accumulation. Far better to
dismiss the whole attack at one stroke by declaring that it is
all based upon the "elementary fallacy" that you can com-

pare satisfactions. Such a dismissal has, to be sure, the trifling disadvantage that it makes talking or thinking about
economics almost completely pointless. But for the economists in question that disadvantage is far more than balanced by the fact that it also makes any attempt to modify
the system equally pointless. For, of course, if it is impossible
to tell whether anyone is better off than anyone else, there is
no point whatever in trying to alter their conditions. What a
serviceable discovery!

To push the argument as to the incommensurability of
satisfactions to its logical conclusion leads, then, to a manifest *reductio ad absurdum.* But this does not solve our problem. How *can* we measure or compare educational facilities,
hair-do's, loaves of bread and pounds of butter? How can
we make heaps of these utterly different kinds of satisfactions
and compare the size of the heaps? Is not the answer to the
dilemma that we can *compare* these things, even if we cannot accurately *measure* them? Even if we cannot find a common, quantitative unit in terms of which to measure the size
of aggregates of the diverse satisfactions which *are* the
commodities of contemporary life, we may nevertheless be
able roughly to compare their magnitudes. At any rate, we
seem in practice to be able to do so. We may not clearly
know what we are doing when we add up into a money
total the list of satisfactions obtainable by a British worker
paid the representative British wage in 1956, then add up
the list of satisfactions obtainable by a representative British
wage earner in 1856, also into a money total, correct the two
totals for changes in "the price level" and then compare
their magnitudes. We do not know what we are doing,
since this process of correction for changes in "the price
level" by means of an "index number" itself consists of comparing the money unit (pound or dollar) with a list of the
prices of certain representative commodities or satisfactions.

(It is rather as if a draper first measured off his material with his footrule and then measured off the footrule with the material.)

Nevertheless, and in spite of these logical deficiencies, the calculations which have resulted from these queer statistical goings-on do appear to be meaningful. For instance, when we say that a 1956 representative British wage earner commands over £2 worth of commodities or satisfactions for every £1 worth commanded by an 1856 representative British wage earner, in pounds of constant value, we do seem to be making a meaningful statement. No doubt there are all sorts of philosophical "inarticulate major premises" lurking behind our statement. No doubt we are assuming that command over double the amount of commodities does give more satisfactions, *i.e.*, does make people happier. But at the standards of life in question this appears, to me at least, to be an incontrovertible assumption. For if it is not so why do people make such gigantic efforts to increase their command over commodities? Indeed, it is the assumption upon which all economic life is based.

In practice, then, rough-and-ready comparisons of standards of life are as possible as they are manifestly indispensable; they are possible so long as we do not try to make them exact. We are in this matter about at the stage of savages who can look at three peaks of a mountain range and say, with fair assurance, that peak A is higher than peak B, but lower than peak C, although they have no means of measuring the height of any of them. But, of course, we must only expect very broad and approximate results from such methods. It is possible to say that the heap or list of commodities acquired each week by a representative British wage earner is today larger, not smaller, than it was in Marx's day. It will be useful to make rough estimates of the degree to which it is larger, *i.e.*, that it is two and one-half times larger, in the sense that it is not just a little larger nor yet again twenty times as large.* But, if we begin trying to get such comparisons down to exact figures, if we attempt to say that one heap is 69.5% as large as the other, we shall soon be talking nonsense. That is why it is necessary to be vague.

Moreover, it will manifestly be much easier to compare the "heaps of satisfactions" enjoyed by people of the same sort living in similar environments, for they will tend to acquire similar heaps. Quite good approximate measurements of the comparative satisfactions of contemporary wage earners in, say, Britain and America may be possible, for their ways of life are relatively similar. In the same way, we may be able to do fairly well with comparisons between the standards of life of, for instance, British wage earners now and in the relatively recent past—up to 100 or 150 years ago. So long as the lists of satisfactions are generally similar, the simple money totals of income, merely corrected for changes in the price level, will not serve too badly. But if we go further afield either in space or time: if we try comparing the standard of life of American wage earners with South Sea Islanders or contemporary Britons with mediaeval villains, we must be content with the very roughest approximations, for their respective ideas of satisfactions are and were so very different.

USE WHAT UNITS YOU CAN

We are now in a position to realise how much was lost when the dying Ricardo had to abandon the quest for absolute

---

* There is a further complication. As soon as we reckon in "satisfactions," it will not do merely to measure different gross or net national products *per capita*, even if we consider that we are able to do so. The gross and net national product may be made to grow by methods so Draconian that total satisfactions may undeniably decrease simultaneously, *e.g.*, the British enclosures or the First Soviet Five Year Plan.

value. For, I repeat, if either he or Marx, or anyone else, *had* been able to find "absolute value," *i.e.*, some one measurable thing in the units of which we could reckon off all economic magnitudes, why, then the root problems of economic science would have been solved at one stroke. But, since the labour-time footrule is unable, as we have seen, to measure an increase in the national product by means of an increase in the productivity of labour, we must use the methods of the contemporary economic statisticians in spite of all their difficulties.

It would be hasty, however, to conclude from this that man-hours of socially necessary labour-time are a worthless unit of measurement for all purposes. They will not give us meaningful totals of such magnitudes as the gross national product. But for the purpose of throwing light upon the social *distribution* of the national product they may be useful. Mrs. Robinson, for example, writes that for some purposes one should take money and for other purposes man-hours as one's unit of measurement. "But if you cannot use money, what unit of value do you take? A man-hour of labour-time. It is the most handy and sensible measure of value, so naturally you take it. You do not have to prove anything, you just do it." (*On Re-reading Marx*, p. 23.)

This sturdy British empiricism seems justified. The chief use of the man-hours unit of calculation will be to throw light on the distribution of a given product among the different classes. For here the absolute magnitude of the total will not be the essential matter; and it is true that the total has been exclusively formed by, and *in that sense* is exclusively formed of, man-hours of socially necessary labour. It is valid, therefore, to say that if the rent, interest and profit (the unearned income) taken from the national product at any given time amounts to, say, 20% of the total, then those who work by hand and brain do 80% of their work for them-

selves and 20% for the recipients of this unearned income.*
But for the purpose of adding up the total national product,
or any part of it, such as the part which forms the standard
of life of the population, we are driven back upon a money
total with all its deficiencies.

Thus we reach the conclusion that when the economic
statisticians add up their totals—whether of gross national
product or of the national standard of life or of their other
economic magnitudes—they are doing so in terms of unknown units. They are adding up "we-don't-know-quite-
whats" and hoping that they will form a meaningful quantity. But is this really so shocking a proceeding as it seems at
first sight? Would it seem as shocking to contemporary physical scientists as it would, no doubt, have seemed to the physical scientists of 100 years ago? After all, do not contemporary
physical scientists spend much of their time successfully manipulating quantities of more or less unknown substances?
Without speaking of the nuclear fields, is this not true even of
such an everyday, domestic matter as electricity? We base
our economy on electrical power, we measure it off in various
kinds of units, but the physical scientists still cannot give us
an answer if we ask them what electricity is. Is it not the
same with value? Perhaps the real way of arriving at a true
understanding of the nature of value is precisely to go on
manipulating our quantities (whatever they may be) and
seeing to what extent the results turn out to be meaningful
and to have predictive power. We shall never find any such
thing as absolute or intrinsic value, or "the substance of
value," for it turns out that value is purely social, *i.e.*, a
relationship between people rather than a relationship between things. As a matter of fact, Marx himself declared that
value was "a non-material property . . . something the real-

* Though, of course, these recipients may have usefully accumulated, instead
of wastefully consumed, much of this 20%.

ity of which is exclusively social." (*Capital*, Vol. I, p. 28 of the Eden and Cedar Paul translation; see also *Value, Price and Profit*, p. 43 of the Allen and Unwin 1953 edition.) Unfortunately, however, he usually, though not always, treated value as if it were "composed" of man-hours of socially necessary labour-time, just as a Newtonian scientist thought of matter as composed of hard, "billiard ball" atoms.

We have now come back to the questions which so troubled Ricardo. For what contemporary statisticians are doing is what Ricardo thought of attempting in his letter to McCulloch of June 13th, 1820 (see footnote p. 60 above). He there suggests that the theory of the distribution of the national product might be independent of the theory of value. But to make use of that suggestion would have meant finding some unit other than man-hours of labour in terms of which to work out his magnitudes. And how was Ricardo to do that, long before the problem of average prices expressed by index numbers could be effectively tackled either in theory or practice? As a matter of fact Ricardo (Mr. Sraffa informs us) some years before he wrote the *Principles* had attempted something of the sort. In his *Essay on the Influence of a Low Price of Corn on the Profits of Stocks,* he proposed, in effect, to take corn as the single commodity in the units of which everything is to be reckoned. He does so because, he suggests, in the overwhelmingly important case of agriculture, corn is *both* the product of the whole process *and* the stuff in which real wages are paid. Thus by simply deducting the number of bushels of corn which the farmer must pay to his labourers from his total harvest, we can get his gross profit. If then we can reckon how much of this gross profit he will have to pay away to his landlord, we have got a theory of the distribution of the national product—and got it without all the headaches of a theory of value.

We can only comment that *if* the entire economy were devoted to producing and consuming corn and nothing else, this would indeed be the solution of the problem. Malthus soon knocked Ricardo off this theory by pointing out that even the agricultural labourers of their day got paid some sugar and some clothes, etc., as well as corn. Nevertheless, and however drastic were the simplifications of Ricardo's "corn-ratio" theory, as Mr. Sraffa calls it, it was the germ of the index number method which everyone now uses. That method does not get over all the difficulties any more than does the "corn-ratio" theory or the labour theory of value. What we can say about it is that it seems worth trying out.

In any case it is far more agreeable to the British empirical tradition to try the thing out even before we fully understand it, and as a means of getting to understand it, than to let ourselves be baffled by what may well turn out to be a largely verbal problem. The use of modern statistical methods can scarcely give worse results, after all, than the two other approaches which are available. To deny, as the more extreme of the orthodox economists do, that standards of life are commensurable leads to blank reaction under the guise of scientific scrupulousness. (It leads, for example, to the perfect *reductio ad absurdum* that unemployment cannot exist.) On the other hand, to attempt to use the Ricardian-Marxian conception of man-hours of socially necessary labour leads both to inability to discuss the rise in the productivity of labour and to the dogmatic assertion that wages can never rise above subsistence. To follow the economic statisticians may be to rely upon a logically indefensible position. But if the use of their methods begins to show results, the logic will surely look after itself in the end. In fact our experience as to what the results will be of the statistical measurement of economic magnitudes, and the efforts at the control of the economy which are based upon it, is still short. But it is not unpromising.

The real difficulties of its application are not logical but political. The Ricardian-Marxian use of man-hours of socially necessary labour-time as the unit of calculation led to an almost exclusive concentration upon the distribution of the national product among the different social classes. For their methods were apt for that purpose alone. The concentration of the men of the marginal-utility school and their successors on the fluctuations of price led towards a disregard of both the total size of the national product and its division among the social classes. For their methods were unable adequately to display either factor. Today's statistical methods have led in practice to a concentration of attention upon the size and growth of the national product, at the expense of attention to its division among the social classes. For, although these methods are suitable to the display of both magnitudes, they have been used on the whole by the majority of their discoverers and developers for the former, and more respectable, as against the latter, and more radical, purpose. In the hands of the most "right wing" of those who use the new methods, the doctrine preached has almost been that, if one looked after the growth of the national product, its distribution would look after itself. For this reason a revival of interest in the object of study of the founding fathers of the science, namely, social distribution, is now appropriate, even if we abandon their traditional tool of the labour theory of value and try out the new statistical methods.

Which factor matters most, the size of the gross national product or its distribution among the different social classes? Can we possibly give any other answer to this question than the platitudinous one that both factors are enormously important? To the wage earner what matters is the size of his real income—his slice of the cake which is being cut up at the national tea party. But obviously the size of that slice can be increased either by the existing cake being cut up more equitably, or by a larger cake being cut up in the same proportions, or by any combination of the two methods. Moreover, we shall find that the matter is more complicated than that. There is no doubt that the speed at which the national product grows is bound up with the question of how equally or unequally it is cut up. The advocates of a more equitable distribution believe that more equal slices will make the cake grow all the quicker; the advocates of unequal slices believe exactly the reverse. We shall be much occupied with this matter, both in this and later sections of the study. It is perhaps the most practically important economic question of the mid-twentieth century. We shall find that no simple answer, such as that a more equitable distribution will tend to increase (or decrease) the total to be divided will suffice. One policy of distribution will have one effect in certain conditions, over the short run, at certain times, and the opposite effect in other conditions, in the long run, and at other times. The social and political environment, "the climate of opinion," and other non-economic factors may well be decisive in this extremely important matter.

CAN ECONOMICS BE TRANSCENDED?

These considerations will cause us to question whether economics can ever be a true science in and by itself. We shall be increasingly inclined to conclude that economics will turn out to be merely one aspect of an all-embracing, but as yet embryonic, science of society as a whole. Many of the most disastrous miscalculations, both of the orthodox economists and of the Marxians, have arisen from pursuing theorems with inflexible logic in social and political environments to which they no longer apply. (That is why the expression of economic views by a layman like myself, who can attempt to mate such economic knowledge as he has with fairly varied experiences as a working politician, may not be useless.)

We cannot acquit the Marxists, also, of failure to re-integrate adequately their necessary abstractions of economic theory with the complexities of an ever-changing social and political environment. Yet Marx did make an attempt—and a heroic one at that—to do just this. Marxism is a first attempt at a sociological method of analysis, or system, of which economic theory is merely one part. Marx came to economics via philosophy and the theory of history. His economics were, above all, the application of general sociological thinking to the particular environment, namely, early capitalism, which he saw around him. The three volumes of *Capital* are in a sense no more than a huge "particular case" of the much more generalised view of the world which he had put forward, very briefly, as a younger man in *The Communist Manifesto*, the preface to *The Critique of Political Economy*, and which he continued to exemplify in his historical pamphlets. This was Marx's "vision" of the nature of human society in Schumpeter's sense of that term. *Capital* was the attempt to "arm" that vision with analytic proofs, in the same sense that Keynes' vision is contained in *The Economic Consequences of the Peace*, and his attempt to arm it with analytic proof is contained in *The Treatise on Money* and *The General Theory*. Moreover, there is little doubt that Marx intended to come back to these wider sociological considerations in *Capital* itself. For the manuscript of the third volume breaks off with the sociological question: "What constitutes a class?" (*Capital*, Vol. III, p. 1031, Kerr edition.)

Thus Marxism is an indivisible whole, a seamless robe, and we do it violence when we consider its economic aspects alone, although in exposition we have to do so from the simple necessity of beginning somewhere. Nevertheless, we should never forget that Marx was perpetually trying to transcend economics and lay before us a grand panorama of how human society worked *in every aspect*. The development of a hundred years has shown that his attempt did not, and could not, succeed, except as a very rough first approximation, which if applied uncritically can lead to enormous errors. But that must not blind us to the heroic nature of the attempt. In the vast, unsystematic, ill-proportioned, unfinished body of Marx's writings, in which some essential parts of his "summa," such as the materialist conception of history and the theory of class struggles, are nowhere systematically set out, or are set out in a few pages of a preface to a work devoted to something else, and in which other parts, such as the labour theory of value, have whole volumes devoted to them, we yet confront the rough-hewn monument of a giant.

That Marxism attempts to transcend economics and to lay the foundations of a truly all-embracing science of society is one of the reasons why men and women will both live and die for it. For it gives them an indispensable sense of understanding the otherwise terrifying flux of contemporary events. However often its failures to account adequately for the real development of events may be pointed out, Marxism will not lose its appeal unless it is itself transcended and comprehended in a more realistic, more flexible, but equally comprehensive, science of human society. Nothing less than this will serve. An account of the real interconnections of society, not only in its economic, but in every other, aspect, sufficiently realistic to make possible at least rough predictions, and a measure of control founded on those predictions, is today the only thing which will in the end satisfy us.

It may be objected that such a comprehensive science of society would invade the province of religion itself. But this is to exaggerate and misunderstand what its scope would be. There is no reason why the most devout believer in transcendental religion should not desire that the society in which he lives should be brought under comprehension and control. On the contrary, there is surely every reason why he should passionately desire to abolish the interminable human misery and degradation which an uncomprehended and uncontrolled society has always involved. And in fact some of the foremost of those who have attempted, in Britain, to make sense and reason prevail in the British economy have been devoutly religious. For example, in the immediate past Sir Stafford Cripps strove, by direct political action, to make the British economy serve the needs of the British people. Anyone who worked with Cripps, as I did, during the years in which he was Chancellor of the Exchequer saw how his socialism and his driving impulse to make the British economy *rational,* far from being in conflict with his religious faith, served that faith, so far as the things of this world are concerned, and did not impinge upon it in respect of his unquestioning transcendental beliefs.

What must be agreed is that any comprehensive science of society would have much to learn from the religious tradition. The fact is that on one whole aspect of social reality—the subjective, human side—the scientific approach has been until very recently almost absurdly weak. Religious tradition has shown an incomparably deeper insight into "human nature." By the use of powerful symbols, and clothed in all the glory of the main aesthetic achievements of the race, it has given the only remotely adequate account of man and his positive reaction on his environment—a good half of what has to be comprehended.

Contrary to what is so often alleged, Marxism was the first attempt from the rationalist side to give due weight to this subjective, active, reaction of man on his environment. Marx and Engels continually criticised eighteenth-century rationalism for its deficiencies in this respect, for its "passive" concept of man as a creature entirely formed by his environment. He was, on the contrary, they emphasised, a creature formed by, and forming, his environment in reciprocal interaction. Nevertheless, neither Marx, Engels nor their successors ever got very far with their account of what man on his subjective, positive side was really like. They modified the eighteenth-century rationalist concept of an "economic man" who was continually pursuing his *individual* economic interests, and nothing else, to the extent of postulating economic classes which pursued, with the same exclusiveness, their group economic interests. But that was about all. Subjective psychology had not yet even been born. Freud's attempt to account rationally for the manifestly vast irrational element in human motivation had not begun. Anthropology was only just beginning. The extreme complexity of human motivation had still only been revealed in the glimpses afforded by art, literature and religious teaching.

Even today the possibility of describing, sufficiently adequately to be of practical use, this subjective side of things is often disputed. And certainly it has not yet been fully accomplished. Be that as it may, the realistic scientific method has been *applied* to society and its interconnections. Once that has happened, and once that application has begun to show some predictive power, however approximate and crude, it is doubtful if men will ever again be satisfied with anything else. The prestige of the scientific method, since it is now rapidly bringing our physical, as distinct from our social, environment under our control, is now very great. Unless we give up the struggle altogether and, our spirits broken by new social catastrophes, relapse into a new age of darkness, we are committed to the attempt to apply the scientific, realistic method in the social field also.

Only now, however, are we beginning to see how immense a task that is. To apply the scientific method to our immensely complex and above all rapidly changing society, and yet to avoid creating another rigid system, must be the work of many minds. Such intellectual co-operation has been shown to be feasible in other fields. Again the real difficulty is political, not intellectual. Profound class prejudices, which have by no means yet been fully brought into consciousness, so that they may be offset and discounted, distract and blind both the specialists and the social philosophers who would be necessary to such a task. Yet until intellectual workers who have become fully conscious of their own political bias, and can therefore discount it, tackle this major theoretical task of our times, Marxism, for all the roughness of its approximations and the huge miscalculations which result from them, will hold the field. It will hold the field because it alone even attempts to occupy the field.

METHOD, SYSTEM OR MYTH?

Another factor upon which the success or failure of any such attempt would turn would be this. The result aimed at must be the discovery of a flexible and effective *method* of social analysis, and not of the elaboration of another rigid system, purporting to account for everything, and to account for it once and for all. It is often claimed for Marxism itself that it is such a flexible method, that it avoids, with its dialectical approach, all the rigidities of "a system." Marxism, no doubt, *ought* to be just such a method. As Schumpeter has pointed out, many of its main concepts, such as historical materialism, the theory of the conflict of classes, and some at least of its economic concepts, are, or ought to be, simply instruments of analysis, and in any other field than the bedeviled field of sociology they would, long before this, have become highly developed and refined.*

* *Op. cit.*, p. 440. "If we get from Marx an ideologically warped definition of classes and class antagonisms, and if in consequence we get an unsatisfactory description of political mechanisms, we nevertheless get something very worth having, namely, a perfectly adequate idea of the importance of the class phenomenon. If in this field there existed something like unbiased research, Marx's suggestions would have led long ago to a satisfactory theory of it."

The tragedy is that Marxism has become, above all during the mental ice-age of the Stalinist period, a fixed "system" of the most extreme rigidity. And, as we have seen, this system has grown to have less and less application to contemporary Western reality. The ossification of Marxism had set in, however, long before the Stalinist, or indeed the Leninist, period. Already the German Marxists of the Social Democratic period were unable to wield the massive instrument of their theoretical inheritance; they let it set into a system as rigidly conservative as the communist version is rigidly revolutionary.

Nor can it honestly be said that all this has been due, merely, to the failure of unworthy *epigoni*, properly to comprehend the work of their master. In Marx's own hands his methodological concepts often tended to freeze into a "system." This suggests that they were themselves but first, rough models of the instruments of social analysis which will be needed. Consequently what will have to be done is to evolve new instruments of social analysis, taking full account of Marxism, rather than to attempt another "revision" of Marxism itself.

Something more difficult to deal with rationally obtrudes itself into the discussion at this point. Experience has shown only too plainly that more powerful than either "a system" or "a method" in actually affecting men's actions has been what is often called "a myth." What has often happened, notably in the case of Marxism, is that what has started as an attempt to develop a method of social analysis has become a system, rigidly and dogmatically describing, with ever-diminishing accuracy, the ever-changing social world. And then a third stage has occurred. The system has finally become "a myth." It has become something which, though now only loosely and indirectly connected with reality, is charged with profound emotional significance. The very rigidity, the very incomprehensibility, the very irrationality of the-system-become-myth secures for it the blind and passionate allegiance of millions. It stirs men to action; true their actions cannot accomplish what they wish, for they are distorted by the distortions of their myth. But if the myth has had its origins in the vision of a major prophet, they do accomplish *something*. Men set up under the power of their myth a new society of one kind or another. But the character of that society will still remain outside the control of their conscious volition.

"Practical men," who take little account of methods of social analysis or of systems, pay great attention to such myths. For myths, they believe, are what "get things done." So they do. But the wrong things. From one point of view, no doubt, that does not matter. If our objective is simply power, then the myth's correspondence with reality is a secondary consideration. What matters is its emotive force. And so the "practical men" lay hold on the myth—any myth which they notice to be capable of moving men to action—and attempt to ride to power upon its band waggon.

Well, that is all right and no doubt inevitable. But the results must always be as we see them. Because at best a partial, one-sided, fragmentary insight into the social process has been achieved, the action, be it never so heroic, which results from the acceptance of the myth produces very different results from what anyone expected. Only too often it produces no real results in terms of actual human development; one set of "practical men" with their myth are merely succeeded by another set of "practical men" with a different myth. At best the new order of things which comes into being turns out to be tragically—or comically, whichever way you feel it—different from the promise of the myth. All of which prompts the question: in what sense are "practical men" practical?

The sole escape from the meaningless turning of the wheel of social development upon which the practical men and their followers are bound must be by way of the discovery of methods of social analysis which will give results sufficiently close to reality to make them a real guide to action.

WHERE MARX WAS RIGHT AND WHERE
HE WAS PROVED WRONG

To return to Marx's conceptions of what the development of capitalism and the fate of the wage earners must be. When he said that the wage earners would sink into ever-increasing misery—that the sum total of "the mass of poverty, oppression, enslavement, degeneration and exploitation" would grow and grow—he undoubtedly envisaged that the actual, concrete heap of commodities which the wage earners received each week would get even smaller than it was in the hungry eighteen-forties. And there he has proved entirely wrong. How profoundly right, however, he was to concentrate our attention on this question. How refreshing is his Johnsonian insistence that it is better to have two loaves of bread than one; that it is better to have shoes and schooling for your children than none; that milk and meat are better than a diet of potatoes; that a good home is better than a hovel. How right he was to assume that if we do not know that much we do not know anything. What well-merited scorn he would have poured on sophisticators who pretend that we cannot tell whether one man is better off than another. How justified would have been his scorn at the bogusly "spiritual" claim that the standard of life and the distribution of the national income do not really matter because, truly, the higher things are not material. (We will listen to that argument from those alone who have voluntarily reduced their own standard of life to subsistence level.) How sensibly he concluded that a certain material basis at least is indispensable to any form of the good life, however conceived.

Marx was right, too, in believing that his whole prognosis of the future of capitalism turned on the question of whether the wage earners' standard of life rose or fell, and that the capitalist system, *operating in the political and social environment which he alone knew,* contained a strong tendency to hold down the wage earners' standard of life to a subsistence level and so reserve the whole of the ever-growing surplus for the rich to spend or accumulate.

How right Marx was about all this. But, on the other hand, how wrong he was proved to have been in supposing that this tendency of capitalism could not be, and in some circumstances would not be, overcome and reversed by other, and essentially non-economic, forces. This error sprang from his partially deductive, anti-empirical approach, which made him believe that he had determined and defined the value of labour-power as subsistence; that this was an irrefragable law which in the nature of things could not be abrogated so long as capitalist relations of production persisted. Marx based his practical political predictions on this supposed "law." How vastly important, then, on Marx's own showing, must be the consequences of a mistaken prediction on a matter so essential to his whole system as this.

7 ▪ THE REAL DEVELOPMENT

"RELATIVE IMMISERATION"

The fact that the prediction of ever-increasing misery has
been falsified by the real development of events has been
noticed not only by anti-Marxists but also by some Marxists.
The anti-Marxists have, I repeat, simply pointed to it in
order to deny that there is any tendency in capitalism towards an ever-worsening distribution of the national income.
In doing so they have fallen into errors grosser than those of
Marx.

The Marxists, on the other hand, have tried to explain the
mistake away. We must postpone discussion of the first and
most important of their explanations until a subsequent volume of this study. Briefly this explanation is that, although
it may be true that the standard of life of the wage earners in
the leading capitalist countries has risen, instead of fallen,
yet this is only a local and temporary exception to the general
rule that capitalism as a world system must produce ever-
increasing misery. For it is asserted that this is precisely
what it has done in the case of the hundreds of millions
whom it has enslaved in the colonial possessions, and semi-
possessions, of the leading capitalisms. And it is further argued that it is the vast profits derived from the exploitation of
these peoples which have alone enabled the major capitalisms to raise the standard of life of their own wage earners.

This is an aspect of that Leninist theory of the character of the latest stage of capitalism which we have already noted. As a part of the theory of imperialism, it will be more conveniently treated in the section of this study which will be devoted to the relationship of the latest-stage capitalisms with the underdeveloped parts of the world. Suffice it here to say that we shall find that, while it is undoubtedly true that colonial possessions, and imperialism generally, have greatly helped the leading capitalisms, the figures simply will not bear the interpretation that this was ever the only, or even the main, explanation of the rise in their wage earners' standard of life. Moreover, this conclusion is strongly borne out by the fact that in the most recent period the major capitalisms have relinquished, voluntarily or involuntarily, by far the greater part of their empires without suffering any deleterious effects upon the standard of life of their peoples.*

Our first task in this chapter is the more limited one of considering the second way in which Marxists have attempted to deal with the impossibility of reconciling the doctrine of ever-increasing misery with the facts, for this will lead to a consideration of what the real development in the distribution of the national income has been. This is the doctrine of "relative immiseration," which was forcibly argued by an able second generation of Marxist economists, notably in Austria. These Marxists said that, although it was true that the standard of life of the wage earners in the major capitalisms had gone up, instead of down, yet their *share* in the

---

* We shall, of course, have to deal with the contention that these relinquishments of sovereignty are mere shams and that the imperial tribute of superprofits still flows undiminished to the latest-stage capitalisms. It will be found that even on the basis of figures given by the most extreme exponents of this view, as for example Mr. R. P. Dutt in his recent book, *The Crisis of Britain and the British Empire* (Lawrence and Wishart, 1953), such superprofits, while they still exist, are simply not of the order of magnitude to sustain the argument.

total national product had declined. If the wage earners were not worse off absolutely, at any rate they were so relatively.

This, as we have seen, is not what Marx said. Nevertheless, it is an important point. In the first place, however, we must disentangle two separate aspects of it which are constantly confused. Are we discussing the question of whether the share of wages in the national income has declined, or are we discussing whether the general distribution of the national income has become more or less equitable? For these two issues are increasingly distinct. Originally the question was asked in the form: has not the share of wages declined? We must dispose of this question first. Then we can take up the more comprehensive question of whether the whole share of the wage earners in the national income, which they do not obtain exclusively in the form of wages, but also, and increasingly, in the form of social services of various kinds financed by redistributory taxation, has declined or increased.*

The answer to the first question—has the share of wages, as such, declined?—was, at the time it was first asked—yes, it had. The figures indicate that the share of wages in the total national incomes of the major capitalisms tended, on the whole, to decline rather than increase in the second half of the nineteenth and the first half of the twentieth centuries. In Britain, for example, it appears to have been around 50% in Marx's day: to have declined to about 40% in the early years of the twentieth century; to have stayed about there till 1939, and then (including, as you must, the pay of the Forces) to have gone back to around 50% by the end of the Second World War. (See Jay, *op. cit.*, pp. 34-

* "The clearest way of analysing changes in income is to proceed step by step, starting with the division of the national product between wages and other incomes, and then allowing in turn for changes in undistributed profits, of taxation, and prices, until we end with the distribution of 'real' disposable income." Dudley Seers, *Has the Distribution of Income Become More Equal?* Bulletin of the Oxford Institute of Statistics, Autumn, 1955.

35, for a review of the authorities for these statements. Some of them differ in detail.)

THE SHARE OF WAGES AND SALARIES

The development since 1911 is well set out in the following table taken from the post-Second World War edition of Mr. Douglas Jay's book (*op. cit.*, p. 31). The earlier figures are taken from Mr. Clark's *National Income and Outlay* (Macmillan, 1937), p. 94, and the recent ones from the White Paper on National Income and Expenditure (M,D, 1623).

	(In millions of pounds sterling)						
	1911	1924	1929	1932	1935	1938	1944
Wages	728	1399	1486	1333	1520	1735	2930
	39.5%	42.1%	41.8%	42.5%	40.5%	37.6%	35.2%
Salaries	288	841	944	890	937	1100	1473
	15.6%	25.4%	26.6%	28.3%	25.0%	23.8%	17.7%
Profit and	623	834	821	590	949	1326	2376
Interest	33.8%	25.1%	23.1%	18.8%	25.4%	28.7%	28.5%
Rent	203	246	302	325	339	380	384
	11.1%	7.4%	8.5%	10.4%	9.1%	8.2%	4.6%
Pay of Forces						78	1171
						1.7%	14.0%

We must, of course, add to wages the pay of the Forces for 1938 and 1944. So by 1944 the total share of wages had risen again to around 50%. On the whole, then, wages, as such, have taken somewhat under half the total national income—at one period 10% less—over the past 100 years. All

the vast effort of collective bargaining has done no more than
prevent their share from dropping. Is not this *prima facie*
evidence that there must be some strong, natural and inherent tendency at work for the share of wages to drop? And is
not this very much what we should naturally expect? Is it
not natural that, as society gets more "capitalistic," as what
Marx called "the composition of capital" changes, and a
greater and greater part is taken in production by machinery, and a smaller and smaller part by labour, the share of
wages in the national income should tend to go down and
that of rent, interest and profit—the remuneration of capital
—to go up? This is a natural economic tendency set up by
the continuing rise in the level of technique in general and
of the process of mechanisation in particular.

It is true that this is a highly complex business. The mere
fact that fewer and fewer workers are needed on the factory
floor is not itself conclusive. Someone has to build the machines which are displacing them. Someone has to adminis-
trate, manage, do the accounts, and generally control the
increasingly thinly manned factories—and also distribute and
sell the goods they are producing. Accordingly, the number
of workers employed in the machine-building and capital-
goods industries and in the office staffs has gone up. Moreover until recently mechanisation had made much slower
progress in these spheres. But now mechanisation, having
begun to drive the worker off the factory floor, is pursuing
him into the tool room, the office and the shop. Therefore all
this can, surely, do no more than postpone and qualify the
general tendency.

We shall be much concerned with this progressive change
in what economists sometimes call "the structure of production" in subsequent chapters. For this lengthening out, as
it were, of the productive process, under which employment
comes increasingly to depend upon the capital goods industries, renders the system more and more inherently unstable.

Here, however, we are merely concerned to notice the underlying tendency to decrease the share of wages in the national income. The logical end of the process (which will never, of course, be reached in practice) is automatic production in which there would be no wage earners at all (except a few maintenance men). This was the state of things immortalised by M. René Clair in his masterpiece, the film *À Nous la Liberté*. And it is perfectly true that in a capitalist society, run on uncompromisingly capitalist principles, an economy of automatic processes would be a *reductio ad absurdum*. For one of the first principles of capitalism is that no one must be paid an income unless he provides one of the factors of production. So if the factor, labour, is no longer required, it need not be, and must not be, paid. But that would mean that just at the moment when there was little difficulty in producing almost everything, hardly anyone, except the circa 10% of property owners, would be able to buy anything.

It would not, however, be particularly profitable to push our investigation into the share of wages, as such, very much further. For the fact is that the share of wages in the national income now tells us less than might be supposed about the total share of the wage-earning class, and in general about the distribution of the national income. For instance, the reader will already have noted from the above table that the share of rent, interest and profits also dropped in Britain in those periods in which the share of wages declined. The increase went entirely to salaries, which are a form of high wages paid at monthly or quarterly, instead of weekly, intervals. This is, no doubt, a financial effect both of technical change and of that ever-growing separation of ownership and management which we listed as the fourth characteristic of the latest stage of capitalism in Chapter 1.

Mr. Colin Clark has been good enough to supply me with interesting figures, which he will be publishing in due course, showing what he calls "labour's share of the net product" at various periods in various countries. It is essential to note that these figures (a) put salaries in with wages, (b) exclude agriculture, a sphere of production in which, Mr. Clark writes, "the division of the product is much less favourable to labour than the division of the product in industry," and (c) credit working proprietors with an "imputed wage" equal to "the average wage per head of the whole body of wage and salary earners." The figures of "labour's share of the net product" computed in this way are as follows:

United Kingdom			Australia	1938-9	66.1
	1843	63.0		1952-3	75.9
	1880	63.2	Austria	1951	74.2
	1911	59.5	Belgium	1951	61.6
	1924	70.5	Canada	1938	72.0
	1938	72.2		1952	74.2
	1952	74.4	Chile	1940	54.6
	1953	72.6		1950	57.4
United States	1919	71.9	Finland	1938	81.5
	1929	71.9		1952	83.0
	1939	76.3	Netherlands	1938	64.5
	1949-51	76.8		1949	69.6
	1953	80.1	New Zealand	1938-9	65.1
France	1929	59.0		1951-2	78.2
	1938	72.5	Norway	1930	60.7
	1952	84.7		1939	60.2
Germany	1913	63.2		1950-2	56.8
	1928	65.9	Puerto Rico	1939	70.0
	1936	56.6		1951	74.1
	1953	70.7	Switzerland	1938	58.8
Ireland	1938	74.7		1949	71.2
	1952	78.9		1952	73.9
Japan	1934-6	55.1			
	1951	67.9			
Mexico	1939	67.2			
	1949	51.2			

Comparison with Mr. Jay's table will show that for the United Kingdom in 1944 the share of wages, salaries and pay of Forces add up to some 68% of the net product. This is broadly consonant with Mr. Clark's figures of, for example, 72% in both 1938 and 1953 as "labour's share" calculated on his basis.

But again the share of wages + salaries + income of working proprietors (with agriculture excluded) is not by any means a satisfactory basis for a calculation of the distribution of the national income. Wages and salaries are ceasing to be the only source of income of the wage-earning population. The whole system of social services, received partly in money, as in family allowances, pensions, etc., and partly in kind, as in education and the National Health Service, has become an important factor. Thus what we have really got to do in order to consider the theory of "relative immiseration" is not to take the share of wages, or even wages plus salaries, as such, but to estimate the distribution of the national income, however received, as between individuals and discover whether it has become more, or less, equalitarian. If it has become less equalitarian, then it can no doubt be said that there has been "relative immiseration," even though the actual, absolute standard of life of the population has more than doubled, as it has. If it has become more equalitarian, then there has been no relative immiseration, but, on the contrary, the wage earners have not only raised their standard of life absolutely, but have increased their share in the national income.

HAS THERE BEEN A REDISTRIBUTION?

We have seen that if we think only in terms of wages, then we find that there was at one time a tendency for the share of wages in the national income to decline, and that at best that share had by 1945 only been restored to the level of a hundred years ago. But surely, the reader must be feeling at this point, if we turn our attention to the broader issue of the general distribution of the national income we shall find a totally different story. Surely we shall find that, far from there having been "relative immiseration," the share of the national income going to the mass of the population, more especially after taxation has been taken into account, has increased and the share going to the rich has correspondingly decreased. That is certainly a most widespread assumption in certain circles. Every member of the British upper and middle classes, if asked whether the net spendable national income had been redistributed over the past 100 years in favour of the wage earners, and against themselves, would answer with a most emphatic "Yes." Far from supporting the theory of the "relative immiseration" of the wage earners, they suppose that there has been a most cruel "relative immiseration" of the middle and upper classes for the benefit of the wage earners!

In fact, the figures are far less clear-cut than that. It would be out of place to attempt a review of the statistical evidence, more particularly as that task has been most competently done in Chapter IV of Mr. Jay's aforementioned work. And Mr. Jay's conclusions are as definite as they will be unexpected to many people.

Mr. Jay's first conclusion is that *in Britain right up to 1939 there had been little or no redistribution of the national income in favour of the mass of the population, either through trade union pressure or budgetary changes. (op. cit., p. 44.)* What had actually happened up till 1939 was that the wage earners' standard of life had risen just about in step with the rise in the total national income, their share remaining about constant. After 1939, however, appreciable redistribution took place. It took place mainly during, not after the war.

What the work of the Labour Government between 1945 and 1951 achieved was, on the whole, to maintain this new and markedly, although not enormously, more equalitarian pattern of distribution in peace time. But this, if it proves permanent, was, as we shall see, no small achievement. If my readers are sceptical of these conclusions, they must study the authorities for themselves. (Especially Mr. Clark's *National Income and Outlay; British Public Expenditure*, Joseph Sykes; The Colwin Committee's report on the same subject; *The Distribution of the National Capital*, G.W. Daniels and H. Campion.) There are minor differences of opinion between the authorities on this or that particular point, but there is no doubt about their broad conclusion that the distribution of the national income had up till 1939 remained broadly constant.

Moreover, a second and equally important conclusion emerges from the figures. Not only had the pattern of distribution remained unchanged, but it had remained unchanged at a much higher degree of inequality than is usually realised. It is not easy to define clearly this exact degree of inequality. But as, once more, readers can see for themselves if they examine the statistical evidence, *the broad pattern of distribution which emerges from the figures is that at the end of the period under discussion, as at the beginning, some 10% of the population got about one half of the national income and the other 90% of the population got the other half of the national income.* Mr. Jay sums up the evidence for this remarkable conclusion, which is so contrary to what is usually supposed, as follows:

"The pre-1939 picture confronting us, therefore, in this country is of a community in which nine-tenths of the individuals receive only 40-50 per cent of the income, just as they had twenty-five years before. Their average standard of living had risen, though not radically, during the interval. But it had risen mainly as a result of a rise in the total national income, and not of a redistribution achieved either by trade-union pressure or Budgetary changes." (*op. cit.*, p. 44.)

Mr. Jay's method is to give the crude pre-tax figures and then to estimate the effect of (a) deductions from incomes by way of tax and (b) addition to incomes by the public expenditure of the money so raised. He concludes, it will be seen, that up to 1939 the *net* redistribution effected by taxation, even as against the pre-tax figures, was very much slighter than is usually supposed. This was mainly because of the expenditure of so large a part of the Budget upon non-redistributory items such as interest on the national debt and defence. This is in broad agreement with the conclusions reached by Mr. Barna in his *Redistribution of Income through Public Finance in 1937*. Mr. Barna considered that in general, at that time, the taxes on the rich paid for defence and the national debt interest, while the mass of the community paid by taxation on themselves for their own social services. No doubt it may be said that but for this defence expenditure a real measure of redistribution would have been effected. The fact remains that it was not.

It is very difficult for people to believe the established facts of inequality as it existed in pre-1939 Britain. The following passage from pp. 32 and 33 of Mr. Jay's work, which is itself based upon that of Mr. Clark, gives the main facts:

It is reasonable to take the figure of £250 per year as the upper limit of working-class incomes before the war (*i.e.*, before 1939. J.S.). This roughly corresponds with the health and unemployment insurance maxima and with what was commonly taken to be the income of the best-paid working man. Now the number of persons receiving incomes of under £250 a year is shown above to be about 17,600,000 and the total number of persons receiving incomes to be just under 20,000,000. There were, in fact, in 1929, about 17,600,000 working-class incomes in this country, each of £250 a year or less; and about 2,300,000 middle-class and rentier families receiving over £250 a year. At the time, that is to say, about nine out of ten income-receivers or families had a working-class income.

These figures are perhaps the most eloquent and significant comment on modern industrial society that can possibly be made. It is quite erroneous to speak of the "community" or the "public" in this country; as if the population consisted of a large mass of persons with moderate incomes, and a few extremely rich and extremely poor above and below them. It is also erroneous to think of the working class as if they represented one-half or perhaps two-thirds of the community, and their interests had consequently to be balanced against those of the middle classes in determining political action. It is equally erroneous again to think of society as consisting of a vast majority of practically destitute persons and a small minority living in great luxury, with nobody in between. In fact, in Great Britain, before the war, 17,600,000 out of 20,000,000 persons, or about nine in every ten, were working class, though not necessarily of course all manual workers; and 12,000,000 of these received an income scarcely above the subsistence level. Another small but substantial group, of somewhere about 2,-000,000, received a middle-class or professional-class income ranging from £250 to £1,000. And finally there was a tiny group of 300,000 very rich persons, whose aggregate income made up a very considerable proportion of the total national income.

Our society was one, in fact, which displayed considerable poverty and very great inequality. The poverty is best revealed by the figure of 12,000,000 persons living on an income of less than £125 a year. Many of these "persons," it must also be remembered, though not all, are really families. The extent of inequality is summarized in the following way by Mr. Colin Clark (*National Income and Outlay*, p. 110):

Speaking of the years 1929-35, we can say that one-tenth of the whole working population, with incomes over £250, took 42 per cent of the whole total of personal incomes, or just under half of it if we allow for the fact that the greater part of the non-personal incomes, in the form of undistributed company profits and such, accrued for the benefit of the rich. A small class, comprising 1½ per cent of the population, with "four-figure incomes" and upwards, took 23 per cent of the whole total of personal incomes.

The only qualification to be borne in mind—although it is an appreciable qualification—is that out of incomes distributed in this way "the 10%," as Mr. Jay goes on to show, paid out of taxation which fell on them the bulk of such general national services as defence, police, administration, etc., some of which services were, in my view, for the benefit of everybody.

It is fashionable in the nineteen-fifties to discount as merely of historical interest the miseries endured by the main mass of the British wage earners right up till 1939, as coldly measured by the above figures. Yet this is *very* recent history. (Moreover can we really be certain that it is only history?)

It is indeed true that the improvement of the last twenty years, partly as the result of the degree of redistribution which we shall try to assess immediately, and partly, since 1949, of the resumed rise in the total to be distributed, is very important. Moreover, figures of income underestimate it. For it was in this period that the British wage earners first managed to obtain a ration at least of that extremely valuable good, leisure. It was in this period that both the five-day week and annual holidays with pay became general. It may be that this limitation in the hours of work (it had begun long before 1939) would have seemed a more startling development to Marx, Engels and their contemporaries, even than the rise in the wage earners' real incomes. Marx laid enormous emphasis on the blind drive of capital to increase the hours of work up to, and beyond, the limit of the humanly endurable, as the one remaining way in which, with wages by definition at subsistence, and a given technique of production, surplus value could be increased. The incontrovertible fact that this whole tendency has been reversed and hours of work considerably reduced, without the abrogation of capitalist relations of production, might have seemed to him almost a contradiction of nature. Nevertheless —and allowing for not inconsiderable offsets, such as the amount of overtime which has to be worked in the nineteen-fifties in order to maintain the contemporary standard of life of the wage earners—the thing has happened. The mere simple fact that the wage earners have today two whole days of rest a week and an annual holiday with pay marks a long stride in their upward struggle out of their status as mere animate means of production, as Marx described them in his day, and as they remained to a very great extent right up to 1914, to the fully human status of ends, *for the sake of which* production is undertaken.

Nevertheless, when all this has been duly taken into account, as it must be, let us not go to the other extreme and appear to imply that the standard of life of the British wage earners now leaves little to be desired. That would be an error at least as gross as the error of denying that there has been improvement. All things are relative. Compared to their own standards of a hundred years ago, or to the standards of many hundreds of millions of other workers today, the standards of the British workers in the mid-twentieth century are incontestably high. But compared to the standards of, for example, many American workers, of the existing British upper middle class, and compared above all to what possessing classes have always and unanimously considered to be indispensable for a good life, they are still very low. The main mass of the less skilled British wage earners still live lives cramped and narrow indeed, as compared with the lives which the British middle classes demand for themselves as a matter of course. The wage earners still have housing which varies quite arbitrarily from the excellent to the abominable, stinted educational opportunities, horrible urban environments and bleak poverty in old age. It is only "primary poverty," in the exact sense of a sheer inability to buy the necessaries of tolerable life, however well one's income is laid out, that has been, virtually, abolished.

To what extent, however, is the remaining poverty of the British wage earners a consequence of the inequitable distribution of the national income? May it not be a consequence of a sheer physical inability of the British productive system, at its present stage of development, to afford a flow of goods and services which would raise the general standards of the British wage earners to a more ample level? That is a question with which we shall be much concerned. Its discussion will be first broached in Chapter 9 below.

THE 1938-1949 PERIOD

The above quotation from Mr. Jay's work probably affords the most faithful and balanced statistical picture available of the British pre-1939 distribution of the national income. The question is to what extent has it been modified by the nineteen-fifties? Mr. A. R. Prest in his article in the *Economic Journal* for March, 1948, made the best-known attempt to show uninterrupted series of figures of the national income from 1870 to 1946. His Table II, p. 59, should be consulted for this purpose.

But much the most detailed work on the distribution of incomes, of which I am aware, has been done, for the period 1938-1949, by Mr. Dudley Seers and published in his pamphlet, *The Levelling of Incomes since 1938* (Basil Blackwell, Oxford, 1951). Mr. Seers' conclusions as to what has happened to real, post-tax, incomes (*i.e.*, to "what incomes will buy" in the sense discussed in the last chapter) are as follows:

> The major change is an effective transfer of some 10 per cent of the real produce* from distributed property income to wages, this change having far more influence in reshaping the pattern of real income than any other. (*Op. cit.*, p. 55.)

There was, then, a genuine redistribution of income in favour of the wage earners as a result of the Second World War and the first majority Labour Government. The possibility of the wage earners not only holding their ground but actually increasing their share under capitalism was demonstrated. Mr. Seers considers that there have been three main causes for this shift. In the first place a smaller portion of profits was distributed after the war, and the share of fixed incomes fell sharply. As we shall see in a moment, this tendency for profits to remain "undistributed" to shareholders and be ploughed back into the business may very easily be reversed, and indeed has been partly reversed after 1951. The fall in the share of fixed incomes is, of course, an effect of the rising price level—an effect of inflation. But inflation, although a powerful redistributory agent, redistributes what it takes from the *rentiers* as much or more *towards* profits as towards wages.

Second, direct taxation on the large incomes has greatly increased. This redistributory factor was the result of the political, rather than the industrial, pressure of the wage earners.

In the third place, Mr. Seers considers that there have been movements of *relative* prices favourable to the wage

---

* By "the real produce" Mr. Seers does not mean the gross national product or total national income (which, I repeat, are the same thing), but that part of it which comes into the hands of private persons. He calls it elsewhere "personal incomes."

earners, largely because of food subsidies. In other words, the prices of the sort of things wage earners buy have gone up less than the prices of the sort of things which the rich buy. This, too, has been, on the whole, the result of the political rather than the industrial pressure of the wage earners. Mr. Seers' analysis suggests that in contemporary conditions such specifically political pressure is a factor of high importance.

If, however, the first conclusion to be drawn from Mr. Seers' work is that actual redistribution in favour of the wage earners is possible, our second reaction to his analysis may well be a contrary one. A 10% "switch" of what there was to divide: a 10% "switch" from the, on the whole, high, property-derived, incomes to the, on the whole, low, wage-derived, incomes may seem an unexpectedly modest amount of redistribution to form the basis of the "social revolution" which, it is often said, has taken place in Britain since 1939.* And so it is. The actual amount of redistribution in favour of the wage earners which has taken place in Britain is much more modest than the, no doubt quite natural, lamentations of the "property interests" would suggest. It is a most remarkable fact that all our complex and far-reaching, redistributory measures and policies, ranging from steeply increased taxation of the rich to enormously increased trade-union strength, based upon continuously full employment, were needed to effect this fairly modest result. Have we not here come upon further evidence that a strong counter-tendency towards an ever more *unequal* distribution, such as Marx diagnosed, is running strongly beneath the surface of capitalist society?

Before, however, we suggest that the feelings of depriva-

---

* We cannot, of course, exactly identify property-derived incomes with the incomes of "the 10%" or wage incomes with the incomes of "the 90%." But by and large the *considerable* property incomes do go to "the 10%" and few of "the 90%" have any substantial supplement to their incomes from property.

tion of the property interests are altogether misplaced, we must look more closely into Mr. Seers' figures, dropping altogether our first approximation of taking into account merely wages, and looking at the incomes from all sources of the different interests. Table VIII of Mr. Seers' book summarises what has happened (*op. cit.*, p. 55):

TABLE VIII. Percentage share in post-tax personal income at 1938 prices

		1938	1949
Wages	. . . .	37	47
Salaries	. . . .	23	21
Forces' Pay	. . . .	2	3
Total Work Income	. . . .	62	71
Social Income	. . . .	6	9
Mixed Income	. . . .	12	10
Distributed Property Income	. . . .	20	10
		100	100

It will be seen that real wages have gone up by exactly 10% of the total to be divided. Social services have gone up from 6% to 9% of the total to be divided. Forces pay is up 1%. So the wage earners' share has probably risen by something between 10% and 15%. But now, if we look at the last item of the Table we see that distributed property incomes have dropped from 20% to 10% of the total to be divided.* Therefore, in 1949, those who derived their incomes from the ownership of property appear at first sight to have had no more than half as large a command over commodities as they had had in 1938. This corresponds much more closely

---

* It so happens that the real total to be divided was approximately the same in 1938 and 1949. So at this stage we can concern ourselves exclusively with distribution.

to what they evidently *feel* has happened to them than the equally correct statement that there has been a 10% "switch" to the wage earners. The reason why both statements are true is, of course, that property-derived incomes, though much higher individually, go to so comparatively few people that, taken together, they were not more than 20% of the total even in 1938.

However, we must immediately qualify, as Mr. Seers is careful to do, the implication that the rich are now only taking half as large a share of the national cake as they were before the war. In the first place, 1949 was probably about the high point of the equalitarian policies of the previous ten years. In the second place, "personal incomes," Mr. Seers makes clear, exclude a most important "hidden asset" of those who derive their incomes from property, namely, the "undistributed profits" of companies. It is true, of course, that such undistributed profits do not come directly into the hands of the shareholders of the companies concerned, to be spent. But, on the other hand, they do substantially increase the value of the shares held. And this increase in share values may sooner or later express itself both in increased distribution by way of dividends to the shareholders and, above all, by capital gains, which are in Britain untaxed. And so it has proved. After 1951, and the return to office of a Conservative administration, there has been a most marked increase in dividend distribution and a still more marked, indeed an almost unprecented, rise in the capital value of share-holdings. Thus by 1955, even though the full figures are not available, it is certain, from common observation, that the real expenditures—from incomes, "expense allowances" and capital gains taken together—of the rich have most markedly recovered from their 1949 level.

Therefore our impression remains that redistribution in favour of the wage earners was zero right up to 1939. (Unless one counts as redistribution the fact that by 1939 the rich were paying for past and present defence expenditure. If one considers, as I do, that in the nineteen-thirties such expenditure was for the benefit of the whole community, no doubt there is here some redistributory effect. On the other hand, such an argument would be much more difficult to sustain in regard to interest on the national debt.) Second, the figures bear out the impression that redistribution has been quite modest (of the order of a 10% "switch" from property-derived incomes to wage-derived incomes) even since 1939. This impression should only be qualified to the extent of noting that, because of the disparity of their numbers and shares in the total, even a 10% gain in the wage earners' share implies a sharp drop in the property owners' share.

THE PERIOD SINCE 1949

It is probably premature to say very much about what has happened since 1949. But Mr. Dudley Seers in the autumn of 1955 published an important paper entitled *Has the Distribution of Income Become More Unequal?* in the *Bulletin of the Oxford Institute of Statistics*. This paper analyses the figures given in the *National Income Blue Book* published in 1955. Very broadly his conclusions are that there has been a slight counter-redistribution of real income from the wage earners to the property owners, especially since 1951. What appears to have happened is that the property owners have taken (by means of revisions of taxation, capital gains, increased dividend distributions and other measures favourable to themselves) most of the considerable increase in the national income distributed in those years, thus increasing the absolute levels of their real incomes most markedly, increasing a little their share, and leaving the real incomes of the wage earners rising slightly in absolute terms, but declining slightly as a share in the total. If this counter-redistributory tendency continues and intensifies over a considerable period, it will serve to show how exceptional were the relative gains of the wage earners between 1939 and 1949, and how easily the distribution of the national income may begin to slip back into its old pattern. And this would be still further evidence of the strong undertow of the system towards an extreme maldistribution of income.

CONCLUSIONS FROM THE FIGURES

Over the whole of the last 100 years there was, then, in Britain no "relative immiseration." (American figures were broadly similar.) Not only did the workers' standard of life more than double, but their share in the national income did not decline. But, on the other hand, the rooted middle- and upper-class conviction that they were being mulcted for the sake of the wage earners is also found to have had but little foundation in fact right up to 1939. And even in the last fifteen years the extent of redistribution has been a good deal less than is usually supposed.

And this is really very remarkable. For the measures of apparent redistribution in favour of the British wage earners which have been applied over the past one hundred years are indeed many and substantial. There has been, in the first place, an immense increase of direct redistributory taxation on the rich. That increase has comprised the institution of an income tax: the increase of its rates from 6d. to 4s. 6d. in the £ in 1939, to 10/- in 1945, and to 8s. 6d. today; the institution of a surtax of progressively increasing weight on all incomes of over £2,000 a year: the institution of Death Duties rising to 80% on the really great fortunes: the institution (since 1939) of heavy profit taxes on companies, etc. It is true that by no means all this money has been transferred from the pockets of the rich to those of the wage earners. Much of it has been spent upon defence and upon interest on the national debt. And this latter part of it has been largely paid back into the same pockets as those from which it was taken. Nevertheless, the redistributory effect of progressive direct taxation on this scale would undoubtedly have been very substantial, *if other things had remained equal.* In fact, the most that can be claimed for it up to 1939 is that it succeeded in shifting the burden of defence on to the shoulders of the rich. No doubt this was a measure of redistribution, of a kind, as against what would have happened without redistributory taxation. But what a modest net result it was for such apparently drastic fiscal measures!

Moreover, taxation is only one of the two major redistributory factors. The other is the growth of trade-union strength. Practically the whole growth of the power of the wage earners to bargain for an increase in their wages falls within the last 100 years. From relatively puny societies of craftsmen, the trade unions have become nationwide cartels for the sale of labour-power at the highest obtainable price, solidly confronting, since 1939 in conditions of full employment, the employing interests.

It can hardly be wondered at that such substantial new elements in the situation as these have made the richer classes of Britain feel as if heavy sacrifices indeed have been demanded of them. Nevertheless, the fact of the matter is that up till 1939 they had lost little of their share of the national income. They, like the wage earners, got almost the same share of a substantially larger cake. And what a share it was! I repeat that that same pattern of 10% of the population getting nearly one half of the cake and 90% getting the other half persisted with marvellous tenacity right up to 1939, and that even now (1956) it is probable that the degree of redistribution has been, from the wage earners' point of view, modest and, from the property owners' point of view, a good deal less than he is accustomed to protest.* What can the explanation be? How can such substantial measures of redistribution as Britain has progressively adopted have done no more than hold the pattern constant up till 1939, and change it moderately in the direction of greater equality since then?

WHICH DIAGRAM?

In my view we have here evidence which should go far to settle the question of where Marx was right and where he was wrong. The failure of all the redistributory measures of the last 100 years to do substantially more, right up to 1939, than to hold the distribution constant shows that Marx would have been right if he had diagnosed an innate tendency, instead of an irreversible law, for the share of the mass of the population to worsen under capitalism. And this, after all, is a conclusion of the highest importance. For it flies in the face of the assumptions, implicit rather than explicit, of the main body of orthodox economic doctrine. Running through the thought of the less extreme of the orthodox economists of the past 100 years (the more extreme have been unwilling to concern themselves with such things, as we have seen) has been the doctrine that the share of the wage earners, and the mass of the population generally, will

---

* We must not for a moment suppose that official figures, which show, for example, that only a handful of persons now enjoy incomes of over £6,000 a year after tax, give any clue even to the actual rate of expenditure of the rich. By a wide variety of devices, such as expense allowances, the regular spending of capital gains, avoidance of inheritance taxes, numerically quite significant numbers of "the 10%" spend on an altogether different scale to this, as common observation will confirm.

automatically *maintain, or even increase,* itself, in competitive capitalism, without any need for political or industrial pressure, and that, thus, the general standard of life will rise at least in step with the rise in productivity.

The concept which has emerged from their writings is something of this sort. It is assumed that, for example, money wages (and other working-class incomes) will remain constant if nothing is done to "interfere" with them. Then the ordinary workings of competition will push down the general price level as the costs of production fall with the improvement of technique. Therefore, with money wages constant, real wages and other working-class incomes will steadily rise. Thus there will be an automatically rising standard of life for the population as a whole. (An assumption that the money incomes of the general population will rise in step with the fall of costs of production, the price level remaining stable, is only another version of the same idea.) In Marxian terminology this is the assumption that "the rate of exploitation" will remain constant, with wages and other working-class incomes rising in step with the growth of productivity. Marx, as we have seen, made the converse assumption that the rate of exploitation must continually rise in step with the growth of productivity, wages and other working-class incomes remaining constant at subsistence.

The question is, which of these two diagrams of the way the system will work in competitive conditions corresponds with reality? I cannot believe that the most fruitful way of answering such a question will be by logical argumentation. The thing is, surely, to look and see what has happened over the past 100 years. At first sight the predictions of the orthodox economists seem to have been fulfilled. The share of the general population—the 90% who have usually got about half the national income—has in fact remained about constant (and has lately improved somewhat) and so their standard of life has risen with the rise in productivity. But

when we look more closely and see *how* that has happened
we may reach an exactly opposite conclusion. For this has
happened, I repeat, only as a result of the most drastic and
far-reaching interferences with the workings of the system,
all of which have had the effect of artificially, as it were,
increasing the share of the 90% of the population. How can
we resist the conclusion that, in the absence of this drastic,
long-continuing and cumulative redistributory pressure on
the system, the share of the general population would have
dropped steadily, so that their standard of life would not
have risen, or would not at best have risen anything like in
step with the rise in productivity?

But this is not quite the end of the argument. It may be
said: Ah, but these democratic political and trade-union redistributory pressures were not the only "distortions" to which
the system was exposed. It was also exposed to all manner of
monopolistic distortions which had the effect of preventing
the natural play of competition from driving down prices as
costs fell and so increasing real incomes. There is certainly
no need to deny the existence of such monopolistic—or as we
have called them oligopolistic—distortions; on the contrary,
their growth is a main subject of this part of the present
study. And, of course, it is true that it is partly their existence
which has made the growth of democratic political and
trade-union counter-pressures so imperative if the balance
was even to be held. Therefore the issue becomes the highly
abstract one of what the tendency *would have been* in a
capitalism at once perfectly competitive and perfectly free
from democratic political pressure.

At this point, however, the argument begins to lose
all touch with reality. I may merely record my view that in
such highly abstract conditions Marx's diagram would be
found to be much the nearer to the truth—at any rate, in
societies with rapidly growing working populations. But in
the real world there never have been, and never will be, such

virginal capitalisms. And the broad fact is that in real-life capitalisms it has taken the utmost efforts of the 90% of the population to prevent their share of the national product from falling, and so to enable their standard of life to rise with the rise in productivity.

> " 'Well, in our country,' said Alice, still panting a little, 'you'd generally get to somewhere else—if you ran very fast for a long time as we've been doing.'
> " 'A slow sort of country,' said the Queen. 'Now *here*, you see, it takes all the running you can do, to keep in the same place.' "

Capitalism, it has turned out, is a Red Queen's sort of country from the wage earners' point of view. They have to run very fast for a long time in order to keep in the same place *relatively* to the other classes. But, on the other hand, if they succeed in doing that, they do get to somewhere *absolutely*, in the sense that their standard of life rises in step with the rise in productivity.

CONCLUSIONS

All this is evidence that capitalism has in fact an innate tendency to extreme and ever-growing inequality. For how otherwise could all these cumulatively equalitarian measures which the popular forces have succeeded in enacting over the past 100 years have done little more than hold the position constant? Is it not clear that, if the workings of the system had not been continuously modified, it would have produced just that ever-sharper polarisation which Marx diagnosed as its essential tendency? Economic and social polarisation, with ever-increasing misery at the bottom and limitless wealth at the top, has not in fact occurred. But it has taken the whole vast social reform movement of the past hundred years to prevent it. If the system had been left to itself, if the advice of its theorists had been taken and everything had been left to go whither it would, the destination must have been that final revolutionary catastrophe which Marx foresaw.

There was nothing basically wrong, then, with Marx's economic insight. It was his political judgment which was at fault. He failed to see that other, essentially political, forces would arise in the advanced capitalist societies which would balance, and, in the end, even begin to outweigh, the inherent tendencies of the system. Our next task will be to describe these forces, their origins, present condition and future prospects. Moreover, if these forces alone prevented the realisation of ever-increasing misery in the former competitive stage of the system, they will be indispensable in order to prevent catastrophic social polarisation in the present, latest stage of capitalism. Finally, we shall advance the view that the forces tending to modify the natural development of capitalism can only fulfil their function if in future they do more than hold their own. They must overreach their own immediate purposes, modify the very nature of the system, and, sooner rather than later, transcend it altogether.

8 ∎ THE ECONOMIC CONSEQUENCES

OF DEMOCRACY

THE DEMOCRATIC IMPACT

There is no mystery about what has caused the standard of life of the wage earners to rise roughly in step with the rise in the national income. Many other factors, such as the rise of productivity, have been a necessary condition; nevertheless the operative factor, without which the rise would not in fact have taken place, has been the growing power of the people. And by "the people" I mean that 90% of the British population who have usually received (as we have seen) about half the national income.* It is this which has prevented the innate tendencies of the capitalist system from working themselves out in the ever-increasing misery of the wage earners.

There will be no need to do more than list summarily the main methods by which democratic political pressure has raised the standard of life of the British wage earners. For they are familiar. They fall into two broad categories. There is, on the one hand, legislation which directly benefits the 90%, either in cash or in kind, at the expense of the 10%. In Britain the long list of social services, in so far as they

---

* It is fair to note that, as we have also seen, the 10% have provided for accumulation and defence out of their half. How much there really is to distribute will be discussed in the next chapter.

are financed by progressive taxation, from compulsory universal education in the eighteen-seventies, to the National Health Service in the nineteen-forties, fall into this category. On the other hand, there is the equally long list of measures which have enabled the wage earners to organise and assert a measure of bargaining power against their employers, and so help themselves. In this category fall Lord Shaftesbury's original Factory Acts, the Trades Boards and other minimum-wages acts, and, above all, of course, the stubbornly resisted series of acts which have in the end fully legalised trade unionism. It is by means of measures of these two types, enacted to a greater or lesser extent in all the advanced capitalisms, that democratic pressure has falsified the prediction of ever-increasing misery.

American development has, at first sight, been very different. Right up to the nineteen-thirties trade unionism played a comparatively minor role. Yet the wage earners' standard of life rose faster, not slower, than in Britain. Those observers who tend to think of the democratic pressure upon capitalism in essentially trade-unionist terms may suggest, therefore, that this disproves the conception that the mass of the population had to force an increase in its standard of life against an innate tendency of capitalism to reserve the whole of the ever-growing surplus for the owners of the means of production. They may suggest that American experience demonstrates that there is no such innate tendency and that capitalism, on the contrary, tends automatically to raise the wage earners' standard of life in step with rising productivity. But this is to conceive of democratic pressure in much too narrowly trade-unionist terms. In fact, while American trade unionism was, up to the nineteen-thirties, weaker than British, American political democracy was stronger. American democracy as a whole probably exercised a greater pressure, on balance, on the economy and the distribution of income than British. As we noted briefly above (footnote, page 128), during most of the past hundred years Americans were the only wage earners and farmers who enjoyed a really wide franchise. And it would be a great mistake to think that they did not exercise their political power to redress the balance of the economy. No doubt the farmers, rather than the wage earners, were in the van in such efforts; no doubt some of their efforts were failures or partial failures, such as the soft-money agitations, or the Sherman Anti-Trust laws. But what was perhaps their decisive move, the Homestead Legislation, by which the American people enjoyed access to free land, right up to the eighteen-nineties, succeeded. And this success benefited the American wage earners almost as much as the American farmers. It meant that both could, as we noted, escape right out of capitalist relations of production and "set up for themselves" as independent producers in a way unattainable to British wage earners or farmers, except by emigration.

Therefore, on reconsideration, it does not seem to me that American development affords an exception to the proposition that it takes strong democratic pressure to raise the standard of life of the wage earners and farmers in a capitalist society. Of course, the leaping increase in American productivity made everything far easier than anywhere else; of course, the opening up of the virgin continent changed the character of the social struggle, throwing the emphasis off trade unionism and the direct struggle of the wage earners, and onto the more political struggle of the farmers and independent producers. Nevertheless, one has only to think of what the distribution of the American national income would probably have been like in the absence of democratic institutions; of what the distribution of income would have been like if the railroad barons and the other tycoons of the first, late nineteenth-century, wave of the consolidation of American capital had been unchecked, to appreciate that

American democracy has had just as decisive economic consequences as any other.

We reach the paradoxical conclusion that it has been, precisely, the struggle of the democratic forces *against* capitalism which has saved the system.* It has done so not only by making tolerable the conditions of life of the wage earners, but also by keeping open that indispensable market for the final product which the self-destructive drive of capitalism to a more and more inequitable distribution of the national income would otherwise have closed. Thus democracy has had far-reaching economic consequences. It has determined, within limits sufficiently wide to be profoundly significant, the actual distribution of goods and services between persons and classes of persons. It has gone far to determine, in plain English, who shall be rich and who shall be poor, and how rich and how poor they shall be.

It is useful to notice here that the derivation of such economic consequences from a political cause is a strictly impossible phenomenon in Marx's system, at any rate as that system has been interpreted by contemporary Leninists.† At a later point in this study we shall discuss this major theoretical issue. Suffice it here to note that contemporary Marxist (*i.e.*, communist) thinking continually tends to assume that the interaction between economic and political events, which was Marx's epoch-making discovery, is always one way; that economic development is always causal

---

* Socialists used to ... there was something wrong in this and protest against me ... ring up capitalism." But the experience of what really happ ... an economic and social system like capitalism collapses has taught t ... tter. They now know that their job is to supersede capitalism *without* letting it collapse.

† Quite a good case can be made out that Marx himself, and certainly Engels, admitted such possibilities, but always a little reluctantly and by way of exceptions. See, for example, Engels' letter to Bloch, 21st Sept., 1890, to Schmidt, 27th Oct., 1890, and to Mehring, 14th July, 1893. (*Marx-Engels Correspondence*, Martin Lawrence, London, 1934.)

and political development consequential. It will be a contention of this study that this has proved an enormously oversimplified view. The interaction between the two types of development has proved to be extremely complex and, above all, reciprocal. The contemporary form of democracy (as defined in this chapter) has been bound up with capitalist "relations of production" (*i.e.*, private property in means of production worked by wage earners). But it has been associated with it not only as effect but also as cause. Not only was it necessary to clear away semi-feudal and absolutist *régimes* at the key points (America, Britain, France) before capitalism could fairly get going; but also, as we have seen, political democracy has continued to react upon the capitalist economy. In the advanced latest-stage capitalisms it has altogether prevented the immiseration of the wage earners, allowing their standard of life to rise roughly in step with the rise in the gross national product per head. And in the last two decades in Britain it has actually succeeded in effecting, for the moment at least (1956), a modest but perceptible increase in the wage earners' share in the ever-growing product. However, it is much too early to assert that this latest achievement will prove permanent. (If it does, it will prove of the highest significance.) But even disregarding this latest and still precarious achievement of democracy, it has now been amply demonstrated that the interaction between "the economic base" and "the political superstructure" of society, as Marxists call them, is anything but one-way.

THE NATURE OF CONTEMPORARY DEMOCRACY

A later section of this study will be devoted to the political and historical issue alluded to in the last paragraph. But even in this "economic" volume it will be indispensable to say something about the nature of contemporary democracy. For this form of government has proved itself to be an economic force in its own right. If we are to have any hope of being able to draw a diagram of contemporary capitalism sufficiently accurate to have predictive power, we must make an estimate of the nature, strength and prospects of democracy, the main force with which it interacts. Naturally our treatment of so vast and complex a subject cannot here be either full or adequate. Here the economic consequences of democracy are our primary concern. We are only trying to sum up, very roughly, what is the nature of this major contemporary phenomenon which is unquestionably having profound economic consequences. We shall not attempt here even to raise the question of the nature of political forces and institutions—the State, class interests, methods of rule— as such.

What, then, is the nature of contemporary democracy? This is one of those questions to which we all know the answer so long as we are not asked to give it. We all know, or at least we all think we know, what we mean by saying that, for example, Britain and America are democracies. But we should be hard put to it for a definition. Contemporary democracy is a complex of social and political institutions, and of attitudes of mind built upon these institutions. It is a form of society the very existence of which it is easy for minds cast in a mechanistic mould to deny. It ought, surely, to be possible to refer to some established and universally accepted piece of political theory in order to define what we mean by this concept which, after all, we use every day. But the truth is that this would not prove a very fruitful procedure. If economic theory is in the "awkward age" of a young science, political science is at least as immature. Political science has in fact scarcely emerged from a purely descriptive, classificatory phase of development. Indeed even the observation and classification of real phenomena have only begun. Much of our political thinking is still half in that pre-scientific stage in which elaborate deductions from abstract "theories" hold the field. Hence we shall have to attempt a little political investigation on our own account, in the hope of achieving at least a rather better approximation to reality.

We may deal briefly with the traditional view that democracy means the direct rule of the people. The word did mean this (or rather it meant the rule of the free males of native parentage on both sides) in the Greek *polis* of classical antiquity. And it is the predilection of some of those who give and receive a classical education to maintain that the word should be restricted to this meaning. But if this is what democracy means, then, of course, there is no single democratic society in existence, nor has there been since the fall of Athens.* Thus if we adopted this "definition by pedantry" the whole question would be of purely academic interest. Germany under Hitler and Russia today would have to be regarded as being as much or as little democracies as Britain or America. There would be no question to discuss. Nevertheless, if contemporary democracy does not mean the direct rule of the people, what does it mean? Surely we must mean *something* when we say that Country A is a democracy and that Country B is not. For we often, and rightly, found our policies upon the distinction.

ASPECTS OF CONTEMPORARY DEMOCRACY

I. Representative Government

The best course will be to examine the main aspects of the political systems, as they actually exist, of those highly de-

* I understand that the institutions of certain Swiss cantons still approximate to direct democracy in this sense; the exception illustrates the rule.

veloped capitalist societies of the West which we call democracies.

There is, first, the narrowly political aspect of democracy, namely, representative government. In everyday speech we say that a country is democratic when there exists some established, and actually working, social mechanism by means of which its adult citizens, or almost all of them, elect a Parliament, or Congress, which has substantial power, and which in turn elects and sustains, at its pleasure, an executive government. Such a definition is by no means perfect. It does not, for instance, exactly cover the largest existing democracy, the United States. There the electorate simultaneously, but separately, elects the head of the Executive in the person of the President, as well as the Parliament or Congress, who appoints his Cabinet or Executive Government.

There is no intention to belittle the importance of these different forms of representative government. On the contrary, particular representative institutions, by either frustrating or promoting the effectiveness of a democratic system, may be of decisive significance. But what it is necessary to emphasise is that these differences between Presidential Democracy, with a sharp division of powers (America), and Parliamentary Democracy, with a high degree of unification of power in the hands of the elected Parliament (Britain), do not in practice cause anyone to doubt that both arrangements are forms of the contemporary system of representative government. In just the same way those still more contrasting political forms of Republic and Constitutional Monarchy are also now unhesitatingly recognised as two alternative forms of representative democratic government.

The fact is that all these apparently very different systems of Presidential or Parliamentary, Republican or Monarchic, government are all now seen to be forms, varying interestingly but not essentially, of the same general social category,

namely, representative government, which is itself the political aspect of contemporary democracy. Why is this? In
answering that question we shall discover the importance, in
any consideration of democracy, of fixing our attention on
the real, functioning institutions and organisations, instead
of upon constitutional provisions; of fixing our attention, for
instance, upon the *political parties*, their conventions or annual conferences, their finances and their social roots, rather
than upon electoral colleges, systems of voting, and the like.
For, of course, the real reason why it makes only a secondary
difference whether you elect your executive direct, or
through your Parliament, or whether you have a Queen or a
President, is that what a modern electorate really elects is
neither President nor Parliament, Queen nor Prime Minister. What a contemporary electorate chooses to rule over it is
a political party. This is indeed a cold conclusion; but it is a
fact and it had better be faced. For it is from this, at first
sight, not very hopeful act of choosing one out of several competing political parties (or a coalition of parties) to form a
government that a people obtains for itself those major and
highly tangible benefits which we have described above. For
example: the contemporary British electorate puts either
the Labour Party or the Conservative Party into power; the
American electorate puts either the Republican or the Democratic Party into power; the French electorate puts a seeth-
ing permutation and combination of parliamentary groups,
which in turn puts an endless succession of extremely brief,
but extremely similar, Cabinets into power. And so on. The
contemporary electorate, "the people," do no more and no
less than this; for good or ill this is the political aspect of
contemporary democracy as we practice it in the West. What
is it worth?

THE LENINIST DEFINITION

Let us first consider a definition of democracy made by the man who valued representative government at its lowest. It will be remembered that Lenin described contemporary parliamentary democracy as a system by which the working class chose, every five years, which member of the governing class was to rule over them. As a description of how, in historical fact, representative institutions grew up in nineteenth-century Britain, the definition could hardly be bettered. An election in late nineteenth-century Britain in a working-class constituency was in fact a contest between two members of the ruling class for the votes of the male wage earners. The two contesting members of the ruling class respectively represented, on the whole, a different section of that class: the Liberal candidate representing the manufacturing, and the Conservative candidate, the land-owning, sections. How, then, did highly beneficial consequences for the standard of life of the wage earners ultimately ensue from such a system as that? They ensued, of course, precisely because the process was one in which two members, and in essence two factions, of the ruling class competed for working-class votes. They ensued gradually but inexorably from the irresistible temptation which such a system set up to bid for working-class votes, and so to promise to promote, and sometimes actually to promote, the interests of the wage earners as well as the interests of the particular section of the ruling class which the candidate, and his party, represented.

Moreover, it was not only that the rival Liberal and Conservative bidders for their votes periodically promoted the wage earners' direct economic interests, as for example by means of maximum-hours and minimum-wage legislation, and later by means of the establishment of tax-financed social services. It was even more that the bidders began, competitively, to permit that crucial growth of trade unionism, and working-class organisation generally, which enabled the wage earners to begin the process of acquiring power in general, and bargaining power in particular, of their own. The story of the gradual, uneven, stubbornly resisted, growth of trade unionism from the Cross Acts to the repeal of the Trades Disputes Act in 1906 is, in its parliamentary aspect, the story of the British wage earners choosing that member of the governing class who would, in return for their votes, permit the growth of the wage earners' bargaining power.*

In Britain, in the first half of the twentieth century, Lenin's description began to be increasingly inapplicable. With the replacement of the Liberal by the Labour Party, British representative government began to cease to be a process by which rival factions of the ruling class bid for wage-earners' votes, and began to become a contest between a party based upon the owning and wage-earning classes, respectively. This will prove to be, it seems probable, a far more important, and critical, phase of representative government than any which has preceded it. For at this point in their development representative institutions are likely to be used by the wage earners to attempt to remodel the economic system in their interests.

Nor must we forget how recent a thing is representative government in this full contemporary form, as we know it today. In fact it will be argued that the General Election of 1929 marked its complete establishment in Britain. For it was not until that election that, on the one hand, completely universal adult suffrage was achieved and, on the other, that the replacement of the Liberal by the Labour Party became definitive. Thus it will be said that fully repre-

---

* The final repeal in 1946 of the renewed bout of anti-trade-union legislation was, of course, effected by the alternative method of securing direct wage-earners' representatives.

sentative government was still (1956) in Britain only thirty-five years old. In fact, it will be more realistic to date its establishment from about the end of the second decade of the century. It would clearly be absurdly hasty to suppose that a form of government which was still only some thirty-five years old had yet unfolded all its potentialities. We must anticipate far more profound consequences, economic, social and political, as a result of the maintenance of such a system over the decades than we have yet experienced, if such a system is in fact maintained. Thus representative government in its contemporary form is not, even in Britain, as is often unconsciously assumed, some old, long-established, traditional way of life. Many of its institutions—Parliament, Cabinet government, general elections, party contests, and the rest—are indeed of varying but considerable antiquity. But, half unnoticed and in our own lifetimes, the enfranchisement of the wage earners as a whole has breathed a new spirit into these old institutions, so that they are now filled with new purposes and face new tasks and new obstacles.

The economic task, which British representative institutions, in their stage of growth, succeeded, on the whole, in performing, was to put enough pressure upon capitalism, in its earlier competitive form, to force it to raise the wage-earners' standard of life, roughly in step with the rise in national production. Their new economic task, now that they have fully developed, will be so to remodel latest-stage capitalism as to make possible the continued rise in the workers' standard of life at a pace sufficient to prevent economic and social crisis. It will be argued below that if we could assume the maintenance, unchallenged, of our representative institutions, and of the democracy of which they form the central part, there could be little doubt of their capacity to perform these further tasks. But the assumption is a major one. For the strains and stresses, internal and external, to which these institutions are likely to be subjected, in the performance of their new tasks, will be heavy indeed. Will contemporary democracy, this newly developed and still daringly experimental system of government, be able to sustain such an ordeal? Will our contemporary representative institutions prove so deeply rooted that they can perform the immense task of remodelling the economic and social system in accordance with the will and interest of the wage-earning 90% of the population? We shall not be in a position to deal with these questions till Chapter 12 below. And even then we shall find that the only honest answer is that the political struggles of our times will turn, in the West, upon the democratic attempt to do just this. Whether it will succeed or not no one can foretell, but the duty of all democrats is to throw themselves into the attempt.

REPRESENTATIVE INSTITUTIONS AND PARTY DICTATORSHIP CONTRASTED

In order even to approach this question, it is necessary to look realistically at our representative institutions as they are actually functioning amongst us in the mid-twentieth century. It has been said that what the British people actually choose, every four or five years, to govern them is a political party. But what that party in fact does, having been chosen, is to establish a government, sustained by its parliamentary majority. And that government will have the general character, colour, tendencies—it will point in the same direction—as the party which has established it. Therefore, what in fact, by means of the mechanism of competing parties, the British electorate does is to choose a government of one or other of two alternative political tendencies. At the moment in Britain, for instance, it chooses a government either of the Labour-Socialist tendency, or of the contemporary, reconstructed, post-Second-World-War, Conservative tendency. The electorate, far from being able even to attempt to govern itself in the old Athenian sense, can do no more, but no less, than this. Again, what is it worth? Experience shows that such a system of representative government, if it can be maintained, is worth almost anything. This conclusion will, surely, only surprise those who are comparing the actual workings of British, American, Scandinavian, West German, French or Italian, representative institutions, with some cherished ideal, instead of with the alternative forms of government actually available to twentieth-century man. Those alternatives are variants of the other possible form of twentieth-century government, namely, party dictatorship.

As this study proceeds we shall have occasion to study both the communist and the fascist forms of this alternative to democracy, namely, government by party dictatorship. It is no part of our argument to maintain that these forms are identical or even similar in content. On the contrary, the social purposes served by the communist and fascist forms of absolute party rule are very different. Nevertheless, they do undoubtedly use the same political mechanism, namely, absolute party rule, as their solution of the problem of how to rule a modern community and how to conduct a modern economy.* Therefore we can in this respect contrast them with government by means of representative institutions. And, if we do so, how can we judge them to be anything but grossly inferior?

It is not that government by party dictatorship is incapable of great economic achievements. On the contrary, in its fascist form it drove German capitalism in its latest stage into formidable activity, and in its communist form it has achieved prodigies of economic development, albeit prodigies drenched with human blood, but nonetheless epoch-

---

* In its fascist form government by party dictatorship can and does conduct an economy in the latest stage of capitalism, while the communist form of this method of government conducts or controls a rudimentary form of socialised economy.

making on that account. Nevertheless, there is now conclusive evidence that this form of government by party dictatorship, since it is uncontrolled by, and only most clumsily responsive to, the will of the population which it rules, is quite unsuitable for highly evolved communities with literate and politically sophisticated populations. If and when attempts are made to impose it upon such communities, monstrous injustices and violent strains and stresses inevitably arise—stresses so violent indeed that they imperil the very existence of man on this narrow twentieth-century earth.

It is not so much a question of the good or evil intentions of the particular men, or man, who, inevitably, come, or comes, to control such a system of absolute party rule. We have experienced the results both when those men are homicidal maniacs of great ability, as in the case of the Nazis, and when they are (as they were in the case of the first Bolshevik government) possibly the most idealistic,* if fanatical, body of men who have ever come to power in a great state. It would be utterly wrong to say that the results have been similar. But they have had this in common: they have both involved a degree of compulsion by physical violence, and all that goes with it by way of mental constraint, before which the world still reels in horror. The basic reason for this common factor of combined physical violence and mental constraint, in such *régimes* of absolute party rule, is that they lack any mechanism by which their populations can modify, control, or periodically change, their governments. For lack of such a mechanism all such governments, irrespective of

---

* They would, of course, have been extremely annoyed at being described as idealists. Yet their record shows that they held to and served the ideal of communism, as they understood it, with unparalleled fixity of purpose. That was just the trouble. If they had been more opportunist they would, no doubt, have been lesser men, but they would have spared Russia and the world almost inconceivable agonies. Nor is it at all certain that in that event Russia might not have made comparable material progress by other means.

their intentions, commit themselves to courses of action which involve them in a monstrously high degree of mental and physical coercion. Precisely because they are irresponsible, they fail to reflect the complex, ever-changing reality of highly developed modern communities (they are much more successful in simpler societies): their decisions begin to lose touch with reality, to become, in that technical sense, insane. They begin to run amok. They do frightful damage to the fabric of society, not so much because of their crimes, as because of their mistakes. And they make those mistakes because they lack any effective mechanism which can keep them in touch with what the populations over which they rule will accept without total compulsion.

It emerges that the first worth of representative institutions lies not so much in what they can accomplish as in what they can prevent. They are, in the first place, safety devices; they are the steering-wheel and the brakes of the vehicle of government rather than its engine. But they are nonetheless important for that. On a crowded modern road a car literally cannot go more than a few yards without steering-wheel or brakes. And in that sense representative government of some kind or another may yet be found to be indispensable to the successful government, over any long period, of highly developed communities.

If this in fact proves to be the case, it will not be because any mystical wisdom resides in contemporary electorates. "The average voter" does not know everything and does not by any means always know best. But he knows one thing. He knows how much he can stand. And when he can stand no more he chooses an "alternative government" which will, in the main, have won his support by promising *not* to do the things which have become displeasing to him in the existing government. Representative institutions are, in fact, then, an elaborate system of interconnections, of transmission belts, between governed and governing. They do not permit the governed to rule themselves; but they do permit them to choose which of alternative kinds of rulers they will have. And by doing that apparently limited thing they establish a much greater degree of popular control over government than might be supposed. Anyone who has been a member of a representative government knows that the transmission belts thus established between ruler and ruled are by no means ineffective. They do not ensure good government, but they do ensure a kind of government which does not diverge too far from what the population will support. For if the government's decisions do so diverge, there are vigilant and active competitors in the field perpetually urging upon the electors that they have only to change their suffrages to secure rulers who are willing and anxious to abstain from the displeasing decisions and policies.

Thus all the fume and fret of elections, the endless and often empty wrangles of Parliament, and all the other banalities and absurdities of democratic political life, really are serving an indispensable purpose. But it is a different and, in a sense, more limited purpose than is often claimed for them. They do not permit the people to rule themselves. They are a form of competitive process. They are the political analogy to the higgle of the market in the economic sphere. The voters choose that team of politicians who by their record of decisions in the past, by their promises of decisions in the future, by their general attitude and approach to public affairs, and by their association with this or that "interest"—employers of labour, land owners, trade unions, etc.—most pleases, or, more realistically, least displeases, them. It is by means of this elaborate, noisy higgle-haggle of the political marketplace alone that contemporary governments are kept in touch with the complex social reality of highly developed communities. By means of this often despised and derided democratic mechanism alone are we saved, not only from the crimes which, truly, cry to heaven, but also from the mistakes, which are far worse still, of contemporary party dictatorships.

For the rulers, or ruler, of such irresponsible governments cannot, with the best will in the world, keep in touch with the social reality beneath them or him. He will possess indeed an elaborate apparatus in his totalitarian party and his police, not only for forming, but also for gauging, public opinion. But all that will be no substitute for the *competitive* processes of democratic political institutions. Unless there are at least *two* candidates at an election, there can be no real test and trial of what the electors think and feel. And so the dictators stalk on, sometimes diabolic, sometimes benevolent in their intention, but always blind. It is their blindness, rather than their sins, which dooms them to coerce and to terrorise. They kill because they cannot comprehend. The democracies are saved from the ovens of Auschwitz and the ice-camps of the Yenisei by the rough and tumble, the horseplay, the absurdities and the extravagances of British contested elections, American party conventions, French party manoeuvring and all the rest of the strange machinery of competitive representative institutions.

The benefits which functioning representative institutions can confer on a community are thus immense. They do not indeed enable us to re-create the exquisite microcosm of the Greek *polis* on our twentieth-century scale, and thus realise democracy in its ancient sense of government directly participated in by each member of the community. (Whether modern technical developments in telecommunication may in future make something of this sort possible again is a speculation for the future.) But they do provide the all-important connective tissue between governed and governing in the body social. By their basic mechanism of choice between competitive teams of potential governors they enable the governed to exercise a very real measure of supervision and control over the general policies of the governors.

They are, on the whole, the central institutions of contemporary democracy, round which its other aspects cluster, and with which they interact.

THE CONCEPT OF AN ALTERNATIVE GOVERNMENT

We must now begin the process, which will preoccupy us in much of the rest of this study, of looking at the other side of the democratic medal. So far we have emphasised the immense benefits which effectively functioning democratic institutions can confer. Now we must discuss the daunting difficulties which stand in the way of actually making such institutions effective. In this chapter we may merely note the inherent difficulties of contemporary democratic institutions and the high degree of sophistication needed by a community which seeks to employ them. In subsequent chapters we shall be concerned with the way in which democratic institutions can be used to change still further the nature of capitalism, and ultimately to transcend it altogether. We shall discuss, from several different angles of vision, the inherent difficulties of such a task. Then we shall notice the maladies to which democratic forces are susceptible, even if the stage of development of the society in which they operate is high enough to make their success objectively possible.

It is, first of all, important to envisage the complex and subtle problems which must be faced in order to make contemporary democratic institutions function at all. In this connection one of the key questions may be defined as the question of the *quality* of "the opposition of the opposition" in a democratic system. Unless this question can be satisfactorily solved, representative institutions cannot work. For if "the opposition of the opposition" in a democratic system is total, it represents in fact a permanent state of insurrection against the existing government. If, that is to say, the leaders and the supporters of the opposition party have

nothing—neither objectives, methods, loyalties, nor faith—
in common with the government party, they are bound,
sooner or later, to destroy that government, and the party on
which it is based, or to be destroyed by them. They cannot
possibly be expected to alternate with them in power. Nor
can we expect either side in such a total contest to abide by
the decision of some particular general election. Men do not,
and never will, go to their final political, and for that matter
physical, destruction according to the majority vote of an
electorate, which at any one particular election may be arbitrary and accidental. Thus it is of the essence of representative institutions that "the opposition of the opposition"
should not be total and that the government of the day shall
not, for its part, do anything irrevocably to injure its opponents. Unless these limitations are observed, the alter-
nation of government and opposition parties in power, and
so the possibility of choice by the electorate, is impossible.

But, if "the opposition of the opposition" must not be
total, neither must it be nominal nor perfunctory. For if it is,
then again the electorate can exercise no genuine choice. Unless the opposition party represents a genuinely different
tendency, unless it really would put the helm over and steer
the ship on a divergent, although not opposite, course, the
electorate is impotent, and soon feels that it is impotent. We
must conclude that, in order that representative institutions
may work, some means must be found of combining real and
important differences with a much deeper underlying unity
between the political parties which compete for the votes of
the electorate, and so for power. (A pair of traditional British political maxims respectively exemplify these two antithetical necessities. "The business of an opposition is to
oppose"; and, on the other hand, "The Queen's Government must be carried on.")

A high degree of political sophistication will be necessary, then, in order to maintain this national unity in diver-

sity. It is foolish and unfair to expect any such thing from communities which have not long possessed a real measure of social welfare and economic stability. It would not be difficult to point out the countries which are still below the economic and social level of development at which there can be much hope of such a feat. Whenever the standard of life of the mass of the population is below a certain level of human welfare, and the distribution of the national income below a certain level of equity, the masses do not and cannot feel the necessary identification with the national *régime*. Nor, on the other hand, do they feel the necessary hope of being able to modify that *régime* in their own favour without first destroying it. And both these basic attitudes are necessary to the effective functioning of modern representative institutions. In such cases the masses either remain indifferent and sub-political, in which case there will be no real differences between the competing political parties, or there will emerge a party of total opposition—in practice today a communist party.

No doubt many other factors, such as national temperament and tradition, geographical situation, and sheer luck, are also relevant. One should not regard the economic as by any means the sole factor. Nevertheless, it may be suggested, by way of illustration, that the economic and social level necessary today for the effective working of representative institutions might seem to be somewhere below that of Northern, and above that of Southern, Italy. Thus Italy as a whole represents a sort of borderland case of a country which is at or about the indispensable level.* Below such a

---

* Mr. Colin Clark (in a letter to the writer) gives the following figures for Italian real income in 1955 pounds:

> 1938. Southern Italy £75 per year per head,
> Northern Italy £135 " " " "

Since then he estimates average income has increased by 50% (to 1955), with a tendency for the South to catch up with the North. (The British figure for 1955 is usually given at something over £300 p.a. per head.)

level of economic and social development it is difficult to see how representative institutions can function effectively.* In simpler communities the Government is the Government. The very idea of "an alternative Government" is baffling and meaningless. I recollect once being asked by a Russian to explain to him the meaning of a third maxim of British public life, "Her Majesty's Loyal Opposition." I did not succeed.

ASPECTS OF CONTEMPORARY DEMOCRACY

II. The Right of Association

So much for those representative institutions which are the narrowly political, electoral side of democracy. It is sometimes suggested, however, that this is not even contemporary democracy's most important aspect. It may be held that today the organisation of the decisive part of the wage earners into self-governing trade unions is the basic condition of the existence of democracy in contemporary society; that representative institutions are themselves but a superstructure, however important and beneficial, dependent upon an underlying trade-union strength. Moreover, it may be held that representative institutions are a superstructure doomed to be destroyed if ever the strength of trade unionism should fail. It may be held that the trade unions are the real institutions which have asserted that bargaining power which alone has falsified the prediction of ever-increasing misery; that, in a word, trade unions are the essential instruments through which the economic consequences of democracy are made effective. But any argument as to the primacy of this

---

* I hope and believe that India may prove an exception to this judgment. Her peoples are far below the standard of life at which one could reasonably expect them to be able to work a democratic system. Yet they are clearly wonderfully sophisticated, subtle and politically minded. They seem to enjoy the democratic political process. Perhaps they will be able to work it.

or that aspect of democracy would be barren. What it is necessary to grasp is that representative institutions are not some abstract good in themselves; that inextricably associated with them there develop other aspects of contemporary democratic society, of which one of the most important is the *organisation* of the wage earners, primarily into trade unions.

Historically neither representative institutions nor the "right of association" into trade unions, co-operative societies, or any other bodies which the workers may choose to form, can claim primacy. The two aspects of democracy have not only developed contemporaneously, but have interacted continually. It seldom proves possible for wage earners to develop their industrial power in trade unions till they have acquired a measure of political power by enfranchisement. Equally, however, it is the solid pressure of established trade unions, seeking to modify the legal, economic and social structure of the community in such a way as to enable them fully to exert their bargaining power, which mobilises the wage-earning voters into political parties.

In the earlier stages of development it is undoubtedly the right of association which matters most directly to the wage earners. The workers begin to struggle to form trade unions more earnestly, and often actually earlier, than they begin to struggle for the vote. In Britain their emancipation from the misery of their conditions of a hundred years ago is more directly and visibly connected with their ability to organise than with representative institutions. Therefore, for the wage earner, the real meaning and content of contemporary democracy is at least as much dependent upon the right of association as upon representative institutions. That is why the tradition, the "lore," of a labour movement concerns itself even more with the trade-union struggle than with the struggle for the franchise. In Britain, for example, the labour movement celebrates the pioneers of early trade unionism and co-operation rather than the supporters of the reform bills of the 'sixties and 'eighties.

We sometimes celebrate those pioneers of trade unionism and co-operation with more sentiment than knowledge or understanding. But, for all that, can we ever too greatly honour these men and women? For they laid the essential basis of modern democracy. In the mire of Tolpuddle and the murk of Rochdale, in a hundred other British back streets and country lanes, the social atoms began to fuse. These for the most part anonymous men and women then and there began the long, painful process by which the hitherto help-less wage earners were to forge for themselves the organisa-tions and institutions which could alone enable them to ap-pear as actors instead of patients on the pages of history. Nor was that development accomplished without almost unbe-lievably stubborn perseverance and immense self-sacrifice. The sheer doggedness, level-headedness and good sense of the nineteenth- and early twentieth-century British workers in using the means that were open to them, constituted a kind of heroism no less noble, and far more fruitful, than that of their continental comrades who died upon the barri-cades. For they gave social and economic content to the polit-ical democracy which, by the middle of the twentieth century, had been established in Britain.

Whoever has failed to understand the extreme importance of the right of association and all that goes with it—of all that is often called "working-class democracy"—has failed to cross the true Rubicon of modern political thought and feel-ing. He has remained upon the other side of that sometimes invisible, but deep, stream which divides the world of the wage earner from that of the property owner. He has re-mained in the realm of abstract principles, of more or less unreal and papery schemes and constitutions, and of "eco-nomic laws" which are thought to apply equally to million-aires and paupers. Paper constitutions are indeed important, or, more precisely, they *become* important as soon as the wage earners achieve a sufficient degree of solidarity, of organisation, of consciousness of their own aims and interests, to fill out those otherwise empty abstractions with the content of their social purposes. But it is the organisation of the wage earners that counts. It is typical of even the most brilliant of those members of the property-owning classes who have not made an emotional identification with the cause of the wage earners to be blind to all or much of this. They remain naïvely individualist, unable to comprehend that it is only by means of the opposite of naïve individualism, that it is only by means of social coherence, by means of organisation and solidarity, with all the sacrifices of personal irresponsibility involved, that the many-millioned and otherwise atomised and impotent class of wage earners can possibly use those very liberal institutions which the upper-class individualists so much value. It is only by travelling down the road of organisation, solidarity and co-operation that the true individualism, the true liberty, which is, undoubtedly, the goal of the whole journey, can possibly be reached. Unfortunately these paradoxes, or dialectical propositions as the Marxists would call them, though sensible and even obvious enough, when you come to think of them, are usually still a closed book to those who have never looked at things from the wage-earners' point of view.

Marx and Engels, on the other hand, may be said to have seen little but the working-class side of democracy. They were passionately eager to help the British workers, amongst whom they lived, to form their organisations. But, naturally enough, it was the trade-unionist side of the movement for which they most cared. They took very little account of the parallel and indispensable movement by which the wage earners were becoming enfranchised. For this process was going on within the upper-class system, by means of the above-defined process of competitive bidding for the wage-earners' votes.

ASPECTS OF CONTEMPORARY DEMOCRACY

III. The Liberty of the Subject: The Rule of Law:

The Diffusion of Power

What may be called "the liberty of the subject" is historically the oldest aspect of democracy. In Britain, long before men attempted to use the government, they successfully attempted to limit it. Long before representative institutions had developed to a point where they concerned the vast majority of the population, enough pressure had been put upon the still largely irresponsible executive to force it to make laws limiting the amount of coercion which it could apply to the subject, and defining the conditions and methods under which this coercion should alone be applied. This is "the rule of law." As it is one of the oldest aspects of democracy, it is also one of the most precious: the twentieth-century horrors which have appeared wherever and whenever it has been abrogated leave little need to remind us of that.

However, this is also a concept of greater political sophistication than is universally realised. A limited government inevitably seems a baffling and even self-contradictory concept to minds which have not experienced our Western kind of historical development. In the same way that the concept of an alternative government is an impossible one for such minds, so is the concept of a limited government. It is felt that any self-limitations of power must be unreliable and unreal; that, in fact, there is nothing between absolute power and absolute liberty. (And that the latter can only be realised in the stateless commune of the future.)

It has been one of the immense achievements of the West to show in actual practice that this is not so. The eighteenth-century democrats who formed, in France, the theory, and in America, the practice of our earlier types of representative government were preoccupied with this issue. Hence their elaborate provisions for the division of powers among different and, if possible, rigidly separated organs of government, such as the executive, the legislature and the judiciary: a preoccupation to which the American Constitution is so vast a monument. This is one attempted solution. But the judicious student of democratic institutions is today unlikely to attach primary importance to such constitutional provisions, either for good or ill. Experience is showing us that it is not the division of powers within the government, but the diffusion of power throughout the community, which matters. It would be possible to have a very arbitrary *régime* indeed, in which executive, legislature and judiciary were rigidly separated, if one narrow section of the population had effective control of all three.

For example, the American government has just such a rigid separation of powers. But if American "big business" were again to become absolutely dominant, and unchecked by any other social forces, as it was in the nineteen-twenties, for example, such a separation of powers would not avail to prevent a tyranny. It is the pressure of the American wage earners and their trade unions, and the American voters generally, which will, in the main, preserve American liberties, not the separation of powers within her government. (This is not, however, to deny that "constitutional safeguards" may play a beneficial role at certain times and places; they may give to an electorate debauched, temporarily, by demagogic reaction time to come to its senses. We have just [1956] seen an example of this in the case of the McCarthy crisis of the early nineteen-fifties.) And equally it is possible for a government to be strictly limited, and scrupulously law-abiding, even if there is little division between its executive, legislature and judiciary, if only power over such a government is shared by, and is widely diffused among, the social classes. The contemporary British government is an example of this fact. The power of the British House of Commons is, since the latest curtailment of the House of Lords' power of delay to nine months, virtually absolute. But British liberties have in fact never been more real. For the House of Commons itself reflects and responds to the diverse, divergent, reciprocating social forces of the whole community. Every section of the British people has found a way of bringing to bear its influence on the making of the government's decisions.

ASPECTS OF CONTEMPORARY DEMOCRACY

IV. Freedom of Speech and Opinion

When we say, "It's a free country, isn't it?" we usually mean that we can say and write what we like. And so, within remarkably wide limits, we really can in mid-twentieth-century Britain. A high degree of such freedom of speech and opinion is another indispensable aspect of modern democracy. This is at once democracy's most obviously attractive result and, at the same time, a condition for the effective existence of the other aspects which we have enumerated. There can be no effective representative institutions, right of association or liberty of the subject without a high degree of freedom of speech and opinion. And freedom of speech and opinion will never be long sustained except in a community which is effectively operating representative institutions and effectively exercising its rights of association and its individual liberties.

Such freedom of speech is a glorious thing and we exercise it in Britain today to our hearts' content. A neighbour of mine, for example, recently informed me with due solemnity that in his opinion the British people were "a nation of Judas Iscariots": and this because 51.3% of the electors at a recent bye-election voted in a sense contrary to that approved of by my neighbour. We indulge wholesale in such ecstasies of partisanship in our day-to-day political life, and at the time even half mean what we say. No harm comes of it because in the crucible of all the thoughts, feelings, opinions and assertions being expressed by everyone an indescribably complex cancelling-out process seems to occur by means of which all the nonsense, or half-sense, or one-sided sense, which we all talk and write is rubbed and shaken together and jostled and rebutted and refuted, until a sort of balance of general opinion is struck. Of course that general opinion is not always right. It would not be difficult to point to occasions on which the light of after events has shown it to have been disastrously wrong. But it has the vast practical advantage of *being* the general opinion, of being the opinion to which there is, on the whole, the least opposition and for which there is the most support. Therefore it can be acted upon with the minimum degree of social coercion.

Moreover, this continuous process of free discussion, in which everybody's ideas are chaffered against everybody else's, has another vital justification. If anybody knew the truth about economic and political issues, to anything approaching even the degree of approximation to reality achieved in the older physical sciences, there would be no need and no justification for such a process. But no one does know. The so-called "laws" of economics and politics are incomparably less exact than those of, say, physics. It is, above all, for this reason that we should preserve our precious liberty to speak nonsense, or at best one-sided sense, for no one yet has more than a glimmer of what is sociological sense. And so the only way of preventing ourselves from deviating too far from reality is to allow everyone to speak his mind and thus provide a sort of vast market of opinion in which some sort of consensus, on the basis of which we can act, will emerge.

All this suggests an analogy with the economic market in which innumerable buyers and sellers used to higgle-haggle over their exchanges and so produce "the price" of each commodity. And this analogy contains a lurking implication. It suggests that contemporary economic development holds a special danger to the right of free and effective expression of opinion. Just as a main theme of this volume is to show how the decrease in the number, and the increase in the size, of the buyers and sellers on the economic market has distorted, and bids fair in the end to destroy, that market, so the decrease in the number and the increase in the size of those who have access to effective means of expression is bidding fair to distort, and ultimately destroy, the play of free opinion. Moreover, the same cause is operative. A continuous rise in the level of technique is in both cases making the units of production, whether of commodities or of opinions, bigger and fewer.

The same cause, namely, mechanisation in its broadest sense, is making the *effective* expression of opinion a monopoly, or at best oligopoly, of those who can obtain control over, or at least access to, a handful of great national newspapers and radio and television studios. This technical revolution in the dissemination of opinion, on the one hand, gives us, I repeat, a glimpse of the possibility that something analogous to the direct participation of the whole people of ancient Hellas in the public life of the community may one day become possible again. But, on the other hand, this same development has suggested that nightmare of mechanically manipulated opinion—of "thought control"—of "1984"—which increasingly haunts the contemporary imagination. This, the crucial contemporary issue for freedom of opinion, brings us to the threshold of a discussion of democracy in the latest stage of capitalism. That discussion must be postponed until we have pushed further ahead with our examination of that latest stage itself (see Chapter 13 below).

OTHER DEMOCRATIC AND PRE-DEMOCRATIC INSTITUTIONS

I am well aware that the above highly schematic summary of some of the chief aspects of contemporary democracy leaves out important institutions, and also less tangible things such as traditional social attitudes, which all go to create an effectively democratic community. In fact, it is possible to imagine a society which had established, at least on paper, a universal franchise, freedom of association and freedom of expression, and yet had failed to achieve much of what we value most in our democracies. For there are older, and less obviously political, institutions, some of them dating from a much earlier period than a wide franchise, which play an important part in our democracies.

There is a story of the Emperor Napoleon which shows how acutely he, with his deep, if fitful, political insight, was aware of all this. At the zenith of the Empire Napoleon was reviewing the *Grande Armée* before the march on Moscow. His Marshals showered congratulations upon him as the dense and glittering columns passed by. But he turned away sadly with the words, *"Tout cela ne vaut pas des institutions"*—All that doesn't make up for the lack of institutions. The Emperor was experiencing the terrible bareness of an immediately post-revolutionary *régime*. Almost all the former institutions of France had been rased to the ground. The national room was swept and garnished, but it was devoid of institutional furniture on which its inhabitants might rest. There were too few established patterns of behaviour; men had to think out their most everyday actions afresh.

What enables contemporary democracy to work in the major Western societies is not only the particular mechanisms, such as the franchise, which we have described, but also a rich pattern of long-established institutions, such as a judiciary at any rate formally independent of the government, judges not open to the crude forms of corruption, an honest and conscientious, even if conservatively minded, bureaucracy, universities jealous of their academic freedom (even if they make but sparing use of it). Such things as these are immensely precious. But what concerns us, in this first, "economic" volume of the study is that they are not only slow and difficult of establishment, but that they are also vulnerable. They are vulnerable in particular to the social strains and stresses which must arise whenever there is a failure successfully to conduct the economy. Of course any full-dress account of democracy itself, instead of, as here, of the economic consequences of democracy only, would have to take all these institutions, their historical origins and their probable future roles, into the most careful account. Here we have attempted to sketch only those aspects of democracy as it is essential to envisage for the purpose of assessing its interaction with the economy. It remains to conclude this chapter by summing up the decisive role which contemporary democracy—whatever weight we give to this or that of its aspects—has in fact played in deflecting the course of economic development from what it would have been if the political environment of capitalism had remained what it was a hundred years ago.

ECONOMIC ACHIEVEMENTS AND PROSPECTS
OF DEMOCRACY

It is this many-sided thing, democracy, which has set the
economic system as a whole on to a different course. It is
not any one of the above aspects of democracy which has
done it. It is not the enfranchisement of the wage earners,
nor their organisation into trade unions, nor their rights
and liberties, nor freedom of speech and expression, by themselves or taken separately, which have enabled the mass of
the population to push up their standard of life broadly in
step with the increase in national production. Contemporary democracy as a whole, which is more than the sum of its
parts, has been necessary to this achievement. For contemporary democracy is something more than its particular institutions. These institutions, if they work effectively, create
an all-pervading climate of opinion. And it is above all
this climate of opinion which has profound economic consequences. It is as if this almost indefinable social category,
modern democracy, had leant its soft weight upon the economic system and gradually bent it into a new shape. Lord
Attlee in a letter to the late Professor Harold Laski, which became well known as soon as it was published, expressed
the extreme importance which he attached to the changes in
the climate of opinion which democracy had effected in his
lifetime.

> Although you are a theorist and I am only a working politician,
> I think that I give more and you less attention to changes of
> conception than to legislative achievements. (But see the letter
> as a whole, pp. 159-162 of *Harold Laski* by Kingsley Martin,
> Gollancz, 1952.)

An all-embracing, all-penetrating democratic climate of opinion must be the end product of our democratic processes and institutions. Immersed in this pervasive medium, each of our institutions becomes a different thing. Crown and Parliament, Prime Minister and Cabinet, Army, Navy and Air Force, taxation and representation, political parties and electoral methods, judicial and educational systems—all of them, even when they retain their traditional forms, change their social content as and when they become filled with the impulses of that vast majority of the people who are now at last beginning to play a real part in public affairs.

But, it will be asked, cannot this pervasive force of contemporary democracy modify the nature of the major units of our economic life as well? If its power can remould the nature of Crown and Parliament themselves, cannot it modify also the nature of those giants of industry which we identified as the true *dramatis personae* of contemporary economic life? If our democracy is beginning to remould such vast bodies corporate as the Armed Forces, must it not also be expected to have its effect upon the oligopolies—upon I.C.I. and Unilever and Courtaulds and Vickers and the rest? May it not deeply modify their conduct, structure and relationships, and, if so, may we not expect democracy still further to modify the methods by which, and the purposes for which, the economy as a whole is conducted?

Again this brings us to the threshold of a discussion of democracy in the latest stage of capitalism. When, however, we come to the chapter on that subject (Chap. 13) we shall be concerned with the other and darker side of the medal. The whole character of the latest stage of capitalism is dependent upon whether it can co-exist with democracy or not. If it can, experience indicates that the latest stage can give much more beneficial results to the whole population than ever the old competitive stage achieved. If it cannot, the latest stage of capitalism must increasingly take on the atrocious form of an oligarchy of one kind or another—of which fascism is only the most recent form. Here we have shown how precious our democracy is; there we shall show how precarious it is. Here we have emphasised the far-reaching impact which it has had upon the whole balance of the economy; there we shall see that, in the latest stage of capitalism, democracy's influence must either grow to a point at which it steadily replaces capitalism by socialism, or be itself destroyed. Here we have emphasised how indispensable the pressure of democracy has been in preventing the extreme bias of capitalism in favour of capital from producing catastrophe; there we shall see that in the latest stage this pressure of the democratic forces is far more necessary still, since the system has lost what natural safeguards and self-regulating devices it once possessed.

Moreover we shall have to recognise how limited a thing is our contemporary democracy. Its institutions were only completed in Britain for example within the last thirty-five years. But it is also narrowly limited in space. It is rooted in Northwest Europe, Australasia and North America alone. It may or may not succeed in spreading to other major communities of the world. It may or may not prove applicable to nations and states which have not yet gone through the tremendous process of capital accumulation and development which characterizes almost all the well-established democracies. The truth is that the contemporary Western democracies are no more than small, brightly lit islands in the vast oceans of political time and space. In these vast oceans live the immense majority of the people of the earth, and they are ruled by much simpler and more direct means.

A DEFINITION

A short definition of contemporary democracy, which at least points towards its essential feature—and no definition can do more—is this: contemporary democracy is the diffusion of power throughout the community. And the diffusion of power pushed further and further points in turn towards the elimination of power. For if everyone could have exactly equal power, no one, clearly, would have any power over his fellows. That, of course, is for us a distant ideal; it is the ideal of perfect co-operation in perfect liberty. Nevertheless, it is important to realise that in the multi-dimensional geometry of politics the democratic line approaches, even if only asymptotically, the curve of ideal liberty. No doubt, that is to say, we shall never reach the ideal of perfect liberty by means of democracy. Nevertheless, the chief glory of democracy is that it approximates, however crudely, and even if only as compared with all other methods of government, to that ideal.

In the long meanwhile the main advantages of democracy are in a sense negative. It is a device for the avoidance of the weary, repetitive catastrophes of all forms of tyranny, while yet enabling government to be carried on. Its supreme advantage is safety—safety from the probable crimes, but above all from the inevitable errors, of irresponsible governments. We value it as much, or more, for what it prevents as for what it can achieve.

If, then, contemporary democracy is the diffusion of power in the political field, it has obvious analogies with a diffusion of ownership and wealth in the economic field. We have noted, however, that the natural drive of the capitalist system, in all its stages, a drive to be overcome only with the utmost difficulty, if at all, is to a greater and greater concentration of ownership and wealth. As we saw, it has proved possible, by means of the separation of ownership and management, by high redistributary taxation, and by other such devices, to separate to some extent the concentration of economic power and control (necessitated by the new techniques) from an ever more outrageously inequalitarian distribution of income. But the underlying economic tendency is strongly inequalitarian and centralising, and therefore it is potentially anti-democratic.

Thus the main trends in the political and economic fields are running in opposite directions. The extension of the franchise and its increasingly effective use, the consolidation of trade unionism, and the other factors which we have noted, have diffused political power through the major latest-stage capitalisms to a varying but significant degree. But in the same decades, economic power has been steadily concentrated into the hands of the major oligopolies. Such contradictory trends can hardly co-exist indefinitely. One must overcome and absorb the other, for political power and economic power are, in the last resort, merely aspects of one indivisible whole, namely, power itself. It is this contradiction which has led those who have thought most realistically about contemporary democracy to depict it always in highly dynamic terms. It is a trend or process rather than a state. Mr. Aneurin Bevan, for example, depicts the play of contemporary social forces in his book (*In Place of Fear*, p. 3) in terms of an unstable equilibrium between democracy, property and poverty. "Either," he writes, "poverty will use democracy to win the struggle against property, or property in fear of poverty will destroy democracy."

This hitherto unresolved contradiction between the trend of our political life towards the diffusion of power, and of our economic life towards the concentration of power, is a major factor in the contemporary situation. So far the diffusion of political power has just about succeeded in offsetting the effects of the concentration of economic power. It is this which has falsified the prediction of ever-increasing misery and by so doing enabled the economic system to function. But now economic power is reaching a critical degree of concentration which threatens to become incompatible with the still-growing diffusion of political power. Economic power threatens to submerge political power unless political power can at the critical moment obtain control of economic power.

THE "KNOW-HOW" FOR DEMOCRACY

The democratic forces, using their political power, must be strong enough to bit and bridle the economic power of capital; if they are to succeed, they must know *how* to control the workings of the system while they are transcending it.

9 ■ ACCUMULATION, DEMOCRACY AND EQUALITY

The rest of this volume will be concerned with the interaction between contemporary democracy and capitalism. So far we have seen that it is democracy which has up till now maintained the last-stage capitalisms in an uneasy balance. This and the following chapter seek to display some of the further economic issues involved. Chapters 11 and 12, which take the form of an exposition and evaluation of the work of John Maynard Keynes, open up the subject of the economic techniques by means of which the democratic forces may seek to control the workings, and then to transform the nature, of latest-stage capitalism. The concluding chapters broach the question of the political difficulties which the democratic forces face, and the maladies to which they are peculiarly subject, in the performance of this, their twentieth-century economic task.

THE QUESTION OF ACCUMULATION

The question of the degree of equality or inequality in the distribution of the national income is bound up with the question of the rate at which capital will be accumulated.

This is the question, to put the thing in physical terms, of the proportion of its productive energies which the community will devote to making consumers' goods for its here-and-now satisfaction, as against the proportion it will devote to making new means of production, with which to make still more consumers' goods later on. The experience of the last quarter century in particular goes to show that the whole stability— the very fate and fortune—of latest-stage capitalisms are bound up with this issue.

At this point a definition of the terms used becomes inevitable. We shall use the term *accumulation* to express the whole process of diverting some of the productive effort of the community from producing new consumers' goods for here-and-now consumption and devoting those resources to producing new means of production. It was one of the main, if largely tacit, assumptions of economics that it could be taken for granted that any productive resources so diverted, withheld or saved, would almost automatically be used to make new means of production. For this act of making new means of production the economists usually used the term *investment*. (Note that this is itself a different and narrower sense of the word investment from the one in everyday use: for the act of "investing" £1,000 in, say, Government bonds has only a remote and indirect connection with making new means of production.) Therefore the economists assumed that the whole process of accumulation would always in practice be successfully accomplished. The idea that the negative side of accumulation, namely, the diverting of resources from here-and-now consumption, may happen without its resulting in the positive side of investing these resources in new means of production, did not occur to them. But it can happen. It has proved that a capitalist community may divert or withhold a certain proportion of its productive potential from immediate consumption—and then simply let those resources lie idle. This will be an issue to which we shall have to return again and again. Nevertheless, at the outset of our argument we are not concerned with it. We are concerned with the complete act of accumulation, assuming for the moment that both sides of it are successfully accomplished.

The question of successfully accomplished accumulation has two aspects, each of which is of the highest importance. First, there is the strictly economic or quantitative aspect: what proportion of its productive capacity is society to withhold from immediate consumption, seeking to devote it to producing new means of production? How is this proportion to be settled? Is the contemporary danger that latest-stage capitalisms will devote too much or too little to accumulation? And what are the factors which will tend to increase or diminish this proportion?

Second, there is the sociological, or qualitative, aspect: what social *form* is to be taken by the recourses which are set aside for this accumulative purpose? Are they to take the form of the private profits of a small class of rich men and women? This form of accumulation is closely identified with the private ownership of society's existing means of production, from the use of which the new funds derive. Or should the sums devoted to accumulation be owned by the community as a whole, so that they become a consciously set-aside deduction from the current national income—set aside for the purpose of increasing that income after the passage of time? This form of accumulation is, of course, closely identified with the public ownership of the means of production.

And, finally, which is it of these two aspects of the question which really matters, both to the standard of life, and to the state of mind, of the wage-earning population? Is what matters the proportion of its energies which society devotes, at the expense of immediate consumption, to creating new means of production? Or is the essence of the matter the social form taken by the recourses which represent this share, *i.e.*, whether they take the form of private profit or a socially owned fund?

OVER-ACCUMULATION

To take the quantitative question first. It has been, as we have seen, common ground, explicitly for Marx, and implicitly for every school of orthodox economists, that under capitalism there would be a most unequal distribution of income, and it has been assumed that this would lead to a high rate of accumulation. Indeed Marx's diagram of capitalism depicted a society blindly and monomaniacally accumulative. He had no doubts of the power of the acquisitive drive of capitalism. This, as he said repeatedly, was the one true function of the system. But he foretold that capitalism would push what was in essence attempted over-accumulation so far that the system must break down; it would break down not only because of the political wrath of the workers reduced to subsistence, or below it, but also because of the economic nemesis which accumulation pushed to this point would bring upon it. For the wage-earning mass of the population would be left too poor to buy the consumers' goods the only ultimate purpose of which the ever-growing stock of new means of production was, after all, to produce. (This was Marx's basic explanation of crisis and slump.) Thus Marx believed that attempted over-accumulation based on an ever more extreme degree of inequality was the nemesis of the system.

In the event, the democratic counter forces, pressing for greater equality, have, in such highly developed capitalist societies as Britain and America, prevented the system from rushing on its fate in this way. But this, we concluded, did not mean that Marx's diagnosis of the innate tendencies of the system was unsound. Moreover we shall see that one clear-sighted school of non-Marxist economists have come substantially (and tacitly) to agree with him.

UNDER-ACCUMULATION

It is hardly too much to say, however, that all other orthodox economists, including even so progressive a figure as Schumpeter, have feared, and still fear, that the system will suffer from exactly the opposite tendency. The fear that the democratic counter-pressures will make society too equalitarian to be able to save and accumulate sufficiently to keep it technically progressive. Even Keynes himself, in his earlier period, at the time of writing the *Economic Consequences of the Peace,* still shared, we saw, these opposite fears. At that time, before he had developed his general theory, he too feared, rather than hoped, that society would soon cease to be "so framed" as to produce the maximum degree of inequality and consequently the maximum rate of accumulation. He had not then realised that the rate of accumulation which latter-day capitalist society, left to itself, would attempt would be so high as to be self-defeating. But by the nineteen-thirties Keynes had seen that the real danger was precisely that. To this day, however, almost every other economist is still "viewing with alarm" the effect of democratic pressures working towards equality, and, consequently, a relatively high rate of consumption and low rate of accumulation. They suppose that the flow of new capital will be cut off, that society will cease to accumulate, that the wage earners will waste society's assets by consuming its entire gross annual product on riotous living.

CAN DEMOCRACY DO IT?

In fact, it is most unlikely (subject to the qualifications made below, p. 241) that the democratic counter-pressures upon capitalism will get *too* strong. They are most unlikely to make society too equalitarian and so to cut down the rate of accumulation too far. They have, indeed, disproved the prediction of ever-increasing misery. But it has taken them all their time to enable the wage earners to do much more than hold their own—to hold, that is to say, their relative share in the total national product. The position of the holders of capital is too strong for the main "danger" to be that of the democratic pressures succeeding too well.* For in the latest stage of capitalism, especially, the limits set by competition to the growth of profits have largely collapsed. The tendency of the latest-stage capitalism really is towards ever-growing profits. Stalin's account of the system was only false because he failed to see that the system had been to some extent balanced—hitherto, at any rate—in Britain and America by democratic counter-pressures. For, as we shall see in later volumes, in the case of Germany, the most appalling consequences in fact ensue if the democratic counter-pressure on the latest-stage capitalism is relaxed.

As soon as the conclusions of this part of our narrative are thus set out in summary form, we shall see what an immense rôle they give to democracy. Can democracy possibly sustain such a rôle? Is it realistic to believe that the mere exercise of the franchise, every three or four years, can modify the very structure of the economy in such a way that it will cease to be "so framed" that it drives blindly towards maximum ac-

---

* They face very difficult practical problems in applying their pressure; we shall be much concerned with this perplexing issue as our argument proceeds.

cumulation, cost what it may? Put that way the proposition seems most unlikely. But this is too narrow a definition of democracy. Contemporary democracy is much more than the effective possession of the franchise. In order to exist effectively, contemporary democracy must include not only solidly organised and also genuinely democratic trade unionism, but also such things as the statutory buttressing of the agriculturalists, deeply entrenched traditions of free speech, free assembly and personal liberty. Contemporary democracy must amount to a complex of institutions and social traditions, the whole producing an all-pervading climate of opinion if it is to fulfil its momentous economic rôle. When we see it whole, in this way, its capacity to modify the economic structure of society does not seem so incredible. Its action may seem weak indeed in comparison with the iron compulsions of capitalism. But, like a living thing—so long as life is in it—democracy is immensely persistent and pervasive; it may yet save the day.

At this point in our study it is too early to do more than pose such questions as these. But one thing we may notice already, and that is the folly of looking upon social development statically and absolutely. Everything economic and social is ceaselessly changing—and changing at varying speeds. In particular the political and the economic factors are ceaselessly interacting and modifying each other's development. All is process and becoming. It was Marx who, above all, emphasised the necessity of this dynamic approach if any useful sociology was to emerge; it was Marx (and still more Engels) who inveighed constantly and eloquently against the rigid, anti-historical absolutism of the economic and political conceptions of their orthodox contemporaries. How bitter an irony it is, then, that contemporary Marxism has been put into a Stalinist straitjacket which renders it incapable of taking into account the flow and flux of mid-twentieth-century social development in the highly developed economies of the

West. Common or garden British and American empiricism, for all its inadequacies and banalities, which Engels used to satirise so brilliantly, is now far less out of touch with reality.

In any event, what matters is not to attempt to predict whether the impact of democracy will prove sufficient to modify capitalism, ultimately out of recognition; that none of us can confidently assert. The essential thing is to see that the struggle is being fought out above all in the field of democratic action. The essential thing is to see that the struggle is being fought out in terms of the attempt to preserve, extend and make effective those democratic forces which impinge on capitalism. It is, above all, because the Stalinist in the West will not face that fact that he bars himself from taking effective part in the social contests of our Western time and place.

So much for the quantitative aspect of accumulation. The answer to the question of whether the danger is that accumulation will be too big or too small must be that under capitalism its innate tendency is to become so big as to be self-defeating. Nevertheless, as we shall see immediately, there may be social cross currents and eddies which will introduce important qualifications to that conclusion at particular times and places.

THE PRIVATE APPROPRIATION OF SOCIAL ACCUMULATION

We can now pass on to the second, the sociological, the qualitative, aspect of the matter. We must consider the social form under which accumulation takes place in capitalist societies. The form taken by accumulation in all capitalist societies, whether or not they have reached the latest-stage, is private profit, or rather it is rent, interest and profit; it is private appropriation.

We come here upon one of the main anomalies of contemporary capitalism. For, whatever may have been the case in the adolescence of the system, accumulation is today unquestionably the accumulation of a socially produced surplus. The old arguments that the surplus arises from the "abstinence" (or the "waitings") of individual private persons, are now seen to be largely curiosities. No one who has a grasp of the reality of contemporary large-scale industry can doubt that the surplus which society annually accumulates for reinvestment in new means of production is the result of a social process of production. In that process thousands, or rather millions—indeed in the last analysis the whole community— co-operate to produce. Nevertheless under capitalism this socially and co-operatively produced surplus still in the main takes the form of private profit,* and consequently becomes the private property of a strictly limited number of people who cannot be reckoned as comprising more than 10% of the population.† Moreover it remains as true as ever it was

---

* The total surplus of production over consumption is not, of course, identical with the total of rent, interest and profit—of property-derived income, unearned income, or surplus value, whichever you like to call it. For, on the one hand, quite a lot of property-derived income is spent and some work-derived income is saved. Nevertheless, when we are dealing with broad categories, as we are here, it is indispensable to grasp that the main, essential way in which, under capitalist relations of production, a surplus for accumulation is generated is by "so framing" the economy that a large volume of rent, interest and profit is produced.

† The fact that what may be called the true beneficiaries of the system comprise somewhere about 10% of the population emerged from our consideration of the distribution of the national income in Chapter 7 above. But there is another way of arriving at this conclusion. And the relevant figures had better be given here, since it is often suggested that shareholding in the companies of the country has now become "widely diffused throughout the population." If that were so, it would indeed alter the whole picture. But in fact it is not so. The late Mr. Hargreaves Parkinson's book, *Ownership of Industry* (Eyre and Spottiswoode), is the best authority to use in this connection, because Mr. Parkinson's purpose in writing the book was to prove the wide diffusion of shareholding. He is able to show, indeed, that at the time he was writing (1951) the average holding of ordinary shares in public companies was one of well under £1,000. (£788 for all types of

that in law (if not in fact) this socially produced surplus becomes the private property of the owners of existing capital, to do exactly what they like with. Legally they need not reinvest a penny of it. Legally they could distribute to themselves as shareholders, by way of dividends, the whole of the undistributed profits of companies instead of re-investing them. True they would then have to pay back a substantial part of the surplus in tax. But again legally, they could spend on themselves every penny which, by every kind of device, they could retain. And, as common observation will show, they do manage so to retain and spend a remarkable number of pennies. When all the qualifications have been made the fact remains that the socially produced surplus is still privately appropriated, and always must be so, so long as the main body of the country's means of production is privately owned. This has far-reaching consequences.

The first of these consequences is that so long as this state of things exists the wage earners are bound to see the indispensable process of accumulation as the mere piling up of

shares, £ 865 for ordinary shares taken alone.) However, on the last page of his text he accepts as accurate the well-known *Financial Times* estimate that "there are in Britain rather more than 1¼ million separate investors." This, of course, disposes of almost the whole of the argument of the rest of his book. For that argument had been designed to suggest that "most people" were now shareholders. In fact the 1¼ million shareholders were only 5% of the, circa, 25 million persons with separate incomes.

This sounds as if our 10% of "true beneficiaries" was actually a large overestimate. But, of course, shareholding is still by no means the only form, although it is now the decisive form, in which income-bearing property is held. Nothing even approaching accuracy can be achieved for a concept of this character, since whether, for example, various categories of large earned incomes—such as directors' or lawyers' fees—should be included is a matter of personal opinion. But the 10% figure, since it agrees well enough with the economists' findings of the number of large incomes of all kinds, is almost certainly not an overestimate.

(The explanation of why each separate holding is, on the average, of under £ 1,000, of course, that persons with substantial capital—say, £ 50,-000—almost never invest it all in any one company, but split it up into, say, fifty separate holdings of under £ 1,000 in 50 or more companies.)

profits in the hands of the rich. Keynes may have told them that the rich are bees accumulating the honey of profits for the benefit of us all. The fact remains that the wage earners see that the social surplus passes, initially at least, into the hands of this small class of the rich as their absolute private property. And the rich are under no legal obligation to accumulate by reinvesting it, but can dissipate all of that part of it which they can retain, after a struggle with the tax gatherers, on luxuries, if they so wish. This is one of those manifest scandals which, even if the economic loss involved is not so great as would at first sight appear, can hardly continue indefinitely once its existence is realised.

THE RIGHTS OF PROPERTY

We brush here against the vast and vexed question of "the rights of property." Fortunately we need not embark, for our present purposes, on any enquiry as to the contemporary justification, or lack of it, for different categories of private property. We need not now distinguish, for example, between property in non-durable consumers' goods, such as clothing, the right to which no one disputes, property in dwelling-houses lived in by their owners, the right to which only doctrinaires dispute, and property in means of production worked by their owners, the right to which it is foolish to dispute. We need not do more than differentiate all such forms of property from the form that chiefly concerns us here, namely, income-bearing property in means of production (whether land, capital or equipment) with which the owner has no real working or managerial connection. It is this last form of property—and predominantly its sub-division of shareholding in large, oligopolistic companies—with which we are above all concerned.

The historic justification of the rights of property is that property is the creation of man's own labour; therefore to take it from him is to rob him of the fruits of his labour. This, for example, is how Locke puts it, archetypally, in the second *Essay on Civil Government:*

> Thus the grass my horse has bit, the turfs my servant has cut, the ore I have digged in any place, where I have a right to them in common with others, become my property, without the assignation or consent of anybody. The labour that was mine, removing them out of that common state they were in, hath fixed my property in them. . . . Though the water running in the fountain be everyone's, yet who can doubt but that in the pitcher it is his only who drew it out? (Chapter V.)

Notice, however, that the grass which the philosopher's horse bit, and the turfs his servant cut, do not become the property of the horse or the servant; they become the philosopher's property. Already a social alchemy is at work transforming the right of property from being the assurance that a man will reap what he sowed into its opposite, into the assurance that one man of property will reap what many other men have sowed. (See above, Chapter 2, p. 52, on this reversal of values effected by the appearance of dependent wage labour.)

In the case of contemporary shareholding almost the last dreg of reality has been drained out of this classic justification. The representative shareholder in a large modern company has had as much to do with the creation of either its plant, or its product, as he has had with the creation of the moon. He has usually never even seen the factories or mines the shares of which he has bought; for that matter he may have only a hazy idea of what they produce. He has usually put no more than a small fraction—a twentieth or a fiftieth part—of his total fortune in any one enterprise, and he is frequently "switching" his investments from one concern to another, so that he has only a quite mild interest in the fortunes of any particular firm. Yet this is the form of property which is still defended by the arguments which were, and are, applicable to the peasant's plot or the artisan's workshop. And so slow is society in adjusting its thinking to its own rapid development (especially, of course, when its most influential thinkers do not *want* to make the adjustment) that the wage earners themselves can often still be impressed by these arguments. Some of them at least can still be persuaded to suppose that the defence of the right of certain families to draw, generation after generation, great incomes from shares in the major oligopolies, with which they have no other connection at all than this extractive one, is the defence of the garage proprietor's, or the one-man shopkeeper's, or the peasant's right to the fruits of his labour in creating his garage, his shop, or his farm.

Socialists, for that matter, are much to blame for failing to make the all-important distinction between these different forms of property sufficiently clear. And in the course of this study we must settle accounts with this whole issue. In this chapter, however, all that we are considering is the economic and social consequences of the private appropriation of a socially produced surplus. And for this limited purpose the essential form of property is, I repeat, modern shareholding. So long as this form of property remains unmodified a moral poison is bound to permeate society. For its manifestation is unearned, property-derived income, which will become an increasingly indefensible economic category. In particular it will become increasingly indefensible with the passing of each generation. For it is above all inheritance which cuts the last connection between property-derived income and any function in the process of social production. All arguments about the rewards of enterprise and the like, which may have force for a particular entrepreneur, become simply farcical when the enterprise which, it may be held, is being rewarded was that of an iron-master in the eighteen-sixties, and the reward is going to his great-grandchildren. For this reason recent democratic socialist economists, notably Mr. Hugh Dalton and Mr. Hugh Gaitskell, have laid great emphasis on limiting more and more the right to inherit considerable quantities of income-bearing property. This is undoubtedly a sound view, so long as it is realised that income from inherited property is merely the most scandalous case of the general scandal of the private appropriation of the socially produced surplus by means of private property in the means of production.

HOW MUCH DOES IT MATTER?

How much, however, does the continuance of this scandal matter economically? To Marxists it is, of course, all-important, for it is the essence of exploitation. But a more important question is this: how much does it matter in the minds and hearts of the Western wage earners themselves? The answer must surely be that it matters to them a good deal, but not overwhelmingly. Many wage earners do realise more or less clearly that they and the technicians and executives are the people who produce the social surplus, and resent bitterly the fact that, legally at any rate, it is appropriated by passive shareholders. So long as private shareholding in large, oligopolistic companies, which is now the economically decisive form of private property, persists, the wage earners can never feel that they are genuinely working either for themselves or for the community.

But we must not lose sight of the other side of the picture. The fact is that the *immediate* economic gain of abolishing the private appropriation of the socially accumulated surplus would be by no means so great as would appear at first sight. This is not to deny that the amount of social waste represented by the luxury expenditure of the rich in all latest-stage capitalisms is considerable. It is least important in Britain, more important in America, and more important still, in proportion to the national income, in Western Germany (and, for that matter, in France and Italy). But nevertheless it is not a very large factor in the standard of life which the wage-earning mass of the population of such societies can hope to achieve. For it must be agreed that the leaders of the national economy, the skilled technicians and the high executives (as contrasted with the functionless shareholders) must, at our stage of human development, receive very considerably higher incomes than the rank and file of the community. Moreover, it has now been discovered by trial and error that this must be so, in the contemporary stage of human development, in any form of society, whether capitalist or communist.* Once this is recognised, the fact must be faced that, while the amounts, in lateststage capitalisms, spent by idle and functionless property owners would provide a useful fund for raising the standard of life of the masses, yet they would be by no means sufficient suddenly to transform that standard. The real scandal is the existence of a category of persons deriving very large net incomes (in one way or another) from completely passive shareholding in the main productive enterprises of so-

---

* These differentials in *earned* income are much higher in Russia than in Britain. During my period of office as Secretary of State for War, I had worked out a comparison of the differential as between the pay of a Russian private and a Russian Marshal on the one hand, and a British private and a British Field Marshal on the other. The result appeared to be that the Russian differential was at least eight times as wide as the British, post-tax in both cases.

A few British socialists, Mr. Victor Gollancz for example, in agreement with Bernard Shaw, deny the contemporary necessity for marked differentials in earned income. I wish I could agree with them.

ciety, rather than the actual quantitative loss to the community which their expenditure represents.*

Nevertheless, the long-term, as opposed to the immediate, economic gain of abolishing, or even markedly diminishing, unearned property-derived income might be very great. This would be so if the resultant saving (in real terms, the productive effort thus released), instead of being distributed to the mass of the population, was used to increase investment. Let us say, purely for the sake of argument, that the rich are receiving (net) 10% of the gross national product by way of property-derived income, half of which they spend and half of which they save and re-invest. If, then, the 5% of the national product used up by the rich in the spending of their unearned incomes was added to investment, it would permit, over the years, of a rapid acceleration in the rate of growth of the national product. It would not indeed *double* the rate of investment, for, as we shall see immediately, the savings of the rich are today far from being the only source of investment. But it would, over, say, a decade, make a very useful difference. This, however, presupposes a way of making sure that the extra accumulation thus effected actually would be used, *i.e.*, invested. Moreover it presumes a progressive *abolition* of the functionless, unearned, property-derived incomes of the rich, as distinct from their mere mitigation by taxation. And I for one cannot imagine any way of effecting that abolition except by the transference of their income-bearing property to society.

* Thus the differentials in *earned* income in contemporary Britain may well be on the low, rather than on the high, side. But this fact is habitually confused with the continued existence of very high *unearned,* property-derived, incomes, the huge differential effect of which taxation can do no more than mitigate, as we have seen.

SEMI-COLLECTIVISED ACCUMULATION

Writing in the nineteen-fifties, it is necessary to add a further qualification to the classical socialist objection to the private appropriation of the socially produced surplus. In capitalist societies of the latest stage, such as Britain and America, an important part of the social surplus never in fact reaches the hands of the individual owners of capital, although it still nominally becomes their legal property. In the first place, a really considerable part is now taxed away again, pooled in the hands of the state, and used as society thinks best. On the whole this tax-diverted part of the surplus tends to be spent upon current consumption, usually by way of either social services or defence. And conservatively minded writers accordingly see in the taxation of profits and of large incomes in general a squandering of the seed corn of the community. But their arguments can never be taken on their merits so long as their suggestion for preserving the seed corn is—to continue the agricultural analogy—to let the landlords keep it as their absolute private property to do what they like with. Moreover, there is nothing inevitable about the state using its part of the social surplus for consumption after it has diverted it by tax. It can be, and in Britain recently on occasions has been, used, directly or indirectly, for accumulation, *i.e.*, it has been used to add to the community's stock of productive resources.

Second, the great corporations, which have become the decisive units of production, are increasingly inclined to refrain from distributing a part of the remainder of their surpluses (after tax) to their individual shareholders. Increasingly they themselves use a part of their surpluses for developing their own means of production. This semi-collectivised process of accumulation on the part of the great corporations may well become an even more important factor than the pooling of surpluses in the national budget by means of taxation. As these pages were being first drafted in May, 1954, the largest of all British privately owned companies—Imperial Chemical Industries—issued its annual report. It showed that in the years 1945 to 1952, I.C.I. had invested in new productive equipment, stock, etc., £213 million. Of this £153 million had been drawn from "sources within the company," *i.e.*, from non-distributed surpluses of one kind or another. Only £60 million had been raised from the market. Nor would it be true to say that all of this latter sum of £60 million represented the capital of individual rich men which they could have spent on luxuries instead of reinvesting in I.C.I. A great part of it unquestionably represented semi-collectivised surpluses of another kind, *i.e.*, funds of insurance companies and similar institutions. Or again, we can take a much more general illustration from America. In 1953 the profits of all corporations appear to have been some $43 billion before tax. Of this sum $23 billion went in corporate taxes, $10 billion was held back by the corporations as undistributed profits and presumably reinvested, leaving only $10 billion to be distributed to individual shareholders. (*Economic Report of the President 1954,* Chart 23, p. 43.) This is an account of an economy in which the function of accumulation is in a state of transition.

Such developments of the latest stage begin to point beyond the confines of the system itself. For example, we are at once prompted to ask why the directors of the boards of the oligopolies accumulate in this way, if the process benefits them, individually and financially, but remotely, if at all? The answer is no doubt complex, but in the main, surely, it must be that they accumulate in order to enhance the power and success of their organisations; they accumulate in order to be the directors of a concern of the first rather than the second magnitude. They accumulate for fear that their corporation will lag behind in the race for technical improvement, and may thus ultimately be swallowed up by a rival. And if at first hearing these seem but weak motives compared to real, old-fashioned self-enrichment, the answer must be that they have not proved so. Our experience is that the oligopolies accumulate very determinedly. It evidently matters extremely to their directors that "their show" should expand and succeed even if they will continue to get much the same salaries, expense accounts and privileges after it has done so. Old-fashioned competition has been metamorphosed into a complex kind of rivalry. Moreover, since their motive is the acquisition of prestige and power, rather than wealth, their motive for expansion is an unlimited one. "Keeping up with the Joneses" is a trivial matter compared with "keeping up with the I.C.I."—or with Duponts or Fords.

THE AMOUNT, NOT THE FORM

For all these reasons it is becoming clear that what chiefly determines the standard of life of the mass of the population is not the social *form* taken by accumulation, *e.g.*, whether it be private profit or a social fund, but its *amount*. In other words, at any given level of national productivity, what in the main determines the national standard of life is not whether accumulation takes the form of private property or a social fund, but whether the rate of accumulation is set high or low. The higher it is set, the lower will be the standard of life (other things being equal) at the given moment; but the higher (other things being equal) will be the standard of life attainable in the future. Conversely, the lower the rate of accumulation, the more of our products we shall be able to consume now, but the slower we shall enlarge our productive capacity.

The importance of the amount rather than the form of accumulation has been brought into our consciousness by the fact that the communist societies of our day, which have abolished the private appropriation of the social surplus, are nevertheless maintaining a higher rate of accumulation than any other societies of which we have evidence. Thus, if we ignore for a moment the form which accumulation takes, the communist societies undoubtedly deduct from their wage earners a larger proportion of their product than do the capitalist societies. Can it be said, then, that they "exploit" their workers even more than do the capitalists? That all depends on whether the question of the *form* or the *amount* of the deduction from possible present consumption is considered the main thing. To the Marxist the decisive thing is that none of the vast sums deducted from possible consumption in Russia, for example, go into the pockets of Russian owners of the means of production in the form of private profit. They are all used to build new steel works, power stations, atom plants, etc., etc., potentially at least for the ultimate benefit of the Russian people as a whole. On the other hand, a sceptically and conservatively minded Western wage earner might comment that in fact the considerably smaller proportionate deduction made in the form of private profit from *his* possible consumption was not, in the main, used for the luxury spending of the rich, but did get used for building new means of production;* that he was confident of getting his share of the final products of these new means

---

* We shall find that the worst trouble under capitalism is that not only does some of it get diverted into luxury spending by the rich, but that at intervals some of it does not get used at all. We shall be much occupied by this aspect of the matter as soon as we remove our temporary assumption that the diversion of resources from consumption does always in fact result in investment in new means of production. (See below.)

of production, as a result of using his weapon of democratic pressure; that for his part he was more concerned at the *amount* of the deduction than the form; that he would rather have, say, 20% taken from him for private profit than 40% for a social fund.

Nevertheless, their tremendous rate of uninterrupted accumulation will undoubtedly stand the communist societies in immensely good stead in the long run, even though it means that they have hitherto had to hold down the standard of life of the mass of their populations more rigorously, and more tyrannously, perhaps than capitalist societies have ever done. This fact is illustrated not only by the forty years' history of Russia since the Revolution. The gigantic nations of Asia are, in the middle of the twentieth century, beginning the processes of industrialisation; China is engaging on that process in a predominantly socialist form; India in a semi-capitalist form. And if, on the whole, many people fancy that China will succeed in industrialising herself more rapidly than India, that is precisely because they think that the communist dictatorship in China will squeeze a higher rate of accumulation out of the Chinese people than can be secured from the Indian people by a mixed process, which is partly capitalist and partly democratic socialist.

Paradoxical conclusions emerge from these considerations. On the one hand, bitter experience in the first half of the century has taught us that the innate tendency of latest-stage capitalism is to attempt to maintain an extreme degree of inequality, and, associated with it, so high a rate of accumulation as to lead to periodic slumps and crises.

But, as we have seen, the degree of inequality has now been somewhat mitigated, on balance, by the pressure of the wage earners acting through democratic institutions. The wage earners, who have become conscious of what is happening, are now apt to grudge every penny put aside for accumulation, because it takes the form of totally unjustified unearned income. Thus the profound paradox might arise that, as the influence of the wage earners grows, and in spite of the fact that classical capitalism's supreme tendency was to accumulation *à l'outrance,* the contemporary democratic capitalisms might be, to some extent, immobilised by the play and balance of their own social forces. Under the pressure of wage earners resentful of the out-of-date social form taken by accumulation, namely, private profit, they might accumulate too intermittently or too sluggishly to hold their own in the race with the ruthlessly accumulative communist societies. In that case the ironic situation would have been reached that it was precisely the fact that accumulation took the sociologically indefensible form of private profit which was making adequate and successful accumulation difficult.

BEFORE AND AFTER THE HUMP

Indeed it has been argued that democracies, even if they have become socialist democracies, will never be able to match the rate of accumulation of the dictatorships. For, it is suggested, their electors will always see to it that their governments devote a very high proportion of their gross national products to immediate consumption. I believe that this contention has force for societies in one stage of economic development, but that it has much less force for societies which have reached a more developed stage.

This brings us to a concept used by modern economists—particularly Dr. Thomas Balogh—the concept that there is a "hump" in the process of the industrialisation and general modernisation of a community, a "hump" which it is arduous and painful in the extreme to surmount. But once this hump is surmounted—and by whatever methods—the community will be able to develop, and in particular to accumulate, with far less difficulty. Till communities are "over the hump" the process of capital accumulation is both imperative —if appreciable progress is to be made—and at the same time extremely painful for the population. For the bitter truth is that in such circumstances accumulation, under no matter what kind of social system, can only take place at the direct expense of the existing standard of life of the mass of the population. The manhours of labour necessary to build the initial, basic industrial equipment of the country in question must be diverted somehow from the task of providing the existing supply of consumers' goods and services. This must mean, unless circumstances are especially favourable, an initial fall in that standard.* It would be asking much of an electorate to ask it to vote itself such a fall in its own, by hypothesis, meagre standards of life, however much the economists were to prove that this was the only way to raise those standards, at any speed, in the long run. Thus it may well prove to be true that it is very difficult to combine a socialist economy and democracy in communities which have not yet surmounted the "hump" in the process of industrialisation—in, that is, what are often now called undeveloped countries. (And they comprise, let it not be forgotten, the larger parts of both the capitalist and the communist worlds.) But then experience shows that it is also very hard to combine a capitalist economy and democracy at this "pre-hump" stage of economic development. After all, we never even tried to establish democracy in the contemporary sense in Britain until we were well over the hump, somewhere about the third quarter of the nineteenth century. It is the fact of underdevelopment, not the particular economic system, whether capitalist or socialist, which makes it difficult for democracy to function in a "pre-hump" society.

* It may be that societies such as India with large quantities of unemployed and underemployed labour will provide an exception to this rule, if they can find a way of rapidly setting their people on to work.

Once, however, the initial hump of industrialisation has been surmounted a very different situation arises. A high rate of accumulation becomes at once less imperative and far easier to achieve. The level which is achieved becomes a matter of social preference. If the level is set on the low side, all that will happen is that the present standard of life will be high, but its rate of growth over the decades relatively slow, and vice versa. Such countries as America, Britain, Australia and New Zealand, Western Germany, Sweden, Holland, Canada—and more precariously France—are over the hump. In the communist world Russia (and perhaps Eastern Germany and Czecho-Slovakia) alone has even approached it; but Russia may now (1956) be nearly over. It will be extremely interesting to see whether or not Russia begins to develop democratic institutions if and when she comes down the developed side.

On the whole, then, the prediction that democracies, once at any rate they have begun to transform the social form taken by accumulation into a consciously set-aside fund—once they have begun to become socialist, that is to say, for this is one way of defining the essence of the transition—will prove spend-thrift, and so cause their countries to fall behind in the race of economic development, will, I believe, prove to have little force, at least in the case of highly developed communities. For all that the acceptance of a high rate of accumulation will do to their populations is to impose an initially slower increase of their standard of life than would otherwise have been possible; it need never mean an arrest of that rise or an initial fall. Once accumulation predominantly takes the form of a publicly accounted for, continually discussed, social fund, instead of the large unearned incomes of irresponsible individuals, the difficulty of securing support for a high rate of accumulation will become much less. After all, we are at present asking the wage earners to abstain from consumption in order to provide high incomes* to the rich which they need not legally use for accumulation at all, but are quite free to dissipate in any form of luxury spending. (And, after all, in some cases that is what does actually happen.) After the transformation of the form and method of accumulation, it will not, I believe, prove difficult to convince modern electorates that a high rate of accumulation is in their long-run interest. Even the simplest peasant knows the necessity of putting aside the seed corn.†

Evidence that this is so is provided by the example of Sweden. Sweden is by no means a fully socialist democracy. Nevertheless she has now (1956) been ruled by Social Democratic governments, with socialistic and equalitarian tendencies, virtually without interruption, for twenty-five years. And yet in 1956 Sweden is accumulating at an exceedingly high per cent of her gross national product.‡ Again, the

---

* By "incomes" I mean in this context the actual amounts which the rich do in fact, by one means or another, retain after tax. And these amounts are still high.

† An additional reason why the problem may not prove as intractable as had been supposed has recently been advanced. It is now suggested that really advanced industrial societies *need* a lower rate of accumulation than has hitherto been supposed. Mr. Colin Clark is now (1956) an advocate of this view. It is suggested that technical progress is now being carried forward by means of discoveries and developments which save capital, per unit of product, quite as much as they save labour, so that we need worry our heads much less than had been supposed about this whole matter of setting aside resources for accumulation. This is a convenient view. But surely it should not be pressed too far? Mr. Clark points out that in future non-material forms of development, such as qualitatively superb educational facilities, may be more important than new material equipment. No doubt. But then it costs far more to build, equip and staff a first-rate new university than to build a first-rate new power station. Whatever the objects of expenditure, it will, surely, be necessary to divert resources which could have been used for immediate consumption, if rapid development is to be achieved.

‡ The Swedes actually claim a rate of 33⅓% per annum. If these figures were really comparable in their method of calculation they would be much higher than either the current British or American rate. But I am informed that there may be certain offsets.

rate of accumulation instinctively established by the British Labour Government in 1945-1951 was much higher instead of lower than that which British capitalism had established in the nineteen-thirties.

There is a final reason why the basic problem of accumulation should be manageable for socialist democracies. The wage earners learned by agonising experience in the inter-war years that maintaining a relatively low rate of consumption, in order to make possible a high rate of accumulation, may not, under capitalism, result in a rapid growth of society's powers of production at all. It may produce, instead, chronic mass unemployment. For the resources "saved" from consumption may not get used after all for the creation of new means of production; they may simply be left idle. It is this monstrous contingency, even more than private profit, that "puts off" the present-day electorate from accepting a high rate of accumulation. As soon as this has ceased to be a possibility, the electorate will be much more favourable to a high rate of accumulation. On the other hand, it is this very characteristic of latest-stage capitalism which more than anything else complicates the problem of its transformation by democratic means into a predominantly socialist society.

10. THE MAINSPRING

CAPITALISM NOT SELF-REGULATING

We must now drop the simplifying assumption of the last chapter. That assumption was that the diversion, withholding or saving of a portion of the available productive effort from being used for immediate consumption, will automatically result in that effort being used for investment, *i.e.*, for the creation of new means of production.

We now encounter the crux of the problem of contemporary capitalism. The fact is that under capitalism investment by no means always or automatically follows the diversion of resources from consumption. True, investment, in the end, cannot be accomplished without such diversion: you cannot use resources of production for making new machines if they are already being used to produce consumers' goods. But, within that limit, the actual level of investment is independently determined.* It is undertaken by a different category of persons, actuated by different motives; it may well be dropping when the diversion of resources from consumption is increasing. Or, conversely, those who decide the level of investment, since they move independently, may attempt to set it at a level higher than is made possible by the amount of

---

* As we shall see, the link was supposed to be the rate of interest. It is a most defective one.

resources which are being diverted from consumption, and, although they cannot succeed in this, their attempt will have disastrously inflationary consequences.

Mrs. Joan Robinson in her important work on this subject, entitled *The Accumulation of Capital* (Macmillan, 1956), sees investment as the prime mover of the whole system.* What in the world, then, determines the level of investment? Mrs. Joan Robinson, in a striking passage, declares simply that we do not know! She writes: ". . . as to what governs the level at which it" (investment) "gets itself established we know very little. We know that it varies widely from period to period and from country to country, but any attempt to identify causes of variation in such influences as a tradition of vigorous competition among entrepreneurs (as opposed to a lethargic spirit of live and let live), a rapid rate of technical progress, or a high propensity to retain profits (amassing reserves to finance investment without borrowing) is in danger of confusing symptoms with causes. On the other hand, it is not very satisfactory to have to rely for an explanation upon a 'capitalist spirit' due to Protestantism or goodness knows what. Economic analysis requires to be supplemented by a kind of comparative anthropology which is still in its infancy as a scientific study." (*Op. cit.*)

Mrs. Robinson is here feeling the need of some kind of *summa*, transcending, although including, economics and laying the basis of an inclusive science of human society, a *summa* at which Marxism is at present the sole attempt (see p. 147). She is confronted with the fact that her analysis has led her to conclude that the true prime mover of a capitalist economy—the decision to invest—is determined by causes

---

* She goes so far as to conclude that the level of investment is itself the main determinant of the degree to which productive effort will be diverted from immediate consumption. For the profits, distributed and undistributed, made in the system as a whole, will be determined by it. So, if the spending of the rich remains constant, that will set the degree of diversion for consumption.

which are largely outside the scope of economic analysis. Once the classical assumption that investment would—except for short-lived crises—always use up all the productive resources diverted from providing for immediate consumption had to be abandoned, the presumption that capitalism contained a self-regulating mechanism had to be abandoned also. Once the level of investment was shown to be an independent variable which could, and did, set itself—from whatever causes—at a more or less arbitrary level, an imperative need for a conscious, overall control of the system was established.

THE MAINSPRING

Mrs. Joan Robinson's new work gives the latest and clearest analysis of why capitalism even in its earlier competitive form always had a tendency to instability. No one who reads her pages can doubt that economic activity in both competitive and latest-stage capitalisms, if they are left to themselves, must oscillate widely, with all the disastrous social, political and human consequences which such wide oscillations must have. This is at bottom because the mainspring of such societies, the power of which activates all their other parts, is the investment decision of entrepreneurs (individual or collective). Under unmodified capitalism that mainspring is wound up by the motive of profit-making. Investment in new means of production will take place, that is to say, when entrepreneurs believe that it will be profitable so to invest, and not otherwise. But for the reasons which we have sketched, and which Mrs. Robinson analyses in the greatest detail, the very consequences of investment are bound at intervals to make further investment appear unlikely to be profitable. Whenever that happens, the level of investment will drop, and this will "stall" the whole vast economic engine of contemporary society.*

Thus the motivation of production emerges as the key issue. In so far as that motivation remains exclusively the making of profit, extreme instability (or possibly long-term stagnation) is inevitable. This has proved to be by far the most serious defect in the capitalist system. It was not the inequity, it was the *instability*, of capitalism which went far to wreck the world in the first half of the twentieth century. Great, advanced, highly developed, wealthy societies simply cannot live with a system the mainspring of which is subject to sudden and arbitrary stoppages, to stoppages which bring ruin to hundreds of millions of human beings. The first, essential economic task of socialism is, then, the provision of some more dependable motivation for production in general and for investment in new means of production in particular. What society must have is something more dependable than can be provided by the inevitably widely fluctuating expectations of private profit-making. What has to be done is to provide some way in which the system's mainspring, namely, investment in new means of production, can be undertaken at a rationål rate, without interruption, and independently of fluctuation in the expectation of profit-making. If—but only if—that can be done, much of the rest of the economic mechanism can, if this is thought convenient or expedient, be left in private hands to be operated under the hope of profit and the fear of loss.† For the primary impulse which will be imparted by the devotion of a steady and adequate part of the available productive resources to the production of new

---

* Mrs. Robinson seems to me to have come near, at least, to giving the first rigorous account of the mechanism which has always hitherto caused economic activity in a profit-motivated economy to oscillate more or less rhythmically; to giving, that is to say, a satisfactory explanation of the trade cycle.

† In my view it will prove neither convenient nor expedient so to leave them in the long run.

means of production can be relied upon to transmit itself to every part of the huge and intricate mechanism.

DEMOCRACY AND THE MAINSPRING

But how can this be done? To make the original, primary economic decision, which is to invest or not to invest, independent of the profit motive would seem to be incompatible with the existence of capitalism. And so, in principle and in the long run, it is. Nevertheless, a remarkable process appears, in the middle of the twentieth century, to be taking place in the major latest-stage capitalisms. This is partly because the fateful decisions to invest or not to invest are no longer made by the same category of persons who made them in the previous, competitive stage of capitalism. At that stage the prime mover of the system was the individual capitalist owner-manager, of whom the Lancashire mill owner was the archetype. It was upon the decisions of some hundreds of thousands of such men, engaged in fierce competition with each other, that the system depended. In that stage of development there was at least some justification in the classical economist's assumption that those who made its investment decisions would in fact always invest up to the possible upper limit set by the amount of productive resources diverted, withheld or "saved" from immediate consumption. For the sheer thrust of the system in its heyday—the sheer *élan* of nineteenth-century profit-making—was so great that over the decades this was roughly true. About once each decade there was, to be sure, a crisis, in which the rate of investment suddenly dropped sharply and slump ensued, but within a few years at most this was overcome and a new wave of investment carried the system forward to a new peak of activity.

In contemporary latest-stage capitalism, as we described it in Chapter 1, all this has been changed. The men who make the fateful decisions to invest or not to invest, on which almost everything else will be found to hang, are today, in the first place, the directors of the large oligopolies and public companies. And, as we have just noted, they make their decisions from an extremely complex mixture of motives, of which the desire to maximise the profits of their shareholders is only one. Moreover, these directors of profit-making companies are today flanked by an important body of men who are members of the boards of nationalised and publicly owned industries and other public authorities. And they make their investment decisions from different motives again. On the other hand, there still remains, of course, a diminished but still important sector of the economy in which the small owner-manager predominates, and where the investment decisions must be made from strictly profit-seeking motives.

But another and still more important change in the nature of society as a whole is tending to make this great, main decision of contemporary economic life partially independent of the expectation of profit. Once again, the social pressures set up by contemporary democracy are at work. Without, in the main, taking the existing means of production out of private hands, a new motivation for the production of new means of production is unmistakably making its appearance on the contemporary scene. To some extent—to *what* extent is one of the crucial questions of our time—investment is being undertaken and maintained, whether or not the particular entrepreneurs (individual or collective) concerned can or cannot foresee a profit from it.

This is not so much because either governments, or public opinion, are consciously aware that the maintenance of investment is all-important. What is felt is, more simply, that there must not be another slump. So far not everyone feels even this. A few of the richest and most influential of the members of "the 10% of real beneficiaries of the system," especially in America, still, I suspect, think in their heart of hearts that drastic oscillations of economic activity are inevitable, and may even be desirable. And considerable strata of the wage earners are still fatalistic about the prospect of mass unemployment recurring. Nevertheless, the workings of the contemporary democratic mechanism, with its hard-fought competition between the parties, as we have sketched it above, does appear to have produced a genuine determination on the part of the governments of the leading capitalist democracies to avoid wide economic oscillations, if they possibly can. Nor is that determination, on the part of the politicians at least, difficult to explain. To put the matter crudely, their political skins are at stake. No political lesson stands out more starkly from the experience of the first half of the century than that in a democratic latest-stage capitalist society any government which permits slump and mass unemployment to appear is doomed. Enough, at any rate, of the wage earners have come to the conclusion that the horrors of mass unemployment can and must be avoided, to ensure that.

When, however, governments turn to the question of *how* instability and slump are to be avoided they find that at bottom the issue resolves itself into the question of how investment is to be maintained. If, of course, the means of production, or even a decisive part of them, had passed into public hands, the thing could be done, in principle, simply by instructing their managers to maintain, come rain or shine, the proportion of the national productive effort being devoted to producing new means of production; that is what, again in principle, is done in the contemporary communist societies. But can the same thing possibly be done when the decisive part of the existing means of production remains in private hands, to be operated in the expectation of private profit?

Clearly in these circumstances the mainspring of the economy can only be kept permanently wound by more indirect means, if at all. The owners—or more realistically today the managers—of the means of production must be *induced,* since they cannot be ordered, never to let the level of investment drop. And how can that be done? Experience shows that it can be attempted, at any rate, in many different ways, of varying degrees of indirection. For example, contemporary governments can, and do, attempt to control the economic climate, as it were, so that by artificially stimulating ultimate consumers' demand—in round terms by giving people money —it always will seem profitable to the entrepreneurs to invest. Or, again, governments can supplement the investments of profit-seeking entrepreneurs by themselves investing, either by way of creating new means of production or by creating "public works."

Subsequent chapters will be largely concerned with the theory and practice of such attempts. Here let us simply take note that in the decade which elapsed after the end of the Second World War (1945-1955) the governments of the democratic latest-stage capitalisms have not only made attempts to act along these lines, but have been remarkably successful, on the whole. Indeed in the sense that they have often provided for a fairly serious excess of total demand, instead of the previous deficiency, they have been oversuccessful. This has led some people to suppose that the whole trouble is now overcome, as a result of the action of the new political and social pressures on the system. But this is a superficial verdict. The fact that for the moment (1956) the tendency is towards an excess, instead of a deficiency, of demand does not mean that the tendency of the system to instability has been overcome. On the contrary, the inflationary difficulties from which Britain, for instance, now (1956) suffers are only, at bottom, symptoms of the persistent instability of the system in a converse form. This will become painfully apparent if inflation is allowed to get beyond a certain point, for in that event it will probably turn into its opposite of slump, if only because the drastic measures which will then become necessary to arrest it will be almost bound to over-reach their purpose. We shall discuss these immediately practical issues in a later section of this study. Here we may merely note that the change in the political balance of forces within our societies has recently changed the super-ficial character of the problem and, it is becoming possible to hope, begun its solution.

Moreover, whether this qualified success, over what is, after all, the short period of a decade, is a result of skill or luck or the cold war, is another matter with which we shall also have to concern ourselves. Be all that as it may, these attempts at avoiding the sickening oscillations which have hitherto characterised capitalist development represent a more drastic—though largely unconscious—departure from capitalist principles than is usually realised. For they alter the basic *motivation* of production. When a government, fearful of the retribution of the electors, seeks to control the level of investment, it is introducing, whether it knows it or not, a new overall social purpose for economic activity. Such a government is saying to the entrepreneurs, in effect, "Whether or not you think it will be profitable for you to invest in that new steel works, those new factories, or other objects of investment, either you or we or someone else must be induced or cajoled or forced into doing so (or conversely, in an inflationary situation, must be induced *not* to do so), for otherwise we simply can't face the electors." Moreover, as we shall notice later, the democratic mechanism, in its role of applying pressure upon the economy in the equali-tarian direction, has succeeded in, as it were, building cer-tain stabilisers into the capitalist societies of the latest-stage. Of these perhaps the most important is the high direct taxa-tion of large incomes. We shall see how this stabiliser works in due course.

IS LATEST-STAGE CAPITALISM MORE OR LESS STABLE?

All this raises the question of whether latest-stage capitalism has in fact become more or less inherently unstable. Are we not now suggesting that the contemporary form of the system is after all showing a greater rather than a less degree of stability than the earlier and more competitive form? The issue is, to some extent at least, a verbal one. It may well be that if we treat all the democratic institutions which we have been discussing in the preceding chapters as *a part* of contemporary capitalism: if we treat trade unions, representative institutions with a universal franchise functioning effectively, freedom of speech and of assembly, and the whole mental climate which such institutions produce, together with all the heavy, moulding pressure which they exercise upon the economy—if we treat all this as part and parcel of contemporary capitalism—then it may prove true (I am inclined to believe it will) that our contemporary *society*, taken as a whole, will prove a more stable, controlled, manageable, organism than did nineteenth-century, *laissez faire* capitalism. At any rate, very recent experience, although short, gives us the right to consider this possible.

In this volume, however, I have considered it clearer and more convenient to treat all these political institutions and forces as something separable from, and external to, contemporary capitalism as such, and reacting upon it. Not only would any other method of exposition have proved almost impossibly confusing and complex, but also the method of exposition actually used is, I think, justified by the fact that there have been several instances of latest-stage capitalist economies which have existed in societies which had no such democratic political institutions, no trade unions, no representative government and no freedom of speech or assembly. Nazi Germany is, of course, the obvious example.

No doubt it would have been more Marxist to attempt to treat the contemporary economy and contemporary political institutions—"the foundations" and "the superstructure"— as one indissoluble whole. But mainly for the reason just given—because experience has shown us that one can in fact appear without the other—I do not think that it would have been realistic to do so. This is an exemplification of one of the main arguments of this study, on its theoretical side, namely, that the connection between the economic foundation and the political superstructure of society, while all-important, is in fact looser, and above all more reciprocal, than Marxism in practice will allow for.

In any case, there can be no doubt that latest-stage, oligopolistic, capitalism, without the modifications which democratic pressure has in some cases succeeded in making in it, would be, and has been when and where it has appeared, much more unstable than the earlier stage of the system. It may be convenient to summarise here the main reasons for this, since they are scattered through preceding and following chapters. The essential cause is, once again, the progressive atrophy of competition and the consequent ability of the remaining few sellers to fix prices, within limits, to suit themselves. This, unless counterbalanced, must distort the balance of the economy in the direction of greater inequality in the distribution of the national income, in favour of the owners of the means of production and at the expense of the wage earners and remaining independent producers. This, in turn, must further distort the balance between the metropolitan, latest-stage capitalisms, on the one hand, and the underdeveloped world, on the other. In order to conduct such an economy at anything like full activity it would be necessary to achieve a higher and higher rate of successfully accomplished accumulation and investment. This would mean that a larger and larger proportion of the available productive effort would have to be used for making new means of production, and a smaller and smaller proportion for direct consumption. The capital-goods department of the economy must become ever larger in proportion to the consumer-goods department. The economy would become more and more dependent upon the making of capital goods. The "structure of production" would become a higher and higher, a more and more precariously poised, pyramid.

It may be said that all this is merely a natural and inevitable development, made necessary by higher and higher technique. But if the motivation of production remains exclusively profit-making, such a development must produce ever-growing instability. For to an ever-growing extent the economy will become dependent upon the entrepreneurs guessing, over longer and longer periods, that such and such an investment will be profitable. So long as they guess, and act on their guess, that investment will be profitable, it will in fact turn out to be so. But, again in the absence of counter-vailing intervention, they will inevitably sooner or later guess that further investment would be likely to be unprofitable. For the very effects of all their previous investment will have been to reduce the proportionate size of the ultimate outlet for the ever-increasing flow of consumer goods. At the moment that the entrepreneurs act upon the guess that further investment would be unprofitable, they will make their pessimistic forecast come true also. How can great communities possibly allow their fates to become ever more dependent upon this sort of guessing game?

Moreover, the contention that latest-stage capitalisms, unmodified by democratic pressures, exhibit extreme instability does not rest merely on these theoretical considerations. It rests upon the bitter experience of the first half of the century. Until the democratic pressures effected really considerable modifications in the balance and workings of these systems, which happened in America in the 'thirties and in

Britain in the 'forties (it remains to be seen whether it has happened in the case of Germany in the 'fifties), the latest-stage capitalisms *were* more unstable than ever nineteenth-century capitalism had been. In the estimation of all economists, from the extreme right to the extreme left, there never was such a slump as that which began in 1929. Both for its degree of severity at its lowest points, its duration, its catastrophic political consequences and the slow and partial nature of the recovery which followed it, this has been universally called the Great Depression. Here is strong evidence that, as we noted just now, contemporary latest-stage capitalism no longer possesses, in itself, those inherent powers of readjustment and recovery which the sheer *élan* of nineteenth-century profit-making provided.

Finally, unless contemporary capitalism has become inherently more and more unstable, how can we explain the emergence of an irresistible tendency to create new central authorities and mechanisms for its deliberate, purposive control? Men do not set themselves such major historical tasks as that until they have to. If capitalism were not losing its own powers of self-adjustment, no one would have taken these reforming tendencies seriously. Certainly no one would have actually attempted to do the job of reform. Yet in fact all the various contemporary forms of "planning and control," from Keynes' sophisticated specifics, which we shall next consider, to the more direct proposals of the Fabians, or the more wholly empirical experiments of the American New Dealers, have been attempts to remedy the inherent instability of the latest-stage capitalisms. The only alternative explanation would be to suppose that this whole movement of opinion had arisen quite arbitrarily and unnecessarily out of the whims of a few theorists. That indeed is what the most reactionary authorities of all do say. The best answer to them would be, if it were practicable, to challenge them to try to run a typical latest-stage capitalism on wholly *laissez faire* lines, and to see what happened.

No, the latest-stage capitalisms can only become more instead of less stable as a result of the democratic pressures upon them succeeding in more than counter-balancing their innate tendencies; as a result of these forces actually improving the distribution of the national income and providing adequate, alternative, and essentially social, motivations for investing in new capital goods, whether their use, when they have been made, is expected to be profitable or not. Schumpeter (*op. cit.*, p. 441), in his summary of Marx's general vision, writes of "the Grand Vision of an immanent evolution of the economic process—that, working somehow through accumulation, somehow destroys the economy as well as the society of competitive capitalism and somehow produces an untenable social situation that will somehow give birth to another type of social organisation." We are seeing the fulfilment of the prophecy, but, it may be, in ways which the prophet never imagined. The crucial question is whether the democratic mechanism, working in the above-described highly empirical way, is or is not beginning to provide an alternative motivation for production, capable of constituting the basis for that continuity of economic activity and growth which undiluted private profit-making can no longer provide. What the democratic mechanism is forcing governments, more or less unconsciously, to attempt is, in a word, the socialisation of investment.

We should notice that from a strictly Marxian standpoint it is impossible to conceive of any such attempt being made. This is not because sophisticated Marxists, at least, consider that the economic mechanism for doing so is lacking; it is because the Marxian vision, which is all-embracing and unitary, cannot conceive of a capitalist society creating a government which would even desire to make the attempt to have production carried on for what are, in the last analysis, non-profit-making purposes. We shall be concerned with this issue, which goes well outside the strictly economic field, in subsequent volumes of this study. But from common observation it is evident that, as in the instance of modifying the distribution of the national income, so in this related case of the possibility of controlling the instabilities of the economy, the economic effects of democratic institutions have been gravely underestimated.

11 . KEYNES

We must now turn to the question of how "the 90%" can use the instruments of democracy to control, and so ultimately transcend, the latest-stage capitalisms in which they live. For we shall find that this, although incomparably our most hopeful prospect, is a task of the greatest complexity. The experience of the last twenty-five years shows that it presents major difficulties both in the political and in the economic fields. At this point in the study we are concerned with the economic issues involved. Their consideration will take the form of a discussion of the work of the major non-Marxist economist of our times, John Maynard Keynes. For it was Keynes who evolved one critically important aspect of the economic theory of latest-stage capitalisms, their control, modification and, if desired, supercession.

To write that Keynes supplied a theory of the latest stage of capitalism is in one sense, however, a paradoxical assertion. For he barely noticed its existence. Keynes was only mildly interested in the question of the growing size, and diminishing number, of the units of economic life. The theory of imperfect competition, although it largely emerged from his immediate *entourage* at Cambridge, seems to have made little impression on him. And he neither knew nor cared what Marx and Lenin had had to say about monopoly, imperialism, or the State. Nevertheless, it will not be difficult to show that "Keynesism" is in fact an attempt to comprehend, and then control, the workings of an economy in the latest stage of capitalism.*

KEYNES' CRITIQUE

What Keynes said about capitalism was that it was not, after all, self-regulating. This may sound a comparatively mild indictment. In fact it strikes at the very roots of orthodox economic thought. Far worse still, it undermines the basic claim of the practical men of capitalism. As we have seen, the claim of both has always been that there is a natural law which, left to itself, not only adjusts the countless economic transactions of humanity, but adjusts them in the best way possible. Any apparent maladjustments or injustices which we may observe about us were declared to be either illusory or the result, precisely, of impious interferences with an inherently self-adjusting system.

Moreover, to say that the system was not self-adjusting was to say that it needed the conscious control of some authority to enable it to work. And this, the defenders of capitalism felt, was an appallingly dangerous thing to say, for it implied that it was possible to control the workings of the system. But, if this were once admitted, it would no longer be possible to say that extreme inequality and instability were inevitable. It would be necessary to attempt to justify such things—to justify them, as the result of deliberate decisions to so "frame" society as to produce them. That is why the

* Of course Keynes realised that things were changing, and recorded the fact as early as his aforementioned pamphlet, *The End of Laissez Faire* (1926). But that elegant little volume records rather a change in economics than a change in the economy. For Keynes history was often the history of ideas, not things.

perfectly sincere protests of Keynes and his followers that
they were loyal supporters of capitalism failed to carry conviction. It was little use for them to protest, when in the late
'thirties they explained their new doctrine, that they only desired to control and modify the system for its own good. The
capitalists did not want to be saved *in that way*. They felt
deeply that if once they were to admit that it was necessary
to control the system, even in order the better to preserve it,
true virtue would have departed from it.

Keynes' biographer, Mr. Harrod, has laboured hard to prove
the true respectability of his subject. But it has been in vain.
In vain does he emphasize and re-emphasize Keynes' anti-
socialism, which was indeed strong; in vain does he describe
how Keynes made half a million pounds for himself on the
Stock Exchange; in vain does he quote, like a testimonial,
a letter from Keynes to Professor Hayek expressing sympathy
with Hayek's more hysterical anti-socialist propaganda; in
vain are Keynes' detestation and contempt for Marxism, and
his ignorance and suspicion of the labour movement, revealed. All this is not enough. It is not enough to prove, as
Harrod can and does, that in many respects Keynes shared
the normal opinions and prejudices of his class and time.
The fact remains that Keynes said that capitalism was not
self-regulating; that it was necessary for some authority consciously to regulate its workings or it would destroy itself.
For that he will never be wholly forgiven.*

---

* Moreover Keynes' attack was upon the coping-stone of the allegedly self-
regulating mechanism of the system, namely, the automatic gold standard.
Schumpeter wrote:

"An 'automatic' gold currency is part and parcel of a *laissez faire* and
free-trade economy. It links every nation's money rates and price levels
with the money rates and price levels of all other nations that are 'on
gold.' It is extremely sensitive to government expenditure and even to
attitudes and policies that do not involve government expenditure directly, for example, to foreign policy, to certain policies of taxation, and,
in general, to precisely all those policies which violate the principles of
economic liberalism. *This* is the reason why gold is so unpopular now

SAY'S LAW

This was Keynes' heresy. But he could never have given birth to it if he had not lived in latest-stage capitalism. This is best illustrated by describing how Keynes broke with traditional economic thought. One aspect of the central essence of that tradition had been summed up by the French early nineteenth-century economist, J. B. Say. Say reduced to a clear-cut "law" the general presumption of the great masters. Say's law is, briefly, that, so long as the system is not interfered with, it will always be perfectly self-adjusting and self-regulating, because, in particular, every act of production always generates the effective demand necessary to purchase its product. Thus, if you start up a new boot and shoe factory, the wages which you pay your workers, the purchase price of your raw materials, the rent to your landlord, the interest to your bank, the profits to yourself, and your other costs, will always put enough money into circulation to enable people to buy the boots and shoes which will come out of your factory. There can never be a deficiency in the total demand of the community. There will always be enough

---

and also why it was so popular in the bourgeois era. It imposes restrictions upon governments or bureaucracies which are much more powerful than is parliamentary criticism. It is both the guarantee and badge of bourgeois freedom—of freedom not simply of the bourgeois *interest,* but of freedom in the bourgeois sense. From this standpoint a man may quite rationally fight for it, even if fully convinced of the validity of all that has ever been urged against it on economic grounds. From the standpoint of *étatisme* and planning, a man may not less rationally condemn it, even if fully convinced of the validity of all that has ever been urged for it on economic grounds." (*History of Economic Analysis,* p. 406.)

It was just this comprehension of *why* men took up particular economic views which Keynes lacked. He often thought that they were committing intellectual errors when in fact they were defending particular social interests.

money in circulation to buy the total possible product of society at remunerative prices. Therefore there can never be slumps, crises or mass unemployment.

Only one thing marred the Gallic symmetry of this law: namely, the existence of slumps, crises and mass unemployment. This trifling defect did not, however, prevent several generations of economists from adopting the law as one of the basic tenets of their system of thought. (For example, one of the greatest and most enlightened of contemporary British economists used to assure Royal Commissions on unemployment, as late as the nineteen-twenties, that the chief difficulty of their investigations was that their subject matter did not really exist.) Indeed, if the British economists did not write much about Say by name, it was, on the whole, not because they doubted the validity of his law for one moment, but because they felt that to some extent he had been laboriously formulating the obvious. The infallible mark of the crank, and the quack, or simply the fool, in economics was held to be any questioning of this law. Such doubters were consigned to an outer darkness where dwelt Gesell, Hobson and Major Douglas. And Say's law is in its widest sense simply an assertion of the general, overall self-regulating character of the system.*

It may well be asked how so wonderful a divergence of thought from reality can have occurred. And indeed the story of Say and his law may well provide, with Malthusianism (see p. 63 above), another illustration, in the textbooks of the future, of the psycho-pathology of sociological thought in

---

* Many orthodox economists before Keynes occupied themselves, indeed, with studying monetary theory and the trade cycle. But as Keynes wrote their studies formed a sort of extemporised annex uncomfortably tacked on to the main body of economic theory. The fact that if this main body of theory was correct and complete there *ought* to be no such subjects as the trade cycle, and, except perhaps in the form of an account of the technique of banking and foreign exchanges, as monetary theory, was painfully apparent.

class-divided societies. Nevertheless it was possible to make some sort of a defence of the whole concept of the overall self-regulation of capitalism, at the time when this concept was first worked out. In the nineteenth century capitalism did exhibit a certain extremely rough-and-ready power of self-adjustment. There were periodic slumps and crises and mass unemployment, but they did not last long. The system's power of recovery and recuperation was as marked as was its instability. If society could stand the oscillations (and it could), the system exhibited an inherent tendency to right itself, as well as an inherent tendency to plunge into slump.

MARX'S CRISIS THEORY

Marx's attitude to this aspect of the economic problem is interesting. He was profoundly struck with the instability of capitalism. In fact, I repeat, he and Engels always confidently supposed that each crisis would be the system's last. Every eight or ten years they became convinced that the new wave of cyclical recession must touch off a universal European revolution. In this respect their political judgment had just as little contact with reality as had the economic theories of Say and his friends. Marx, nevertheless, made the first serious attempt to study and account for the cyclical crises. Vol. II of *Capital* is largely concerned with this matter and a good deal of attention is given to it in the course of Volumes I and III. In particular, the aforementioned J. B. Say (with Senior, Malthus and Bestiat) was one of Marx's prime whipping boys.

What Marx had to say about the famous law was in effect this. No doubt it might be true that there would be no crises in an economy which did its exchanging by means of direct

barter.* There every sale would be a purchase, every purchase a sale, as Say and the other economists said they must
be. But this was by no means the case in a complex society
such as ours, which had to mediate its exchanges by means of
money. For money—the medium of exchange—made it possible for sales and purchases to become disassociated one
from another, for a sale to be made and the consequential
purchase to be indefinitely delayed. Marx put it like this:

> Nothing could be more childish than the dogma that, because
> every sale is a purchase, and every purchase a sale, therefore
> the circulation of commodities necessarily implies an equilib-
> rium of sales and purchases. . . . No one can sell unless some-
> one else purchases. But no one is forthwith bound to purchase,
> because he has just sold. . . . If the split between the sale and
> purchase becomes too pronounced the intimate connection be-
> tween them, their oneness, asserts itself by producing—a
> crisis.† (*Capital*, Vol. I, p. 87.)

That passage contains the germ of Keynes' explanation of
how oscillations, and stagnation also, can and do occur in a
capitalist economy. Nearly all his basic ideas could be derived from it. It has the germ in it not only of the overthrow of Say's law, but also of the concept of attempted
hoarding, and even of the refinements of Keynes' concept of
"liquidity preference"—of ways in which men and institutions prefer to hold not only their new assets, but their assets
as a whole. It lays a basis for his concept of men's growing
"propensity" to save, as against their propensity to spend, as
their incomes increase. And from these concepts derives in

---

* As we sketched in the last chapter, in fact there would be: what money
does is immensely to exaggerate inherent instabilities due to leaving the level
of investment to chance.
† See *An Essay on Marxian Economics* (Macmillan, 1942) by Mrs. Joan
Robinson for a full and technical discussion of all this.

turn Keynes' theory of interest. If Keynes had not had such a horror of Marx (he evidently felt an intense need to deny any contamination) he could have saved himself much of the laborious detours of *The Treatise on Money* and come much earlier to the clarity of *The General Theory,* simply by mastering the relevant parts of Vols. I, II and III of *Capital.* For the root of the whole matter is contained in Marx's realisation of the fact that *money* makes the connection between the two halves of an exchange loose and precarious.

In Volume II of *Capital* Marx traced out the interactions, and possibilities of dislocation, between the industries turning out consumers' goods and the industries turning out capital goods, in some detail. And in Volume III he arrived at what is substantially the Keynesian conclusions as to the rate of interest. He wrote:

> No such thing as a "natural" law of interest exists. . . . There are no "natural" limits for the rate of interest. . . . The minimum limit of interest is wholly undefinable. It may fall to any depth. (Vol. III, pp. 419-421.)

Nevertheless nothing could be further from the truth than to suggest that Marx was a Keynesian. All this analysis of the instabilities of capitalism was to him a secondary matter. He did not expect that these instabilities would prove fatal to the system—except perhaps as the last straw which would break its already enfeebled back at the bottom of a slump. On the contrary, as we have seen, he was convinced that capitalism would be destroyed, not by its instability, but by its inability to raise the standard of life of the masses. He believed that it would be destroyed because it would force the masses down into ever-increasing misery, till it produced their revolt. It is true that the two things are connected. The instability which produces slump is clearly related in some way to the persistent inability of the system to provide a market for its final product. But what that connection was Marx never fully elucidated.

KEYNESIAN CRISIS THEORY

Keynes approached the whole matter from a point of view as antithetical to that of Marx as can well be imagined. While Marx's approach was, above all, historical and sociological, Keynes took up the question of crisis from the monetary side. He noticed that monetary theory had long been an unsatisfactory and detached part of general orthodox economics. Seizing on this anomalous fact, he linked it with the far greater anomaly that, while the main body of economic theory proved the impossibility of slump, crisis and stagnation, slumps, crises and stagnation had not only occurred, but were manifestly getting more and more severe. Might not these two things be connected? he asked. Might it not be possible to remedy the failure of theory to correspond to reality by re-integrating monetary theory with the main body of economic thought?

In one sense Keynes was right in supposing that it was from the peculiarities of the monetary circulation that the possibility of the loss of equilibrium arose. But at a deeper level, as he came to realise in *The General Theory*, the monetary disorder merely reflected an underlying disorder in the system as a whole; it merely reflected the fact that the system was not self-equilibrating; that it had become quite untrue—if it had ever been true in the past—that the system would always come back on to an even keel if it was left alone. But what Keynes never came to realise was that this growing loss of equilibrium was itself the result of that mutation of the system, which the growth in size, and the decrease in number, of its units, with the consequent atrophy of competition, had produced.

KEYNES' GENERAL VIEW OF CAPITALISM

Let us now summarise what Keynes considered was wrong with contemporary capitalism. He saw that both its loss of equilibrium and its tendency to stagnation were above all connected with: (a) the difficulties of keeping a balance between the capital and consumer goods industries, or, as he put it, in monetary terms, the ratio of investment to spending; (b) the degree of equality or inequality in the distribution of the national income, for this largely determined the above ratio; (c) the fact that of all the reputedly self-regulating devices of capitalism, the rate of interest was the least effective.

So far we have said little about the rate of interest. The rate of interest was supposed to be, in effect, the price of capital; at any rate, it was supposed to be the price of virtually safe, non-risk-bearing capital. As such it was supposed to adjust, like any other price, the supply of, to the demand for, capital. But in fact it did nothing of the sort. In the first place, the rate of interest never dropped below a certain conventional minimum, however great the supply of, and however small the demand for, capital might be. For what in practice largely determined the supply of capital was the "liquidity preference" of the rich, *i.e.*, the amount of their unspent money which the rich preferred to keep in more or less readily available hoards instead of tying up in investments. Accordingly, if investment opportunities did not seem very attractive, a decisively significant proportion of the incomes of the rich might be neither spent nor invested.

At first Keynes said that this "missing" part of the incomes of the rich was in one way or another hoarded. (*The Treatise on Money.*) But in *The General Theory* he had come to see that this missing part of their incomes was not so much hoarded as simply dissipated into the air. For, if for any reason there was a marked drop in the "propensity" of the rich to invest, the following sequence of events followed: The liquidity preferences of the rich went up; part of their incomes was neither spent (used to buy consumer goods) nor invested (used to buy capital goods). The rich attempted, indeed, to hoard this part of their incomes. But this was an essentially self-defeating operation. For the demand for both capital goods and consumer goods dropped, of course, by the amount of this unspent and uninvested income. Therefore production as a whole slowed up. A depression began. Profits, along with wages and all other kinds of income, began to dry up. And before long this depression had so cut down the incomes of the rich that they had no longer any margin of income left to attempt to hoard. They were soon either spending or investing all of their now *reduced* incomes. But now the whole economy was running at a lower level. It had a margin of unused resources and unemployed labour. Nor was there any *automatic* tendency for it to regain full employment. On the contrary, another shock to the already shaken nerves of the rich might well set them off trying to hoard even out of their now reduced incomes. Then the sequence would repeat itself, and the economy would drop to a still lower level of activity.*

It was not until something turned up to make the rich feel that it was worth while to invest again that recovery could begin. This part of the Keynesian analysis (it was worked out with great elaboration and refinement of detail)

---

* In current practice the process is more complex still, since the term "the rich" suggests individual rich men. But, as we have noted repeatedly, it is now the "collective rich," the great firms, who do nearly all the investing and a good deal of the saving. Their behaviour is not so very different, however, for these purposes.

might be thought to have applied to capitalism in all stages of development. And so, to some extent, it did. The nine-teenth-century heyday was pitted with extremely sharp slumps. But they were of relatively short duration. For in that period of enormously plentiful investment opportunities, "something"—the Californian or the South African gold rush —the opening up of a new continent—or simply another burst of railway, or steel works, or electrical, or chemical de-velopment—always set the ball rolling again before long. Moreover, there were plenty of individual, *competing*, entre-preneurs to take advantage of these opportunities. If one didn't, another would.

Mature twentieth-century capitalism is in this respect more likely to get stuck in a depression. Even if investment oppor-tunities are no less plentiful, relative to the resources now available, there are far fewer entrepreneurs to take advantage of them. Above all, as we have seen, these remaining en-trepreneurs will no longer be genuinely competitive. They will be oligopolists, partially freed from the fear that if they do not "go in" for some expensive new process, a rival will. If they are in a mood of safety first and high liquidity pref-erence, there may be less to shake them out of it.

OLIGOPOLY IN BANKING

Another aspect of Keynes' picture of contemporary capitalism was, however, much more closely associated with the sys-tem's mutation to the latest stage—so closely indeed that it is astonishing that he did not see the connection. This was his view of what the function of the banks had become. He arrived at this piece of analysis some years before the enunciation of *The General Theory,* but he did not modify it.

Economic theory had assigned a modest rôle to the banks. They were, it was said, mere "cloakrooms" at which people left or deposited such of their money as they had no immediate use for, in the same way that a guest at a hotel leaves his hat and coat in the cloakroom when he goes up to his room. The cloakroom analogy was always a little far-fetched, for it would be a somewhat eccentric cloakroom which proceeded to lend your hat and coat to another guest after you had deposited it, and this re-lending of the money deposited with them was always, of course, of the essence of the bankers' functions. Nevertheless, a hundred years ago, and for the scattered, numerous, competing banks of the period, it was, no doubt, largely true that in essence their function was the indispensable but relatively humble one of receiving A's spare cash and lending it, on short term, to B. It was one of Keynes' major achievements that he finally exploded the contention that this is all that the "big five" joint stock banks and the Bank of England of contemporary Britain, or the banking systems of America or Germany, are doing today. The truth is that, once the number of important banks has come down to the order of magnitude of 10 or 20; and associated with that process a central bank, or central banking system, has got a firm control of the operations of the other banks; *i.e.*, once banking also has become oligopolistic, the very nature of its operations begins to change.

This is an especially significant case of the process which was noted in Chapter 1. Once, we saw, the number of units engaged in any field of economic activity drops below a certain critical number, the old "law," which was basic to competitive capitalism, that the policy of none of them can affect the price which they can get for their product, no longer holds. In the same way, once there are only half a dozen or so banks of significant size, it is no longer true that the amount of money which they can lend is governed by the amount of money which is deposited with them. On the contrary, the exact opposite becomes true. The amount of money which is deposited with them will henceforward depend upon the amount of money which they lend.

This was all argued out conclusively by the British Macmillan Commission on money which sat during the opening phase of the great depression of 1929-1935. Keynes was able to show the Commission that the banks were stationed, as it were, at one point in a *circulation* of money. If the banks cared to pump more money into this essentially closed * circuit, by means of increasing their loans, that same money must flow back to them by way of increased deposits. Mr. Reginald McKenna, the Keynesian chairman of the Midland Bank, used to demonstrate this practically. If at the given time the Midland Bank was doing, say, one-fifth of the national banking business, its chairman knew that, if he increased his loans by £1 million, £200,000 would flow back into his deposits in a few days' time. The other four-fifths of his million naturally flowed back into the other four "big five" banks. So, if these other four banking oligarchs "kept step" with him and each increased his loans by an amount proportionate to his share in the total banking business of the country, £1 million would duly flow back into the Midland's deposits. (He used to impress his subordinates by exactly predicting that this would happen.)

Observe that all this had only become true and calculable as and when the banking system became oligopolistic. It had been by no means true that if, in 1850, "Jones' Bank of Nether Smokeborough" increased its loans by £10,000, any of the money would flow back to it as deposits. "Jones' Bank" did so small and unknown a proportion of the total national banking business that there was no ascertainable relation between its loans and its deposits. The chances were that the

* Unless the money went abroad. See p. 305.

whole of its increase of loans would be deposited in other banks, and in any case it could not conceivably increase its loans sufficiently to make any appreciable difference to the supply of credit available.

The point of this relatively early piece of Keynesian analysis was that he showed by it that it had become possible for the score or so of men who controlled the British banking system to vary at will the supply of credit or short-term capital available at any given time. And, of course, if they could vary the amount, they could vary the price. But the price of credit is the rate of interest, or rather the complex structure of interest rates for various purposes. So what Keynes was "getting at" was that one of the ways in which the economy could be levered out of a depression was to lower the rates of interest. And he concluded that the bankers (including the Bank of England) could do so whenever they were so minded. In a word, the price of the thing in which they dealt, *i.e.*, credit or short-term capital, had ceased to be something given to them as a datum; it had become something which they themselves could, within limits, fix—just as had the price of heavy chemicals, or crude oil, or a dozen other oligopolistically controlled commodities.*

Why was it, the reader may well ask, that the bankers put up so obstinate a struggle to deny the existence of these new

---

* The effect of the oligopolisation of banking, *i.e.*, the integration of banks with other banks, has turned out, at least in Britain and America, to be the really significant process. The alternative form of integration is that by which the German banks, in particular, became closely associated with the major industrial oligopolies. This was the process which occupied the attention of Hilferding, Lenin and the other second-generation Marxists. These Marxist authorities did not live to see the critically important consequences of the quite distinct British and American process which we are considering, namely, the reduction of the number of considerable, independent banks below a certain critical point. It is important to distinguish clearly between the two forms of integration—the one horizontal and the other vertical—for they have different effects.

powers which Keynes showed that they had acquired? (They still, at times, try to deny them.)* It was because their exist-ence confirmed the second thing which Keynes said about contemporary capitalism. He believed not only that capitalism had ceased to be self-adjusting and self-regulating. He also believed that it could henceforth be consciously and purpose-fully regulated and adjusted. And the great majority (al-though not all) of the leaders of capitalist opinion objected to this second Keynesian pronouncement even more than the first. At first sight this is astonishing. For there is not the slightest doubt about Keynes' good intentions towards their system. He really did want to regulate and control capitalism in order to save it. He grasped at the steering-wheel only to avoid the ditch. But he encountered, to his own lasting sur-prise, I think, a profound, instinctive repugnance on the part of capitalist opinion—and even more, at first, in America than in Britain—to any admission that the system could be con-sciously controlled.

The reason for such reluctance is not really far to seek. If once the possibility of control were admitted, who would do the controlling? In whose *interests* would the system be controlled? This man Keynes, it was felt, might mean well; but that was not the point. The country had become a de-mocracy. If once the idea spread that there was no natural law necessitating such things as a margin of mass unemploy-ment and the existing degree of inequality in the distribu-tion of income, the system might indeed be made to work again. But in whose interest would it then work? Surely it was not necessary to be saved *in that way?* Or—and this was the choice of one of the great national capitalist groupings—

---

* Many economists before Keynes had arrived at the conclusion that banks could create credit money, and that the central banks and the banking sys-tem as a whole could do so to an indefinite extent. It was the bankers them-selves who put up so prolonged and obstinate a resistance to admitting their own powers.

if it had indeed come to this, had not democracy become far too dangerous an institution?

We approach here the politico-economic crux of our epoch. Here, however, we must continue our account of Keynes' theory of the latest stage by giving an account of his proposals for the conscious and positive control of the system. By describing these proposals we may throw much additional light on the extent to which Keynes was, although on the whole unconsciously, providing the theory of a profoundly modified system. (In Keynes' own works his critique of contemporary capitalism and his positive proposals for its overall control are not separated even to the extent which I have attempted to separate them in this chapter.)

KEYNES' POSITIVE PROPOSALS

If Keynes' first statement about contemporary capitalism was that it was no longer self-regulating, his second statement was that it could be, and must be, regulated. He was a hundred miles from concluding that the system had got irrevocably out of hand and must go to shipwreck. On the contrary, he believed that *overall, generalised* financial and economic controls were all that was needed to make it work better than ever. Moreover, his kind of controls, he insisted, would leave the essence of the system in existence. Not only did they leave property in the means of production still in private hands, but they left the essential decisions of economic life, such as, for example, when to invest and what to invest in, still decentralised and private. Even the movement of prices and the continuance of as much of the free market as still existed (and it was in *some* respects quite a lot) were not threatened, he protested. In this sense, Keynes was able to show, his proposals were not socialism. They required neither extensive public ownership, nor the expropriation of the capitalists, nor a detailed, centralised plan for the economy.

The essence of Keynes' positive proposals for the conduct of an economy in the latest stage of capitalism is this. He considered that it was possible, while leaving the basic economic decisions to be made, as now, by fairly numerous private individuals, to determine the *trend* of those decisions by means of what was, in effect, an ingenious method for the regulation of the economic climate of opinion. If the economic climate was chilly, so that the entrepreneurs were tending to freeze into immobility, the thing to do was to warm things up a bit. Then you would soon see the investment plans and policies of the entrepreneurs begin to unfold and burgeon out in the warmer air. *Vice versa,* if the entrepreneurs were too active and tending to inflation, it was easy enough to drop the temperature a few degrees and so curb their enthusiasm. Thus the individual capitalists and capitalist firms could still *feel* perfectly free, and, in a sense, would be perfectly free, to make their own decisions. Only a central authority would be all along determining what they themselves would want the general character of those decisions to be. Keynes regarded, it will be seen, the psychologies of the investing classes as sufficiently determinate to make it practicable to settle, all unknown to them, what, on the average, they should do, while leaving them the *feeling* of freedom. For that matter, they would keep the reality of freedom as to the character, if not the volume, of the investments which they would make. In a word, the entrepreneurs were to be manipulated for their own good. We must now describe Keynes' specific methods for "warming" or "cooling" the economic atmosphere breathed by the entrepreneurs so that they might be roused from deflationary torpor or calmed down from inflationary fever.

KEYNES' SPECIFIC PROPOSALS

I. Variations in the Rate of Interest

The first two measures upon which Keynes relied, in order to regulate the economic climate, were, broadly speaking, monetary. If entrepreneurship was flagging, the first and perhaps the most obvious thing to do was to decrease the price of the resources with which the potential entrepreneur could carry out an enterprise, and *vice versa* if the entrepreneurs were being too enterprising. In other words, vary the rate of interest. For, as we have seen, Keynes was convinced that the rate of interest was not now in the least a price which imposed itself upon the bankers and other leaders as a datum, but was something which could be consciously determined within fairly wide limits. This conclusion was bound up with his contentions as to the bankers' control of the volume and price of credit. For, of course, a reduction of the rate of interest, like the reduction of any other price, implied that the supplies of the article in question (in this case the credit supplied by the bankers) would be available in increased quantities in order to meet the increased demand that the reduced prices would, presumably, call forth. Keynes had shown that the bankers, by increasing their loans, could pour an increased supply of credit into circulation, secure in the knowledge that it would flow back to them as increased deposits. Such credit is a legally valid claim to real things, such as supplies of labour and raw materials and the use of productive facilities. Thus there is no mystery about why the issue of an increased amount of it, *if* it is taken up by people wishing to make use of real resources, and *if* there are unused supplies of them available, stimulates the activity of the economy. True the credit is only a bit of paper. But the figures written on it really do represent productive resources.

But there is a limitation to this policy. What if the banks can find no new borrowers, even after they have lowered their rate of interest? And this is likely enough to be the case in practice. By hypothesis we are assuming that the entrepreneurs are in a deflationary, discouraged mood, unable to foresee profitable outcomes for new enterprises. For that is the state of things which the lowering of the rate of interest is designed to cure. But will a reduction in the price at which they can borrow really have much influence on entrepreneurs in such a mood? After all, their interest charges are seldom an important part of their costs as a whole. If they cannot foresee a profit from building a new chemical works when the rate of interest stands at 5%, are they likely to be much more optimistic about it if the rate of interest be reduced to 3%? If they are not, and if, consequently, total borrowings do not markedly rise, then a reduction of the rate of interest will have no effect, for the resources represented by the new credit will never be used.

KEYNES' SPECIFIC PROPOSALS

II. Budgetary Deficits and Surpluses

As Keynes' thought developed, he became more and more impressed with the weight of this objection. He relied less and less upon a mere variation of interest rates to stimulate the entrepreneurs. He came more and more to feel the necessity of providing other channels which could be relied upon to get the additional productive resources working, the total demand of the community correspondingly increased and stagnation overcome or prevented. Naturally, he turned his attention towards the State. For here was another actor upon the scene, in addition to the entrepreneurs—an actor, moreover, who was engaged in economic activities on the widest scale. The State is constantly taking in and paying out money by the thousands of millions a year. Most of its activities, in a wholly capitalist society, are not entrepreneurship in the ordinary sense of starting or expanding or engaging in direct production. But what of that? The money which it collects in taxes and pays out in expenditure is very much a part of the circulation. If "the object of the exercise" is to increase total demand, why should not the State simply pay out more money than it collects, to any desired extent? Thus there arose the whole concept of *deficit financing*. It became an important part of the Keynesian case that so long as there was stagnation and unemployed factors of production, the State should run a budgetary deficit in order to pump new money into the system and set its wheels turning again. (And *per contra*, if the system was overactive and inflationary, and if prices were rising, then the State should run a budget surplus, taking more money out of the system by taxation than it put back into it by expenditure.)

KEYNES' SPECIFIC PROPOSALS

III. The State as Supplementary Entrepreneur

The third remedy in the Keynesian pharmacopoeia is concerned with the possibility of the State itself undertaking direct entrepreneurial functions, if the private entrepreneurs cannot be induced to expand their activities by offers of money at lower rates of interest. Thus arose the whole "public works" side of the Keynesian specific. For clearly another way of getting more money into circulation, and so increasing total demand, alternative to leaving more money in the hands of the tax-payers, is to put more money into people's hands by employing them upon public works of one kind or another. Keynes did not primarily mind what kind of public works these were: almost anything would do so long as it put more money into people's hands. (Thus arose the famous, ironic pyramid building and hiding-banknotes-in-old-coal-mines passages in *The General Theory*.) It was a sign of Keynes' (sadly unappreciated) capitalist orthodoxy that he only envisaged the State as doing the general "clearing-up" type of public works, such as building post offices and roads, or, at the very most, dams and power stations, while leaving the real work of production in private hands.

KEYNES' SPECIFIC PROPOSALS

IV. Equalitarian Redistribution of Incomes

The fourth Keynesian remedy was of a somewhat different type. Consideration of it carries us back to the argument of preceding chapters, since it involves the distribution of the national income. Another way of putting his basic critique was to say that what ailed the capitalist system was a tendency for the total demand of the population as a whole to be insufficient to clear the market of the final products of industry at remunerative prices. And this arose because the rich, naturally desiring to save a much higher proportion of their high incomes than the poor, and periodically seeing nothing worth investing in, attempted to commit the sin of the buried talent, and so led the economy into cumulative depression. Well, then, was not one remedy for this state of things to disembarrass the rich of some of their high incomes, so that they would be relieved of the dilemma of what to do with all that part of their incomes which they did not spend? In other words, would not a redistribution of income from the rich to the poor strike at the root of the trouble? Keynes developed a whole set of concepts to demonstrate this suggestion. He said that the poor had a greater "propensity" to spend and a lesser "propensity" to save than the rich. Therefore a pound transferred from the pockets of the latter to the pockets of the former was much more sure to be put into circulation, instead of hoarded in an access of "liquidity preference." In other words, the more equalitarian the distribution of income, the less, other things being equal, would the community attempt to save. And, quite contrary to the unanimous teachings of the economists, this would be a positive advantage. For the very high rate of saving which would be attempted under an extremely inequalitarian distribution of income would be, in a latter-day capitalism, self-defeating. It would not in practice result in a rapid rate of actual capital accumulation; it would be largely dissipated in attempted hoarding, and so merely result in slump and stagnation. In practice a more equalitarian society, which attempted a lower rate of saving and accumulation, would actually achieve a higher level of investment. For what it did save would all be invested and it would thus avoid the immense waste of slump and stagnation.

KEYNESIAN MODERATION

At first sight these specifics all seem fairly limited modifications of capitalism. Lower interest rates, budgetary deficits in depressions and budgetary surpluses in booms, public works, a more equalitarian distribution of income, presumably effected by redistributory taxation—this sort of thing does not seem to pass beyond modest limits of reform, and Keynes himself was always careful to insist that it did not. No doubt such policies could be called socialistic in the very broadest and vaguest sense of that term—in the sense that they involved a greater degree of intervention and guidance on the part of the Government in economic matters than had once been envisaged. But surely, Keynes was accustomed to plead this was only socialism in the sense of the term that Sir William Harcourt had used, as early as the turn of the century, when he said, "We are all socialists now." Here was little or nothing of socialism in the clear-cut, definite sense of the substitution of public for private ownership of the means of production. Moreover, his policy promised very great benefits to the rich as well as to the mass of the population. It promised that, at the price of a little moderation, the profound, dangerous and painful upheavals of slump would be eliminated, or at least greatly mitigated. And, after all, slumps, although to the rich they do not mean mass unemployment and destitution, as they do to the wage earners, may be unpleasant experiences even for them.

Why, then, did the rich react, on the whole, with suspicion and even hostility to the Keynesian policy? That policy has indeed been implemented to a striking extent, and with decidedly encouraging results, at different times in each of the major contemporary capitalisms. But it has generally been implemented by non-capitalist, or at most semi-capitalist, forces. The true defenders of capitalism did not really approve of it. This was, to some extent, no doubt, the result of mere scepticism as to the possibility of action along these lines, of sheer stupidity and inability to grasp where their own true interests lay. But the capitalists have really had good reasons for their reluctance to be saved by Keynesian policies. If we look more closely at the remedies proposed, we shall find that their implications are much more drastic than they seem to be at first sight. And when we come in later volumes of this study to consider the results of the application of Keynesian measures in America, Germany and Britain, respectively, we shall find that in fact the changes effected by them have been subtle, but nevertheless far-reaching.

"WHERE WAS IT ALL TO STOP?"

Consider first the third Keynesian proposal, that of a redistribution of income, not primarily for the sake of social justice, but in order to make the system work again by increasing the total of effective demand for the final product. It was not so much to the immediate sacrifice of income involved (although that was unpalatable enough) that the real guardians of the interests of the rich objected. It could be argued by Keynes, probably correctly, that the rich would gain more by eliminating slump and stagnation than they would lose by financing increased social services out of higher income tax, surtax and death duties. It was the principle of the thing that was so profoundly objectionable. For the proposal rested on the assumption that it was possible to vary the distribution of the national income at will. But such an assumption ran clean counter to really orthodox, classical doctrine. The distribution of the national income had been regarded as a *function* of the workings of the system. Everybody's incomes—wages, interest, rent, profits, salaries, professional fees—alike arose out of the payments which the producers had to make in order to command the factors of production. Personal incomes *were* "factor costs" seen from the opposite side. The productive process was the cause, personal incomes the effect. And the existing pattern of distribution flowed from a natural law which determined that everyone should be paid what his services to production would in fact command—the worker his wages for working; the capitalist his interest for "waiting," and his profit for "risking"; the lawyer his fee for pleading the capitalist's cause; and the economist his salary for explaining the whole business. But now it was proposed arbitrarily to vary the distribution of personal incomes in order to alter the balance of production. What

could be a more impious proposal than that? It would turn
effect into cause and cause into effect. It was proposed to
make the productive system dance to a new tune, a new tune
arbitrarily given it from outside instead of arising melodi-
ously from its own workings.

Of course the protectors of capitalism were not really concerned with the theoretical impropriety of the Keynesian
proposals. But they deeply felt the danger of any sort of
tampering with the system. Keynes might sincerely wish to
redistribute income only sufficiently to make the system work
again. But what guarantee, what likelihood even, was there
that things would stop there? Once the principle was admitted that it was possible to vary the distribution of the national income at will—nay, more, that it was possible to make
it more equalitarian, not only without ruinous results, but
with positive benefits to the working of the system, what hope
would there be of preserving the existing degree of inequality?

It was the same with the other two sets of Keynesian measures. It was not so much that there was anything fatal to
capitalism about lowering the rate of interest, running a
budgetary deficit in a slump or engaging in public works.
But the whole tendency involved in conceding that such conscious direction and control of the system were possible was
altogether deplorable. *Again, where was all this sort of thing
to stop?* For example, if once it became admitted that interest
was not the payment for a mysterious but indispensable
service to production called "waiting," somehow rendered
by the rich, but was something the rate of which could be
lowered or raised at will in order to accelerate or decelerate
the general rhythm of production, would not the fatal question, why pay interest at all, be raised? In fact, Keynes himself raised that very question and answered that in the end
there would be no reason. He had the bad taste actually

to talk about the "euthanasia of the rentiers." * It was the same with public works. There would be nothing fatal to the interests of capitalism if more of the traditional types of public works were engaged in. No one really minded if the Government built some more roads or post offices, or raked more leaves, or dug some holes in the ground and filled them up again. But might not someone ask one day why, if one could build post offices by means of public works, one should not build houses by the same method; if the Government could pay men to dig holes in the ground and fill them up again, why should it not pay them to mine coal? In short, what if the wage earners came to the conclusion that it was not really necessary to tempt the entrepreneurs with rent, interest and profit, to get the necessities of life produced; that it was possible to produce things by means of a *social* initiative, by consciously making up our minds that they ought to be produced and then producing them?

Were not the true protectors of the system justified a thousandfold in feeling that the remedies of this man Keynes, speak he never so mildly and fair, needed looking at very narrowly indeed? Was not a horrid possibility visible behind and beyond his proposals, each of which looked so innocuous when taken separately? If once it were admitted that capitalism could be regulated and controlled in this way, might not the wage-earning majority of the population come sooner or later to the conclusion that the thing to do was neither to put up with things as they were, nor to go through the fiery furnace of social revolution, in order to establish a wholly new system, but to harness—to bit and to bridle—

---

* He foresaw a period when the well-to-do would simply have to make what savings they wished without being paid anything for doing so. They used to do so in earlier periods, and Keynes gave the example of the father of the poet Pope, who at the end of his life retired to his villa at Twickenham with a box of guineas from which he drew as needed.

capitalism in *its* own interest? Was it not apparent that Keynesism had only to be pushed a little further and a state of things might emerge in which the nominal owners of the means of production, although left in full possession of the legal title to their property, would in reality be working not for themselves, but for whatever hands had grasped the central levers of social control? For Keynes had rashly shown that those levers had only to be pulled and pushed this way and that, in order to manipulate the system at will. And, in a democracy, would not those hands in the end almost certainly be those of the representatives of the wage-earning majority of the population? Might not the end of the story be that the once proud possessors of the means of production would find themselves in effect but agents and managers on behalf of the community? If this was saving capitalism, its true defenders felt, it was saving it in a most Pickwickian sense.*

---

* As our argument proceeds we shall discuss the extent to which this comprehensible antagonism to Keynesism on the part of the defenders of capitalism, when they encountered the doctrine in the 'thirties, has now been overcome. No doubt in Britain, and even in America also, it has been overcome to a significant extent. For the threat of far more drastic things than this has been close. Nevertheless, it remains to be seen if the most conservative circles in both countries have in fact become such good Keynesians as their policies, in 1956, would at first sight lead one to suppose.

12. AN EVALUATION OF KEYNES

An inspection of Keynesian doctrine has revealed that it is, in its implications, a much more far-reaching policy than at first appears. For it involves a recognition of the fact that capitalism, in entering its latest stage, has lost most of its genuinely competitive character, and so its capacity for self-regulation. The system must now be consciously controlled and directed or it will smash itself to pieces. Keynes tacitly recognised that capitalism in its latest stage must work either much better or much worse than before. It will work much better if it is consciously regulated in the interests of the community; much worse if it is left to its own devices. But what Keynes hardly touched upon was the question of *who* should do the regulating. Because he was a liberal Englishman, he more or less tacitly assumed that, if the system was to be regulated at all, it would be regulated in the interests of "the community as a whole." At most he would have unenthusiastically agreed that that interest must in practice today be primarily the interest of the wage-earning mass of the population.

IS KEYNESIAN DOCTRINE ILLUSORY?

At the cost of some anticipation of a principal argument of this study it may be useful to attempt at once to answer the question: Are the Keynesian specifics practical and substantial measures against the worst evils of our times, or are they, on the contrary, illusions and will-of-the-wisps, which can only distract us from our tasks of social and economic reconstruction? The answer is, briefly, that there are no specifically *economic* fallacies in the Keynesian case. This is a far better diagram of the workings of present-day capitalism than that provided by the older economists. It follows that *if* the proposed Keynesian remedies can be applied they will have, broadly, the predicted effects. On the other hand, far more formidable *political* obstacles than were ever faced by Keynes exist to an adequate application of his policies. With the question of whether, and if so how, these political obstacles can be overcome a large part of the rest of this study will be concerned.

This view of Keynesian policy can be well brought out by considering current Marxian or Leninist criticism of it. When Keynes' theories were first published, the Marxist reaction was to dismiss them contemptuously as mere economic fallacies. And this is still the official communist view. More sophisticated Marxist opinion has, however, now modified this critique and has come to the view that Keynes' theories are correct in the abstract, but are academic and unimportant, because the capitalists, who control everything, will certainly never apply them. This is the view set out, for example, by that talented American left-wing economist, Mr. Paul Sweezy, in his book *The Present as History* (Monthly Review Press, New York, 1953). It will be worth while following Mr. Sweezy's argument with care, for it leads straight to the very crux of our contemporary problem.

The answer, Mr. Sweezy writes:

> . . . To the Keynesians does not lie in the realm of abstract economic theory. *If* an American capitalist government could spend $20 billion—and if necessary $30 billion or $40 billion—for peaceful constructive purposes, then the Keynesians would doubtless be right. But the point is precisely that the ruling capitalist class, the very class whose enormous wealth and power is assured by the structure of capitalism itself, will never approve or permit spending on this scale (or anything even approaching this scale) for peaceful constructive ends. Nor is this a matter of ignorance or stupidity. It is a plain matter of class interest, which to the capitalist class (as to all ruling classes in history) appears to be the national interest and indeed the interest of civilization itself.

Mr. Sweezy then details, one by one, the main objects on which the American Government might spend large sums for peaceful purposes.

> Take housing, he writes. "Why not a gigantic program to rebuild and rehouse America? Heaven knows we need it badly enough! But everyone who has passed the age of ten knows the answer: the real-estate interests. They will put up with a small amount of government housing, preferably in the field of slum clearance, but when it comes to anything big they say *No*, and they get the solid backing of all the propertied interests of the country.
>
> Or take social security. Why not a real Social Security program? Here again there is no lack of need. But a real Social Security program would require a considerable degree of income redistribution from rich to poor. And besides capitalists do not *want* too much security—for others. It is bad for morale, dulls the incentive to work, leads to exaggerated expectations and pretensions. Capitalists believe—and not without reason—

that their system requires enormous rewards at the top and poverty and insecurity at the bottom to keep it going. A real Social Security program contradicts both these requirements and will therefore always be opposed to the limit by the capitalist class.

Or take Government investments in industry or public utilities or transportation. There is no end of useful projects which Government could undertake at any given time—if it were free to compete with private enterprise; in fact it is here that the resistance of the capitalists to the extension of Government activities is at its maximum. They regard all branches of the economy that can be made to yield a profit as their own private preserve at the entrance to which they have posted a huge No Trespassing sign. If anything seems certain it is that as long as we have capitalism we shall have very little government investment in the production of useful *and saleable* goods and services.

The British reader will find this passage extremely illuminating, but not quite in the sense which its author intended. Large-scale public housing, a comprehensive Welfare State, a substantial degree of actual production carried on on Government account, either directly or by public Boards—these are exactly the things on which recent British governments *have* spent and invested vast sums of money. And yet this talented American economist lays it down as a "law" of present-day capitalist society that the capitalists can and will prevent any government from doing such things. Clearly something is wrong with his argument. For not only have British Governments done such things, without, as Mr. Sweezy is one of the first to point out, British capitalism having been abolished, but also other Governments, including the American, have from time to time done, if not so much, then a quite appreciable amount of this sort of thing. Is Mr. Sweezy wrong, then, in thinking that the capitalists object to this type of governmental action? No, he is not wrong. Not only have we given above the explanations of why the capitalists do indeed object to these things, but also no one who, like myself, has been a member of a government which did these things, is likely to forget the torrent of protests, lamentations, objections and prophecies of doom which the capitalists and their spokesmen raised against these things being done.

What is wrong with Mr. Sweezy's argument is not that the capitalists will object to the Keynesian specifics. Of course they will. What is wrong with his argument is the defeatist conclusion that that is the end of the matter; that, short of the total overthrow of capitalism and the breaking of *all* capitalist resistance, nothing can be done to which the capitalists object. We are back at the same issue which confronted us in previous chapters. There we saw that what had gone wrong with the Marxist prediction was that it neglected the power which contemporary democracy had developed to raise the standard of life of the masses of the highly developed latest-stage capitalisms. Now we see that even so sophisticated a writer as Mr. Sweezy assumes, almost without argument, that, because the capitalists are bound to be against the Keynesian specifics, it is impossible for them ever to be applied. He might yet prove to have been right if he had said that this consideration made it impossible to believe that Keynesian policies would consistently or willingly be carried out by the capitalists themselves, as Keynes genuinely seems to have expected that they would be. But this does not prevent such policies becoming invaluable instruments in the hands of the forces of a contemporary democracy: of the trade unions, the organised farmers, and the political parties which are based upon them. Moreover, it would be to oversimplify the workings of contemporary democracy to suggest that Keynesian policies will only be pursued by labour, socialist, and other progressive governments which are distinctly based upon such forces. On the contrary, the results of Keynesian policies are so overwhelmingly attractive to the mass of the population, who are the mass of the electorate, that even the most impeccably right-wing governments, such as those, for example, of Sir Anthony Eden in Britain and President Eisenhower in America, at the time of writing (1956) are unable to abstain from them. (For example, the present Conservative Government in Britain is [1956] pursuing a policy which results in appreciably more of the national resources being devoted to housing than were so devoted under the Labour Government. It is duly receiving the shocked disapproval of high capitalist circles, but it counts on receiving the gratitude of the voters.)*

Thus, *so long as effective democracy exists,* in the sense which we defined above, it is untrue to say that there is no possibility of applying the Keynesian remedies. They will be opposed by the capitalists, certainly, but experience shows that they can be imposed by the electorate. Keynesian economic policies, joined with traditional socialist measures of public ownership and social reform, have become indispensable instruments by means of which democracy can effect its purposes. Unless democratic and socialist political parties comprehend and command these policies they will not succeed in transforming capitalism to serve their purposes. Indeed, as our narrative develops we shall see that the maintenance of democracy and the application of more and more drastic economic measures of this type are intimately interrelated. Of course this will throw a heavy strain on democracy. But it will be precisely those democracies which do *not* effectively apply measures of this type which are likely to break down.

* And did receive it in May, 1955.

THE DISTORTION OF KEYNESISM

There is another and less palatable reason why it would be a great mistake to dismiss the Keynesian techniques as illusory. As we noted, those Marxians who are unable any longer to deny that capitalism in the nineteen-fifties is behaving very differently from what it did in the nineteen-thirties, explain that this is simply due to vast expenditures upon armaments. Furthermore, a sophisticated minority of them are ready to agree that this is, in a sense, an example of the application of the Keynesian technique of expenditure upon public works—only the public works are guns, or rather in these days nuclear weapons.

The case of these—mainly communist—critics is, briefly, as follows. "No doubt it is true that *if* a capitalist government supplements the activities of its profit-seeking entrepreneurs by itself spending or investing sufficiently massive sums, it can sustain the economy at a level of full employment. But a capitalist government will be intensely unwilling to do this *for peaceful purposes*. If it produces useful goods and services it will be competing with its own entrepreneurs. If it pays out money to the wage earners or farmers it will re-distribute the national income, directly or indirectly, in their favour and to the prejudice of the property-owning classes. Therefore it will be inhibited from such courses. There exists, however, one object of government expenditure which is not covered by these inhibitions, namely, military expenditure. Such government expenditure fits into the generally aggressive policies of capitalist governments of the latest stage. It is this kind of government expenditure and this kind alone which the capitalist governments have undertaken on a scale sufficient to be economically significant since 1945." The communists thus conclude that they can explain away the whole phenomenon of post-Second World War full employment as being sustained by enormous expenditures upon armaments alone.

Such an explanation is a crude caricature of the complex realities of the contemporary situation. Those realities should be carefully unravelled. In the first place, it is not true that in 1950, when America, Britain and to a lesser extent other capitalist governments first undertook their present large rearmament programmes, they did so in order to stimulate stagnant economies which were relapsing into mass unemployment. They undertook massive rearmament programmes because they, rightly or wrongly, necessarily or unnecessarily, became convinced that unless they did so they would be outclassed and ultimately overawed by the existing massive armaments (it was not "*re*armament") of Russia. Nor were their economies relapsing into stagnation and mass unemployment. On the contrary, the British economy was running at forced draft, just, but only just, able to carry out all its activities without falling into rapid inflation. The American economy had, it is true, suffered a very shallow depression in 1948-49. But the figures show incontrovertibly (they will be given in a later part of this study) that this depression was over and the progress of full employment had been resumed before the outbreak of the Korean war and long before the American rearmament programme began.

Is there then no substance in the view that the Keynesian technique of stimulating the economy by government expenditure may be deflected and distorted into expenditure on arms making? That would be a premature conclusion. From a narrowly economic standpoint, it should be noted, arms making is neither a more nor a less effective form of public works than any other. An extra pound or dollar spent on nuclear weapons is likely to have, other things being equal, neither a more nor a less stimulating effect on the economy than a pound or a dollar spent on building, say, schools or hospitals. But such narrowly economic calculations are, as usual, of limited practical importance. The political, social, psychological effects of spending upon armaments instead of for peaceful purposes are different indeed.

In the first place, no one with first-hand experience of the matter can doubt that it is true that it is in one way *easier* for the government of a capitalist society to spend upon armaments than for peaceful purposes. I well remember the remarkable transformation of opinion which took place in official and financial circles, and in the Press and in Parliament, when, in 1950, the British Labour Government of which I was a member was faced with the necessity, as we considered it (rightly in my view), to undertake a rearmament programme. Up till that moment we had been under the most intense pressure to curtail government expenditure in particular and economic activity generally. Our officials, the City of London, the financial writers in the Press, the spokesmen of the opposition in Parliament—all united to point out that employment was already full, if not "overfull"; that there were no unused resources available for any new activities; that our import bill was very high and being met with great difficulty. Far from it being possible to undertake or to stimulate any new activities, it was imperative, we were urged, to cut down some of the old; it was imperative, it was reiterated, to pare the money incomes of the mass of the population by reducing the social services or to reduce the amount of public enterprise going on, or both. Even cuts which would save no more than £5 million or £10 million were, we were told, indispensable.

Then the question of rearmament came into the picture. Immediately the whole character of the advice tendered to us, both officially and unofficially, was transformed. Immediately an increase of government expenditure, not of £5 million or £10 million, but of hundreds of millions was contemplated without demur. "Oh, well," we were suddenly informed, "all these calculations of the gross national product and all that sort of thing are very approximate. The economy has probably plenty of 'give' in it. Nothing serious will happen if we go ahead and order £800 million-worth of warlike stores." The initiation of a rearmament programme may or may not have been indispensable in 1950. I repeat that in my view it was indispensable, although in retrospect it is easy to see that the size of the programme was excessive even from the point of view of procuring the most effective defences. But it is impossible to resist the impression that arms making was the one kind of government expenditure which was considered in orthodox circles to be really *respectable*. It was the one sort of government economic activity which had nothing left wing about it. And the whole character of the economic advice which the Government received was governed by that fact.

In this case it was not that the former advice that we had previously stretched the economy to its limits was ill-founded. It was true that, for the moment, we were doing about all that was possible; that it was necessary at least to avoid any further inflationary move. What *was* ill-founded was the sudden easy-going optimism that further massive government expenditure could be undertaken, on top of everything else, *if this new government expenditure were devoted to arms making*. What proved in the event to be ill-founded was the assumption that somehow or other this vast new burden could be laid on the economy without causing an inflationary rise in internal prices and without a balance-of-payments crisis. For these symptoms of grave overstrain duly made their appearance in 1951.

The moral of this reminiscence is simply that there is no denying that there is a tendency for the governments of latest-stage capitalisms to devote extra expenditure designed to stimulate the economy to arms making rather than to peaceful purposes. Sometimes, in this unhappy world, rearmament will, in my view, really be necessary on its merits. But unless the governments concerned are awake to the under-lying issues involved they will find that somehow or other arms making, if they are to engage in positive economic ac-tivity at all, will turn out to be the path of least resistance. It is true that there will be democratic counter pressure upon such governments in favour of expenditure for peaceful pur-poses rather than upon armaments. But such pressure, in the short run at least, is, in my experience, apt to be more than offset by the solid weight of "respectable" opinion. There may thus arise a sort of compromise under which enough positive government activity to maintain employment is per-mitted, so long as the larger part of it is devoted to arma-ments.

This is a far cry, however, from the communist allegation that the state of full employment in Britain and America in the nineteen-fifties is sustained by their rearmament pro-grammes alone. In the case of Britain, the allegation is al-most wholly without foundation. Britain is currently (1956) spending some 10% to 11% of her gross national income upon defence, in all forms. The balance of economic and social forces is such that if, for example, she could cut her defence-spending back to, say, 5% of her gross national in-come, the effect on her economy would almost certainly be highly beneficial. The resources thus released would get used in a dozen different ways. The main problem would be to see to it that they did not immediately get absorbed by internal demand, instead of being used to increase exports and so strengthen her balance of payments.

In the case of America the position is not so clear-cut. America in the nineteen-fifties is using some 21% of her gross national income in governmental expenditure (Federal and States) of all kinds, of which some 12% is on defence. This compares with some 10% of gross national income spent for all purposes by her governments twenty-five years ago.

Nor is it by any means certain that if American defence-spending were cut by, say, half, and everything else was left the same, there would be sufficient demand to sustain the economy at full employment. On the contrary, I, for one, should say that a sharp depression would be bound to set in in such circumstances. Therefore, in that sense, it is true that American defence-spending on approximately its present scale is one of the factors which sustains full employment in America. But that is far from saying that, given even a modicum of freedom from the aforementioned inhibitions, it would be impossible for an American government to *replace* the volume of demand which would be destroyed by a major cut in defence expenditure.

On the contrary, there are a dozen different ways, of varying degrees of political "leftness," in which the thing could be done. The defence-spending could be replaced by other forms of government spending—either spending on "peaceful" public works, *i.e.*, houses, roads, dams, power-stations, schools, etc., etc., or it could be replaced by increasing and extending social-service benefits, *i.e.*, pensions, insurances, etc., (and subsidies to farmers), while leaving the tax structure as it is. But if the American Government of the day considered such policies too socialistic, then it could probably effect the same purpose simply by cutting down the taxes on the smaller incomes, thus leaving the desired quantum of demand in the hands of the mass of the population. Indeed the relatively high proportion of the national income which now passes through the Treasuries of the latest-stage capitalisms is undoubtedly a major factor in making them amenable to the control of a central regulating authority. For they can readily be stimulated by cutting down the amount of taxation raised from the mass of the population or damped down by increasing it. It is only if (although this is a quite realistic hypothesis) the American Government which was faced with this situation was so rigidly conservative that it made no effort to replace the destroyed demand, or merely attempted to replace it by cutting taxes on the rich (which would be likely to be ineffective for the reasons given in the last chapter), that a major cut in defence-spending *need* bring on a depression.

In the world as it is, no doubt, there is not much immediate hope of a successful disarmament convention which would permit of a major cut in American defence-spending. Future American Governments are more likely to face the issue in the alternative form of American productive capacity outgrowing the present level of mass demand, defence and other government-spending remaining constant. We shall discuss the vital issue of what is the prognosis for the stability or instability of the American economy in a later section of this study. Here we are concerned merely with the attempt to unravel the elements of real analysis from the elements of caricature intermixed in the communist allegation that if the Keynesian specifics get used at all they will be used for war expenditure and nothing else. And in this connection we need only note the final point that we shall find that not only is the demand generated by American defence expenditure fairly readily replaceable, but also that the general remodelling in the direction of greater equality of the American economy which took place in the New Deal period, is a larger element than defence-spending in the remarkably sustained performance of the American economy since 1945.

To sum up: the communist allegation that Keynesian technique will either not be used at all, or will be used only for arms making, is not true. It is true, however, that the balance of social forces in latest-stage capitalist societies is such that a dangerous tendency exists for government economic activity to be diverted on to warlike instead of peaceful purposes. For the former are in practice more palatable to the forces which are usually dominant in those societies.

That is not, as the communist caricature would imply, either because the "right-wing" political forces and parties want a war, or because they have consciously worked out the theory that the least politically injurious way of avoiding slump is to spend on arms. It was never true of more than a handful of the very worst reactionaries that they consciously wanted war. (Although on occasions that handful has come near to being in a position to effect its purposes.) Today it is doubtful if anyone uncertified really desires a nuclear contest. Nevertheless, the extremely challenging policies of the communist world have, in my opinion, made a tough reaction, including heavy-armament expenditure, an indispensable condition of existence for any societies which do not wish to be more or less forcibly brought under communist control.

This heavy-armaments expenditure has had varying economic consequences in the different latest-stage capitalisms. For the Britain of 1950 it was an unmitigated misfortune. We had not the slightest need of the stimulant of additionally created demand. The rearmament programme made us step on the accelerator just when we needed to feel for the brake. Nor is there any proof that the heavy increase in her defence expenditure from 1950 was necessary to sustain full employment in America. The evidence is on the whole the other way. Nevertheless, it is true that, once the present American level of arms-spending had been reached, it could not be sharply reduced, unless replaced by something else, without the gravest risk of slump. In these cirumstances there may be resistance to the idea of a reduction in arms-spending from those who realise the necessity of replacing it, and the political complications of so doing, if slump is to be avoided. But it should be noted that such resistance does not come from essentially big-business circles. On the contrary, the archetypally big-business elements in the present (1956) Eisenhower administration (such as Mr. Humphrey of the Treasury or Mr. Wilson of General Motors and Defence) are for *reduced* defence expenditure. This is undoubtedly because they suppose (I should guess mistakenly) that they could cut defence-spending and then reduce taxation on themselves and their corporations without causing a slump. Therefore the Right and even extreme Right in contemporary America, far from "depending on the arms boom," struggles to *reduce* American defence-spending to a level which its military advisers consider perilously low. Truly, the real world is much more complex a place than was ever imagined in communist textbooks. Finally, if we desire to demonstrate that rearmament expenditure is not necessarily indispensable to sustain a contemporary latest stage at full employment, we may instance Western Germany, where such expenditure has been nil and employment is now (1956) virtually full.*

KEYNES' ECONOMIC NATIONALISM

It remains in this chapter to consider one more aspect—the international aspect—of the Keynesian doctrine. Keynes' advocacy of overall controls for contemporary capitalism led him into unexpected paths. In particular it led him to become, for the middle part of his career, an economic nationalist. This was a startling development for an English liberal. But it followed quite simply from his recognition that cap-

* The basic communist error in this connection derives, in my opinion, from the Marxist theory of the State. The State, they declare, is nothing but the instrument of the great capitalists. It is inherently incapable of undertaking such activities as the application of the Keynesian techniques for peaceful purposes. If it does apply them, it is bound to apply them exclusively for arms making. Keynes fell into an opposite error. He assumed that the State was just the State, to be controlled presumably by disinterested economists. The fact is that in the conditions of contemporary democracy the State and its vast powers are rather prizes for which all sorts of interests are struggling and competing.

italism was no longer in any sense self-regulating. If it was
not self-regulating, it must be regulated—and regulation
implies a regulator. But what authority is available to perform this task? Obviously there is only the Government. But
the Government of what? "The Government" today means
in practice the government of the contemporary nation-state.
And so Keynes, in common with all other "planners," was
forced to plan for the delimited area of the nation-state. For
this was the only area for which there existed an authority
capable of carrying out his measures. If the rate of interest
was to be reduced, public works undertaken or incomes redistributed, there were no authorities even remotely capable
of undertaking the job except the Governments of the major
nation-states. (It is another limitation of Keynesian doctrine
that the Governments of the less highly developed capitalisms are almost certainly incapable, as well as unwilling, to
perform the functions which he assigned to them.)

Hence there arose, in the early 'thirties, the curious phenomenon of this outstanding leader of British liberalism, a
man steeped in the tradition of Smith, of Mill, of Cobden,
of Gladstone, and of Asquith, suddenly advocating what
sounded to the uninitiated something like a new-fangled form
of the oldest of all Tory doctrines—protection. As a matter of
fact, Keynes never had much inclination towards tariffs as
such, but this was merely because he considered them an
out-of-date and ineffective device. What, he came to see, was
necessary to his policy, particularly, of course, in an economy such as Britain, with its enormously high proportion of
foreign trade, was the power to control the *foreign transactions* of all its citizens. This power included, of course, the
power to control the volume, source, and preferably the character, of its imports. But it must also include the power to
control, not only the *import* of goods, but also the *export* of
money. For it was not true that money was exclusively sent

abroad in order to buy goods or to invest in overseas projects. Its owners might, and at critical junctures habitually did, send money abroad, not in order to buy or do anything, but simply in order to *avoid* conditions at home which repelled them.

Keynes came to see that his policies, above all in Britain, could only work if the economy were not only controlled, but closed; if it were closed, not, of course, in the sense that transactions with the outside world were forbidden, but in the sense that these transactions were made subject to the overall decisions of the Government. In a word, a controlled capitalism means in practice a *nationally* controlled capitalism. And this in turn implies the possibility of the conscious, centralised, social control of such an economy's relationships with all the other economies with which its citizens trade, in which they invest, and to which they can send their money. All this, of course, cuts directly across the classical theory of capitalism at yet another essential point. Capitalism was assumed to be self-regulating, not only within each national economy, but internationally also. It was assumed that the invisible hand which, by the instrument of competition, guided for the best the transactions of every trader, was not stopped at frontiers, or rather it was only stopped by tariffs or other "trade barriers" erected by backward governments which knew not the true gospel. A self-regulating system could be internationalist because it could largely ignore governments, so long as they could be prevented from concerning themselves with economic affairs. Hence arose the dream of Cobden and his generation—the dream of an almost stateless world, regulated alone by the automatic mechanism of the market. It was a far from ignoble dream, but it was a dream. For its major premise was the providential existence of an all-sufficient self-regulating mechanism, and this premise has proved to be false.

INTERNATIONAL KEYNESISM?

Nevertheless, a recognition of the necessity of an authority to regulate the overall balance of latter-day capitalist economies does not in principle demand that the regulating authority should be local and national. It could be worldwide. And in the last years of his life Keynes not only dreamed the dream of such an international regulative authority, but actually attempted to create it.

This part of Keynes' life is recounted in great detail by his biographer, Mr. Harrod. For Harrod is deeply conscious of the indelible stain on the orthodoxy of his subject imprinted by Keynes' economic nationalism of the 'thirties. Hence he represents this phase as an aberration, deplorable but temporary, and amply redeemed by the post-1940 attempt to set up a system of *international* economic and financial planning by means of a comprehensive Anglo-American concordat. This concordat was to be embodied in the "Bancor" plan for a payments union on a world scale, the Buffer Stocks plan, the World Fund, the World Bank and the original version of the American loan agreement. It is not necessary to go into the details of these abortive proposals. But it is true enough, of course, that, if the American and British Governments could have set themselves up as a sort of amalgamated joint economic planning authority, operating Keynesian policies on a world scale—why, then the world might well have become a much richer and more prosperous place than it is. But this is really to say no more than that the logic of Keynesian policy points towards a worldwide application, just as did the logic of self-regulating, competitive capitalism—and just as does the logic of communism.

What was really involved in Keynes' last great essay in persuasion has only to be thus stated, however, in order to perceive how chimerical it was. Goodness knows it has proved no easy matter to achieve and maintain a degree of consistency, comprehension and economic insight sufficient to work the Keynesian policy successfully, even in the case of one national government. What real hope was there of the American and British Governments being able to work together, year in, year out, sufficiently closely and harmoniously to plan the economic life of the whole non-communist world along Keynesian lines? Not only do Keynesian controls involve continual and subtle balancing acts on the part of the planning authority in order to offset the continual shifts in the economic climate, but they also, and necessarily and continually, cut across the affairs of almost every great "interest." They cut across the interests of the capital-goods industries, the consumer-goods industries, the farmers, the trade unions, the part of the population with fixed money incomes, the part of the population with variable money incomes, now favouring one interest, now injuring another, as the cause of overall stability demands. Imagine trying to work such controls by means of international authorities, dependent upon the American Government, which was itself dependent upon Congress.

It is a wonder that so eminently practical a man as Keynes, steeped, by the end of his life, in public affairs, can ever have thought such a thing possible. But here we come on a consequence of his inability to see that his whole policy was really a method of regulating the latest stage of capitalism. For he failed to notice at all a whole other aspect—the external aspect—of the latest stage. We shall devote a subsequent section of this study to this external aspect of the latest stage, an aspect so prominent that the first thinkers to recognise the existence of latest-stage capitalism, namely, Lenin and the second generation of Marxists, picked it out as the essential one. They called the latest stage imperialism. They considered that the decisive effect of the metamorphosis of competition was a strong tendency for a handful of the most advanced capitalist states to carve up the world amongst them as their colonial possessions.

If Keynes had ever been able to bring himself to study Lenin's theory of imperialism, it would have saved him a lot of trouble. But all this was Marxism, and so, as he was accustomed to emphasise, a closed book to him. Hence his last act was seriously to attempt to bring into effect his dream of some sort of international control of capitalism, in spite of the fact that there was no international government in existence to do the controlling. No doubt it was not quite impossible that the post-World War II international agencies in their original form as proposed by Keynes might have been set up. But if they had been, their real effect would have been very different from what he supposed. What they would have meant in practice would have been the transfer of all essential decisions in the economic sphere from the British Government and Parliament to American-dominated institutions. Britain would have ceased to be an independent State in more than name. For that is the only conceivable way in which a single authority, even remotely capable of exercising the indispensable Keynesian functions of regulation, could have been set up for the United States and Britain combined. Thus, when we say that Keynesian doctrine is incompatible with internationalism, this does not mean that it is incompatible with one nation simply taking over another. Keynes was the last man to have advocated the economic annexation of Britain by America; but that in fact was the only way in which the elaborate schemes of his last phase could have been made to work.

This is not to say that economic *co-operation* between America and Britain is undesirable or impossible. On the contrary, it has gone on consistently since 1945 and has, on the whole, been fairly successful. The point is, however, that both experience and the reasoning given above indicate that such co-operation must be, in the main at least, upon an ordinary Government-to-Government basis, without the creation, for the time being, of elaborate international planning organisations. If and when such organisations can be created, they should be under United Nations, not Anglo-American, auspices. In the meanwhile, let us continue those Anglo-American discussions, which have undoubtedly been fruitful, which are indeed so obvious a necessity that they have not been interrupted even when Governments of decidedly different political colourations have been in power in the two countries. For such running inter-governmental discussions limit the independence of both countries to the minimum degree.

There emerges again the fact that the latest phase of capitalism, with its loss of automatic self-regulation, imperatively requires a regulating authority. Now we see that that authority can in practice be nothing but the government of a nation-state, or no doubt the government of some amalgamation of two or more nation-states, should any such amalgamations be effected, and whether they are effected peacefully or by conquest. Thus the latest stage of capitalism has to be organised on a more *nationalistic* basis than did the previous stage, or alternatively, as we shall see, it has to be organised on an imperialist basis.

AN EVALUATION OF KEYNES' WORK

Keynes' work is seen, then, to consist of, first, a critical part, of which the essential content is that capitalism has lost whatever self-regulating capacity it may once have had. But this loss of equilibrium is not clearly linked by Keynes to the mutation of the system from its earlier competitive stage to its latest stage of oligopoly.

The positive part of Keynes' work was a demand that capitalism should now be regulated and controlled by a central authority. Such an authority need not, and indeed should not, actually plan what should be produced in what quantities. But it must see to it that total demand is always enough to clear the market at remunerative prices, and yet not so great as to drive up prices in an inflationary spiral. This it must do by constantly taking counter-measures of a balancing character, designed to offset the oscillations of the system. The principal instruments of its policy should be variations of the rate of interest, budgetary deficits and surpluses, public works and a redistribution of personal incomes in the equalitarian direction. This positive side of Keynes' work requires an authority to do the regulating, and that authority can be, in contemporary conditions, nothing else but the government of a nation-state. In that sense the whole concept of a regulated, directed capitalism is necessarily nationalistic in tendency. But here again Keynes saw no connection between his own conversion to economic nationalism (which can, but need not, become imperialistic) and the transformation which the system was undergoing into an oligopolistic and relatively uncompetitive structure.

How are we to evaluate the contribution of this strange man? His profound weakness was that his outlook remained bounded by capitalism. He was a part of the system and saw it from within. He seldom stepped, even in imagination, outside it. He did not see capitalism as one historically short, although highly important, phase of human development, which had been preceded by other kinds of human societies and would be succeeded by others again. An unhistorically minded man, capitalism was for him reality itself.* Linked

---

* I am aware that this passage appears to contradict that on p. 84 above. But all things are relative. Compared to previous orthodox economists, Keynes did succeed in seeing the system from the outside. Compared to the standpoint of a socialist, he remained within the system.

with this limitation was his ignorance and suspicion of the wage earners. He could not imagine that these uneducated men and women had any contribution to make to the solution of contemporary problems. He was an intellectual snob.* He despised and detested Marx and his whole way of thinking, but he had no very high opinion of his contemporary economists either. He saw his own work as above all the correction of their intellectual errors. He did not realise that his mission was to create, not so much a new theory, as the theory of a new economy.

A letter of his to Bernard Shaw, written while he was at work on *The General Theory,* well expresses his outlook.

J. M. Keynes to Mr. George Bernard Shaw, 1st January, 1935.

Thank you for your letter. I will try to take your words to heart. There must be *something* in what you say, because there generally is. But I've made another shot at old K.M. last week, reading the Marx-Engels correspondence just published, without making much progress. I prefer Engels of the two. I can see that they invented a certain method of carrying on and a vile manner of writing, both of which their successors have maintained with fidelity. But if you tell me that they discovered a clue to the economic riddle, still I am beaten—I can discover nothing but out-of-date controversialising.

To understand *my* state of mind, however, you have to know that I believe myself to be writing a book on economic theory which will largely revolutionise—not, I suppose, at once but in the course of the next ten years—the way the world thinks about economic problems. When my new theory has been duly assimilated and mixed with politics and feelings and passions, I can't predict what the final upshot will be in its effect on action and affairs. But there will be a great change, and, in

---

* He was the greatest "tug," *i.e.*, Scholar of Eton College, who ever lived; he had the quintessential flavour of that particular and select company, a flavour different from the Etonian "oppidan," on the one hand, or the Wykehamist, on the other, and yet partaking of both.

particular, the Ricardian foundations of Marxism will be knocked away.

I can't expect you, or anyone else, to believe this at the present stage. But for myself I don't merely hope what I say,— in my own mind I'm quite sure. (Quoted in Harrod's *Life*, p. 462.)

His inability to understand Marxism was due to a profound emotional inhibition. But he had no doubt of the importance of his own work. And, on the whole, and in spite of his extremely serious blind spots, he was justified in that. In one sense he did succeed in altering the way "the world in general thinks about economic problems." Nevertheless, different categories or classes of persons continue to think about them in the way which their own interests dictate. It was the existence of this profound bias of class which prevented Keynes from, on the whole, inducing the true capitalists themselves to undertake the modifications in their system which he prescribed. What he actually accomplished was something which he did not intend, but which he would, on the whole, I think, have welcomed—if rather wryly. And that has been to help the democratic, and, on this side of the Atlantic, the democratic socialist, forces to find a way of continuously modifying the system, in spite of the opposition of the capitalist interests. Keynes made the greatest single contribution to the technique of democratic transition. In so doing he helped to show the peoples of the West a way forward which did not lead across the bourne of total class war—a bourne from which the wage earners of the West recoil, now that they can see its raging waters. Thus he did, in some measure,

"Cast the kingdoms old into another mould."

And, if they were, in the first instance, only the kingdoms of thought, that in the long run may make his achievement all the greater.

13. ■ DEMOCRACY AND THE

LATEST STAGE OF CAPITALISM

Preceding chapters have been devoted to showing that enough insight into the nature of latest-stage capitalism is now available to make possible its democratic transformation. Moreover it is not to be doubted that democracy, *if it can maintain itself,* will in fact transform latest-stage capitalism, in the end out of existence.

But now we must take account of the other side of the medal. Otherwise far too optimistic an impression of the real prospects of contemporary democracy will have been presented. And to do that would be fatal. For the besetting sin of democrats has been complacency. The attitude of mind of democratic leaders—the mental climate of social democracy in particular—has often been, and often still is, based upon the assumption that democracy is bound, slowly, but smoothly and almost automatically, to affect the progressive transformation of society. In particular it is assumed that there is nothing to hinder a prolonged period of co-existence between democracy and latest-stage capitalism, a period which will pass so gradually into a more advanced form of society as to make the process imperceptible. The experience of the first half of the century shows that this is far from being the case.

A later section of this study will be devoted to describing

the tragedies to which this characteristic social democratic complacency contributed during the first half of the twentieth century. The remainder of this volume will attempt merely to state, in general terms, the incompatible tendencies of latest-stage capitalism and democracy. (At the cost of some anticipation a few notes will be added on the way in which those general incompatibilities sometimes express themselves in contemporary political life.) We shall find that there exist both general and specific incompatibilities. Not only do latest-stage capitalism and democracy possess sharply divergent tendencies: there exists also a specific economic stumbling-block which makes capitalism's transformation by democratic means particularly difficult. The frightful consequences which arose between 1918 and 1945, partly at least because of democracy's failure to remove this economic stumbling-block from its path, or even clearly to perceive its existence, will not be reached in this volume.

CO-EXISTENCE IN TENSION

The general tendencies of latest-stage capitalism and democracy conflict because it is the purpose of the former to concentrate, and of the latter to diffuse, power.

The first question which we have to ask is whether they can nevertheless live together, at any rate for a period. Manifestly they can; they do, in Britain and America, for example. Indeed, our theme has been that it is only by means of their co-existence that a working economic balance can be maintained in such highly developed capitalist societies. Nevertheless, democracy and latest-stage capitalism undoubtedly pull in opposite directions. Their co-existence constitutes a state of antagonistic balance. They co-exist in the same way that the two teams in a tug-of-war co-exist upon the rope.

Such a form of co-existence can hardly be permanent. One force must begin to gain, and at length to gain decisively, upon the other. And so it will be in the end in this example of co-existence in tension. In the end the power of contemporary democracy must encroach upon capitalism until its latest stage also has been completed, or, alternatively, capitalism must encroach upon democracy until this young, vulnerable and experimental method of government has been destroyed. That is why the struggle to preserve and to extend democracy both in time and in space is likely to be a crucial feature of the politics of the second half of the twentieth century, at any rate in those highly developed societies whch are the primary objects of our study.

ENCROACHMENTS UPON DEMOCRACY

The methods by which latest-stage capitalism encroaches upon democracy are subtle rather than direct. It may be asked, for example, whether it is really being suggested that the representatives of British, American or German latest-stage capitalism are likely to attempt consciously to subvert the democracy of their respective societies. Any such direct attempt is unlikely. American and British democratic institutions are relatively deep-rooted and it would take great hardihood to make any frontal attack upon them. It is true that the same cannot be said of those of West Germany. Moreover, the German oligopolies played an important part in the subversion of those institutions in 1933. Nevertheless, even in the German case the obstacles, internal and external, to the resurrected German oligopolies repeating that process would probably prove formidable.

What is to be apprehended is not, then, a direct attack. What is not only likely but inevitable—indeed it is taking place without ceasing—is an attempt, largely unconscious, on the part of capital, highly organised and integrated in the oligopolies, to manipulate and distort, and if necessary frustrate, the workings of contemporary democracy to its own advantage.* Again, there is no need to postulate a high degree of conscious intention. It is often an error to attribute to social forces much self-consciousness. It is rather that the oligopolies, working quite naturally to further their own interests, come into conflict with this or that aspect of democracy and seek to modify it to suit themselves. But the sum of those modifications and manipulations, if they did not encounter successful opposition, would spell out the end of effective democracy.

This is another important "special case" of the process which we have been studying throughout this volume, a special case of the consequences of the reduction of the units in any sphere of the productive system to a small number of large firms. It will be recalled that this process had exceptionally far-reaching consequences in the case of banking (see Chapter 11 above, p. 273). A reduction in the number of banks to the typical handful of oligopolies transformed the very nature of banking from being a humble handmaid of industrial production and commerce, useful for storing and pooling spare surpluses, into a mighty engine of control, capable, if acting in step with the State, of modifying the whole economic climate of the society in question. Now we must note other cases in which the process of "oligopolisation," spreading from the strictly economic field into every part of contemporary society, has critically important consequences. The first of these examples is afforded by the Press and the

---

* An example of these reactions is well described in Mr. Rogow's recent book, *Labour and Industry* (Basil Blackwell, 1955), which gives an account of the struggles between big business and the British Labour Government in the latter part of that Government's period of office between 1945 and 1951. I can testify to its essential correctness from personal experience.

other media of mechanised expression, such as broadcasting and television.

OLIGOPOLY AND THE FREEDOM OF EXPRESSION

The theory of "the free Press," as it was developed in the last century, and as it still dominates many minds, is based on the assumption, usually now unconscious, that the Press will be conducted along the lines of any typical nineteenth-century industry. There will be, that is to say, some hundreds at least of independent firms publishing newspapers in conditions of more or less perfect competition. In such conditions it is no doubt true that there will be a fairly effective freedom of the Press. Any man who can command a not impossibly large sum of capital will be able to start a new newspaper or to buy an existing one, and thus actually to exercise "the freedom of the Press." *

The structure of, in particular, the mid-twentieth-century British Press is, however, extremely dissimilar to this. It is in fact the typical structure of oligopoly. There is in this industry also a handful of really large firms publishing national newspapers and periodicals (and many provincial ones also). And clustering round these giants there are a number —but a diminishing number—of smaller independents, surviving by means of this or that set of special circumstances. Moreover, the major newspaper publishing firms, such as Ex-

---

* For example, it could be argued that it was actually easier for the relatively impotent British labour movement, in its first abortive stage of Chartism, over a hundred years ago, when it lacked the franchise, many of its present civil rights, and possessed incomparably smaller resources, to start and conduct newspapers, than it is for the giant labour movement of today to do so—and that simply because the capital then required was of the order of hundreds of pounds, whereas it is today of the order of millions of pounds.

press Newspapers, Northcliffe Press, Odhams, the Kemsley Press, *The Daily Mirror,* and a few more, are enterprises on the true oligopolistic scale. They employ capital and earn returns which put them into the big class. They exercise a marked degree of control over the prices which they pay and receive. They are tending to limit their, still fierce, mutual competition to factors other than price. They are large public companies with tens of thousands of shareholders. They are controlled by directors and managers. It is very difficult to suppose that they will ever again be seriously challenged by new competitors.

Thus, however strongly they may still compete with one another, these publishing firms collectively constitute a semi-monopoly in the mass dissemination of news and opinion by means of daily newspapers. This does not mean that all major newspapers are anti-democratic or even necessarily pro-conservative. Some important ones in Britain are not. But it does mean that the old assumption that the freedom of the Press existed, and must exist, as long as there was no *governmental* intervention, ownership or censorship, is no longer valid. The freedom of the Press, if it is to be maintained in the conditions of the latest stage, must, like the balance of the economy, be maintained by the exercise of the conscious pressure of the desires and interests of the mass of the population on their newspapers. It must be maintained by those countervailing pressures which we found to be indispensable to the balance of the economy.

Nor is the prospect, in Britain, by any means wholly dark in this respect. Many of the great newspaper proprietors and directors are convinced that they are manipulating public opinion. And so to some extent they are, usually with pernicious consequences. Fortunately, however, in this case, the manipulated are beginning, in various ways, to turn round and manipulate the manipulators. The pressure of the interests and opinions of their readers reacts upon the newspapers. The most direct instance of this is that by which the basic organs of the wage earners, the trade unions, have come to terms with one of the major publishing houses, Messrs. Odhams, for the publication of at least one definitely pro-labour daily newspaper, *The Daily Herald*. But in the long run the silent, largely unconscious pressure of the wage earners, who form the immense majority of the readers of the really large-circulation newspapers, may prove an even more important factor. For in important instances (*The Daily Mirror* and *The Sunday Pictorial*, for example) they have induced major publishing firms to conclude that "it pays to be Left."

The American Press is apparently less oligopolistic than the British—the mere size of the country has so far prevented it, and, in spite of air distribution, may continue to do so. But the same process is in full swing by means of the establishment of major "chains" of newspapers—such as the Scripps-Howard and the Hearst chain, etc. Moreover the much lower degree of political consciousness on the part of their wage-earning readers has allowed the American newspapers and periodicals to remain with virtual unanimity right wing.

In the newer fields of radio and television the position is again different in each country. American radio and television have fallen into purely commercial hands and are becoming increasingly oligopolistic in structure. In Britain, up till 1954, both sound radio and television had been in the hands of a public, non-commercial authority, the British Broadcasting Corporation. Such a public corporation, while extremely conservative in the general sense, had yet given wage-earner opinion a far nearer approximation to equality of representation than it gets, even now, in the commercial Press. But while this chapter was being written the struggle to allow part of the great new medium of television to pass into the hands of private capital was pressed to a conclusion by the existing (1956) British Conservative Government. It remains to be seen how much representation characteristically wage-earning opinion will secure.

Here we have a cardinal instance of how the development of capitalism in its latest stage automatically encroaches on democracy. The dissemination of news and opinion has become a branch of big business and, like other big business, has passed into the oligopolistic stage. As such it becomes the quasi-monopoly of a handful of great firms, just as does the manufacture of motor cars, or chemicals, or steel, or half a dozen other products. But the dissemination of news and opinion is no ordinary productive process. It is closely bound up with the existence of effective democracy. Experience has indeed shown that in favourable circumstances it is possible for democracy to function even when almost all the media of mass expression are in the hands of only one of the main political tendencies. But there is a limit to the monopolisation of opinion which democracy can stand and yet continue to be effective. If *all* the effective media of expression come into the hands of one political tendency—and it will be, of course, the pro-big-capital political tendency—then it is almost impossible for the electorate to make a rational choice. That is why such issues as the control of television are, and are felt to be, of immense importance. These issues, and not, in the main, constitutional forms, will be what really matter in the political struggles of the second half of the century.

WHO CONTROLS THE STATE?

With effrontery, the organs of big capital represent their struggle to maintain, extend and perfect their grip upon all the media of expression as a noble stand against the danger of totalitarian control by the State. Experience of communist societies shows indeed that there is such a danger as this, and that it can be a hideous one. But this is not the danger which faces the people of the highly developed latest-stage capitalisms. On the contrary, our danger is that the virtual monopolisation of the media of mass expression by big capital will distort and finally abort the democratic process.

This whole controversy as to what in fact is the real menace to our democracy and liberty is being conducted in depressingly primitive terms. We shall not be in a position to deal with it adequately until we have dealt with the question of the State, and that will not be until a much later point in this study. But it is indispensable to say here at any rate what the State is not. It is fashionable in Britain at the present time to rail in the most extreme terms against "the tyranny of the State," and to declare that anything, including big-business control of every medium of expression, is better than that. But not a word is said or written to define what is meant by this terrifying bogey "the State." Apparently we are all in extreme danger of being enslaved, not by *anybody*—not by any identifiable person or category of persons—but by a thing, an abstraction, labelled "the State." But *things* cannot enslave us. We can only be enslaved by other *people*. The very concept of the slave pre-supposes the slave-owner. The only function which a *thing*—an apparatus, mechanical or administrative, such as the State—can have is to serve as the instrument *by means of which* a certain, definite person, or, more likely, group or class of persons, may tyrannise over us. To talk as if "the State" could ever enslave us is to sink to the level of primitive, fetishistic thought. It is to fail to make any attempt even to find out what "the State" really is.

But, of course, it would be odd if the upper classes in Britain (the 10% of the population who till 1939 received about 50% of the national income) were not conducting just such a propaganda campaign as this. For they are in a somewhat unpleasant position. For several generations the State has been *their* State. Ever since they first reduced and then eliminated the arbitrary power of the monarchy it has been broadly true that the formidable apparatus of State power has been at their disposal. It would be a great exaggeration to suggest that it has now slipped from their grasp. Nevertheless, over recent decades, and in particular, of course, during the six years of the third Labour Government, they encountered the profoundly disturbing possibility that the State apparatus might become responsive to the wishes of the wage earners, to the wishes of the 90% of the population who habitually received the other 50% of the national income. And, as we saw, a modest, but distinct, redistribution of the national income was actually effected.

Accordingly, the traditional early nineteenth-century doctrine that "the State" is the most hideous engine of oppression ever conceived of by the mind of man has been rediscovered. For so this instrument appears to those who see it slipping from their grasp. Such political naïveté would be amusing if it were not so dangerous. For nothing will ever convince the members of the upper classes that these are their motives. They will take the greatest possible care never to analyse what they mean by "the State," or to become conscious of the fact that what they really fear is not some impossible oppression by a thing, but the influence of the wage-earning majority of their fellow countrymen, exercised, in part, through a democratically achieved control of the State apparatus. They will never face the fact that what they fear is the use of the State to remodel the national economy, and the national life generally, to suit the wage earners better and the upper and middle classes less well. Such clarity of vision would be far too painful. Therefore we must anticipate that from now on almost all respectable opinion will deafen us with propaganda as to the terrible danger to liberty involved in any form of State activity. This propaganda will be the more formidable because, in nine cases out of ten, its authors will be perfectly sincere. They will be convinced that they are fighting the good fight of the men of Runnymede, that they are the heirs of Hampden and of Mill, when in fact all that they are doing is to attempt to prevent the immense majority of their fellow countrymen from democratically remodelling the national institutions to suit themselves.

Such propaganda, conducted as it is, and will be, with all the immense power and influence which the best-off 10% of the population still commands, is extremely dangerous, because it helps to produce a frustration of the process of democratic social change. (And even the bare economic factors make this a by no means easy process.) But if democratic social change were frustrated, then, and then only, would the danger of a tyranny really arise. Then, and then only, would there arise the danger of a governmental monopoly of opinion, either of the Right or the Left. For, if the democratic process were rendered ineffective, so also would be those countervailing pressures which, as we have seen, are indispensable to the present working and future transformation of latest-stage capitalism. In that event the necessary central regulating authority would indeed be ultimately set up, but without democratic control, and it would be used on behalf of big capital itself to tip the balance of the economy into unworkable lopsidedness. Then the economy would break down, as it did in Germany in 1931-32, for example, and *governmental* totalitarianism, either of the Right or the Left, would be inevitable. Thus the continuance of effective democracy depends upon the prevention of big capital's control of the media of expression becoming absolute. And upon the continuance of effective democracy in two or three key societies of the world everything else will be found to depend.

AN OLIGOPOLISTIC SOCIETY

The oligopolisation of the media of expression is an example of a general tendency. Just as the units of production have become few and large, so have almost all the other institutions of the national life. And for the same reason. Modern techniques depend upon large units and central control for their application, not only in the productive process itself, but in administration, and even in such apparently less relevant spheres as political and cultural life.

The next and perhaps most obvious example of this tendency directly affects the labour movement itself. When the firms in an industry consolidate into a handful of giants, the basic wage-earners' institutions, the trade unions, must perforce, if they are to achieve effective bargaining power, follow suit. And this is what has happened. The structure of British and, to a hardly lesser extent, American trade unionism is today a faithful mirror image of the structure of British and American industry. Here, too, there are plenty of remaining small and medium-sized units, but here, too, decisive power has fallen into the hands of half a dozen or so giant organisations—in Britain, the two major general unions, the engineers, the railwaymen, the distributive workers and the miners in particular. There is nothing *of necessity* anti-democratic in these vast and indispensable aggregations of wage-earning bargaining power. Some of them, such as the engineers, for example, have exceedingly democratic constitutions. Nevertheless, it cannot be denied that the difficulty of making democracy real and effective by means of the actual *participation* of the members in the activities and decisions of their organisations increases with their size. Certainly it is felt to do so. Certainly a feeling of impotence and disinterest is only too apt to spread amongst members of any organisation which has reached a size at which the responsible leaders must seem remote and impersonal authorities to the rank and file.

These well-known troubles of large size affect, particularly acutely, the administrative apparatus of government. Their decentralisation into local and regional units, each democratically elected and responsible to bodies of electors from which they are not too remote, has long been the traditional ideal of all democrats. But this ideal contradicts the almost inexorable tendency of modern technique. And in fact we find British local government, on balance, losing rather than gaining power to the central authorities. It has ceased, for instance, to generate its own electricity and it has surrendered its hospitals to a National Health Service. The same obstacles are encountered by the Scottish and Welsh nationalist movements in their endeavour to set up effective institutions of their own.

Finally, in Britain and America political life itself has fallen into the same pattern. Two great parties, and only two, confront each other in the political arena. In a sense this has long been true. But the new factor is that all possibility of effective political action by such vestigial smaller political parties as still exist, or, more remote still, by independent individuals, gets less and less. This development appears indeed to be more directly the result of the British and American electoral systems than of the oligopolisation of the economy. Nevertheless, it is a fact, and it completes the pattern of what it is hard to deny is an increasingly oligopolistic society.

CHARACTER OF FEW AND LARGE POLITICAL PARTIES

It may be worth while to make here a few notes, by way of examples, of how in practice democracy and latest-stage capitalism are interacting in mid-twentieth-century Britain. Naturally such examples will take us on to a different level of discussion; they are of a far more local and temporary application than the other propositions of this study. Nevertheless, they may bring alive these more general propositions.

The first thing to notice is that democracy does not exercise its pressure upon latest-stage capitalism entirely through or by means of the political parties of "the Left." On the contrary, the essential thing is the general pressure of the complex of democratic institutions, and the climate of opinion which they produce, upon society as a whole. For it is one of the most formidable aspects of contemporary democracy that the wage-earning majority of the population may not infrequently be able to constrain even parties of "the Right" to serve their purposes.*

So long as an effective universal suffrage plus effective freedom of assembly, association, and expression are in existence, that process of political competition which was defined in Chapter 8 above may often ensure that parties which essentially represent the interests of "the 10%," rather than "the 90%," have, as a condition of their survival, to further the work of social transformation in the interests of the latter. Naturally this is regarded by those who voice the interests of the 10% as a most regrettable, and indeed scandalous, thing. They deeply deplore the fact that (as we saw on p. 191 above) the competitive processes involved in an election tend gradually to compel *all* political parties to have regard to the interests of the majority of the population. That is why ugly names, such as "vote catching" are invented to describe that process. That is why political leaders who act in a way

---

* "Parties of the Right" and "Parties of the Left" are phrases far too apt and convenient to be ignored. No doubt it would be very difficult to provide a satisfactory scientific definition of the terms. But everyone knows perfectly well what their significance is, and unhesitatingly uses them. It will not be till a much later stage of this study that we shall attempt an elucidation of such questions.

contrary to the opinions of the wage earners (in any particular instance they may, no doubt, be right or wrong to do so) are always called "courageous," "strong" and "statesmanlike," while those who act in accordance with the opinions of the wage earners are referred to contemptuously as "weak," "vacillating" and "demagogic." This type of political name calling is as old as the hills and will no doubt endure as long as classes do. Its only interest is that it reveals the unremitting pressure which the wage-earning majority of the population exercises by means of democratic institutions—a pressure from which no leader and no party is exempt.

The configuration of the mid-twentieth-century political scene in both America and Britain well exemplified this mechanism. In both there were only two effective political parties. In both the party of "the Right," the Republican Party in America, the Conservative Party in Britain, were (1956) in power, but in power with but a narrow margin of superiority, and under a most urgent constraint to secure the support of electorates composed, to an overwhelming extent, of wage earners and farmers. The result was that in both cases there was, on balance, a slowing down, or at most arrest, rather than a reversal, of the process by which the democratic forces had been modifying the structure and workings of the economy in their own interests during the preceding twenty-five years. The right-wing parties found themselves, sometimes to the dismay of their members, tending to do the work of their natural opponents rather than their true supporters.

The best example of all this is afforded by America. Indeed it is often maintained that the two American parties, the Republicans and the Democrats, are "politically neutral" organisations; that each bids for popular support, without any discernible or stable orientation, or any permanent connections with this or that social or class "interest"—such as the great firms, the major trade unions, or the farmers. I do not myself take this view. It appears to me that slowly but unmistakably the Democratic Party is becoming a party of "the Left" and the Republican party a party of "the Right." The now apparently fixed connection of the major trade unions with the Democrats and of immensely the greater part of big business with the Republicans seem decisive evidence that this is so. But the very fact that this question can be argued at all shows to how great an extent the pressure of the American wage earners and farmers works *through* each of the political machines, and not by means of overcoming one of them by means of the other. Moreover, it is perfectly true that the identification of the Democratic Party with the characteristically "Left" interests—*i.e.*, those of the wage earners and farmers—could not have been justified even twenty-five years ago. It is something which is happening rather than something which has happened. It dates essentially from the New Deal and the nineteen-thirties and it is still, of course, significantly qualified by the extremely "right-wing" character of the Democratic Party in the old South and, for that matter, by plenty of highly conservative elements in the party elsewhere.

Traces of "Left" tendencies and affiliations in the Republican Party are harder to find. Nevertheless, they exist. Indeed, such tendencies might in 1955 be considered to be dominant, if we think of "Left" in a sufficiently relative sense. For it is undeniable that, compared to the main congressional, and in many cases local, leadership of the party, the leadership provided by the "Eisenhower tendency" is comparatively of the Left. Moreover, and this is the essential point, this "Eisenhower tendency" can only maintain itself because everyone knows that without it the Republican Party would have no chance of election. Therefore it is, precisely, the electoral pressure of the American wage earners and farmers, acting through *both* parties, which determines the course of events.

In Britain—and even more so in many European countries

—the political scene appears very different. The two British parties actually announce their political character, their ideologies and their social connections, in their respective names—the Conservative Party and the Labour Party. But in fact the difference between the American system and the British is one of degree. It would be eccentric, instead of plausible, to deny the association of the British Labour Party with the wage earners and of the British Conservative Party with big business. Nevertheless, those respective associations are by no means simple or complete. The Conservative Party has a lingering, but still appreciable, association with the land-owning, *as against*, the big-business, interest; more important, it must on pain of inevitable electoral defeat retain the votes of something in excess of one-third of the wage earners themselves. Therefore its actual policies, and even, although to a much smaller extent, its character and structure, must and do adapt themselves to these facts of British political life. Conversely, the Labour Party is constantly subject to the enormously powerful and pervasive influences of a still capitalist society, influences which continually tend to deflect it from the courses which, it might be expected, any party so specifically based upon the wage earners would pursue.

All this reflects itself in the personal composition of the political parties in question. When there are only two of them, each party has to become, in effect, a coalition of men and women of very varying political instincts and opinions— instincts and opinions which must cover at least half of the whole spectrum of possible political attitudes for that time and place. Indeed, each of the two parties in a two-party system will contain members whose attitudes cover an even wider range than this. For the parties will overlap, as it were, over the middle ranges of opinion. This is obvious in the American instance. The Democratic Party notoriously contains right-wing members who have far more in common with the more left-wing members of the Republican Party than with their own Left—and *vice versa*. This is a little less true—but only a little less—of the British Labour and Conservative Parties.

These are the inevitable characteristics of those large and few political parties, which appear, in Britain and America at least, to be the political counterpart to an economy of large and few units—although a direct causal connection between the two phenomena would, I think, be hard to define. On the face of it a comprehension of how political democracy is working, and must work, in such conditions may be a disillusioning experience for some democrats. But that surely will only be so if they have a naïve conception of how the pressure of the wage earners and farmers, acting through representative institutions, in fact makes itself felt. If they suppose that a party of the Left will some day defeat, once and for all, a party of the Right, and then live happily ever afterwards, they will be disillusioned. What they are much more likely to see is a complex play of political life, in which parties and persons are constantly found doing unexpected things, on occasions changing policies—or even places. Contemporary Leninists often make great play with all this in order to denigrate and discredit the democratic process (although contemporary communist parties notoriously perform acrobatic feats of self-reversal which far outdo the backings and fillings of the democratic parties). But in fact all this is the way in which institutions representative of the mass of the population must work. And the fact that they work *through* each of the political parties, instead of merely opposing one to the other, is, on the whole, a safeguard and assurance for the maintenance of democracy. It may slow down the pace of change, but it helps enormously to make permanent each change that is made. If it were not for these characteristics of large and few political parties, such two-party systems as the British and American would probably prove unworkable. Nevertheless, these characteristics of the workings of contemporary representative institutions impose heavy strains and stresses upon both of the political parties in a two-party system. These strains and stresses may be worth describing in the case of the mid-twentieth-century British example (with which I am alone familiar at first hand), since they throw light on the real magnitude and difficulty of the task of contemporary democracy in transcending the latest stage of capitalism. They pose painful dilemmas for both the party of the Right and the party of the Left.

THE DILEMMA OF THE RIGHT

The dilemma of the Right is the obvious one that it is extremely difficult *both* to do enough for the wage earners to retain substantial electoral support amongst them and at the same time successfully to defend the interests of property in its decisive contemporary form of shareholding in the means of production. However, the British Conservative Party, since 1945, has given the world a fascinating example of how the attempt to do just this can be made. The major re-consideration of its policies and attitudes undertaken after the heavy defeat of 1945 marked the party's adaptation to the pressure of the predominantly wage-earning British electorate. The consequence is that the British Conservative party has moved far to the Left of any position which it could have been conceived of occupying as lately as the nineteen-thirties, for example. Nor have the British Conservatives lacked their electoral reward. They were enabled to win, although narrowly, the elections of 1951 and 1955. But they have done so by accepting the greater part—although not the whole—of the considerable change in the character of British society—in the balance of power between the big business and wage-earning interests—effected by the preceding Labour Government from 1945 to 1951.

No doubt for a time this is a possible position for a Conservative Party of so admirably flexible a nature as the British. But will it remain possible? Will it remain a possible position either when serious economic problems force the government in power to go further forward along the postwar British road, or to go back towards the inter-war position? Will it remain possible, moreover, as the warning of the 1945 defeat recedes into a memory? It is already (1956) clear that strains and stresses have been set up within British conservatism. So far they are hardly apparent amongst the practical working politicians. The electoral success of the new policy has been considerable; the warning of 1945 is still near. Leaders like Sir Anthony Eden, Mr. Butler and Mr. Macmillan have learned to swim most elegantly with the democratic tide. They are professional politicians in a very real, and in some ways in a very beneficial, sense. They are genuinely concerned to secure the electoral success of the Conservative Party even at the price of failing to reassert the interests of big business and of the property interest generally.

So far, too, this has been true, on the whole, of big business itself. Considerably concerned by the wage-earners' strength both in the political and the industrial field, those who conduct the great oligopolies have been well content for a Conservative Government to temporise. (What will be their attitude when they are faced with the necessity of making major new decisions remains to be seen.)

Thus symptoms of strain have so far (1956) appeared neither amongst the practical working politicians nor amongst their big-business supporters; but they have appeared amongst the Conservative intellectuals. Amongst, significantly enough, the younger Conservative intellectuals

an unmistakable sign of distress has appeared—of distress at
the necessity for their party to give ground before democratic pressure. Moreover, this sign of distress has taken precisely the form which might have been expected, namely, a
full-dress attack upon the democratic principle itself. For,
after all, it is democratic pressure which is forcing their party
reluctantly to behave in a way contrary to its natural bent.
What could be more inevitable, then, than that some of its
leading writers and publicists should discover that all the ills
of the world are in fact attributable to this odious democratic force? And that is just the discovery that has been
made.

These younger Conservative intellectuals, who for the
most part do not have to subject themselves to the actual
process of "catching votes," are free to say and write what
they really think. And with remarkable unanimity what they
think turns out to be that democracy must be fought. In such
circles nothing could be more wholly out of fashion, more
démodé, more intellectually *vieux jeux*, than any defence of
democracy, more especially in the sense which it has been
herein defined. The fashionable thing is, on the contrary, to
deplore "the tyranny of the majority," to stigmatise any purposive or positive action on the part of the State as dictatorship, and, finally, to clinch the argument with the suggestion
that democracy "leads to communism," *1984*, and all the
horrors of a revolutionary period. It will be prudent to describe this anti-democratic tendency in the words of one of
the younger Conservative intellectuals, so that the reader
may judge for himself both its extent and force. Mr. Utley,
one of the best known of the younger theorists, gave an
informative summary of intellectual Conservative opinion in
the nineteen-fifties in a review of a book by an older Conservative theorist, Lord Percy of Newcastle. Lord Percy's
book, itself entitled *The Heresy of Democracy*, was devoted
to the aforementioned proposition that democracy, in any

thoroughgoing form, all the way from the Augustine
Church to comprehensive schools (which are impartially de-
nounced), must lead to totalitarian dictatorship. This is Mr.
Utley's opening paragraph:

> Democracy is out. The symptoms of this have been multiplying
> for a long time: Mr. Oakeshott generating scepticism from his
> chair, while the ghosts of Graham Wallas and Harold Laski
> glower: the first volume of Dr. L. L. Tallmon's massive analysis
> of *The Origins of Totalitarian Democracy* which appeared in
> 1952: Mr. Isaiah Berlin's pedigree of contemporary tyranny (out
> of Liberty by Rousseau) which the third programme produced
> in the same year, and Mr. Beloff's revival of Mill's objection to
> majority rule in an article in the *Fortnightly* in February 1953,
> distinguished by commendation in *The Times;* all these are only
> random illustrations of the point that those who enjoy sacrilege
> had better look elsewhere than to democracy for their target.
> It is the main theme of almost all intelligent writing about
> politics today that our contemporary troubles arise from the
> eighteenth century and are attributable to the rationalist tradi-
> tion in political theory and the most popular minor theme is
> that majority rule, as an institution, has a permanent and
> increasing tendency to produce either dictatorship or bank-
> ruptcy or both. (*Spectator*, January 21st, 1955).

There is no doubt, then, about the scope and width of this
Conservative anti-democratic reaction, although it is, as yet,
confined to highly intellectual circles. The interesting question to ask is *why,* as Mr. Utley so accurately observes, the
Conservative intellectuals, who provide, he is sure, "all the
intelligent writing about politics today," have thus with one
voice come to the conclusion that "majority rule . . . has a
permanent and increasing tendency to produce either dictatorship or bankruptcy or both"? The fruitful course is, surely,
not to chop logic as to why the alternative to majority rule,
i.e., minority rule, is supposed to avoid "dictatorship or bankruptcy or both." It is rather to point out the fact that these

fatal characteristics of democracy have been discovered just at the moment when majority rule, working, as we have seen, almost as powerfully upon the party of the Right as on the party of the Left, is pushing the economy along paths profoundly unwelcome to "the 10%." The attempt of the majority of the electorate actually to get its will implemented by means of the creation of the sort of economic and social institutions which suit it, is called "tyranny." The redistribution of some 10% of distributed personal income from property to wage earning (Chapter 7 above) is called "bankruptcy." (The very real question of how a rational distribution of income can be introduced without interrupting the flow of national production will be taken up at a later point in this study.) No doubt it is too early, in 1956, to say whether this strongly anti-democratic tide in Conservative intellectual circles will spread into practical politics. So far it is merely a question of the democratic pressure driving the Conservative working politicians in one direction and the Conservative intellectuals in the other. This symptom is no more than premonitory, but it is premonitory of the strains and stresses which are likely to affect, not only the British Conservative Party, but British society as a whole. It indicates that all those whose deepest—if often largely unconscious—motivation is to preserve contemporary capitalism at all costs will have an inclination, now latent, now overt, to turn upon democracy in order to try to strike this weapon, which otherwise must prove deadly to capitalism in the end, out of the hands of the wage-earning majority of the population.

THE DILEMMA OF THE LEFT

It would be a great mistake to suppose that the above strains and stresses are confined to parties of the Right. On the contrary, the difficulties of the party of the Left, in a contemporary two-party system within a latest-stage capitalism, are at least as acute. These difficulties arise from the urgent necessity of actually *using* the democratic institutions progressively to remodel the economy, and indeed society as a whole. For the faith of the mass of the population in these, as we have seen, comparatively recent and untried social mechanisms could easily be dissipated. The wage earners cannot be expected to have, in the main, an abstract or theoretical attachment to these institutions. If they are to value them at their true worth—and it is in fact inestimable—they must be shown that democratic institutions really are capable of gradually remodelling society. If the operation of democracy—if the actual process of changing the distribution of the national income in particular—is continually frustrated and aborted, democracy can perish just as easily from a loss of faith on the part of its own natural supporters as because of the inevitable hostility of those whom its pressures adversely affect.

Thus the party of the Left must be able, decade by decade, to show a certain minimum measure of economic change, on pain of decay. And this will not be easy. Society is stiff and intractable material on which to work; it must be so or it would lack indispensable stability. Only powerful and sustained pressure on the part of the party of the Left can remodel it. It is indispensable to such a party to retain a strong reforming zeal if it is to have any hope of success. And to retain this social *élan* is particularly difficult for a democratic party of the Left at the mid-twentieth-century juncture. Such a party, on pain of certain failure, must be able to throw its full energies into the struggle with the immensely powerful forces which wish to keep society as it is. If the party of the Left is distracted and diverted by other considerations from this, its *raison d'être*, its prospects will be poor indeed.

THE ANTI-COMMUNIST OBSESSION

Moreover, in the mid-twentieth century, nearly all democratic parties of the Left are in fact in danger of being deflected from their struggle with their real opponents on the Right; they are in danger of being deflected into fighting a defensive action on their left flanks.

This potentially disastrous situation arises directly out of the communist misappreciation of the way in which latest-stage capitalism is in fact working in the highly developed Western societies. The economic root of this misappreciation is, as we have seen, Marx's original error in denying that it was possible to overcome the tendency to ever-increasing misery. Onto this root has been grafted a whole system of basic misconceptions of the character of Western society. And out of these misconceptions there has emerged, with rigid communist logic, a whole range of policies which have, in turn, proved hopelessly inappropriate to the realities of the latest-stage capitalisms. Moreover, the spectacle of totalitarian practice in the East has been combined with these insanely perverse communist policies in the West. And this has profoundly affected the thoughts and feelings of the members of the democratic parties of the Left. (It could not have done otherwise.) Indeed it has not merely affected, it has almost reversed, the basic impulses of some of the leaders, and some of the rank and file also, of such parties as the British Labour Party. Some of the most serious and earnest of such men and women have been so repelled by Communism that they have come in fact to care about little else than the anti-communist struggle. Everything they do and say shows that this is the issue which really engages their thoughts and feelings. Compared to it, the struggle with their conservative opponents has become for them a very secondary matter. They have been faced right round, as it were, by the shock of the communist onset, so that their real political front, on which they deploy their main energies and resources, now confronts an opponent on the Left instead of on the Right.

It would be instructive to study in individual cases how this remarkable reversal of roles has come about. For it must not be supposed that lifelong and earnest socialists have thus been converted—as in effect they have been—into conservatives either easily or without extreme provocation. In some cases it is personal experience with communist methods in the trade-union movement which has done the damage. Communist attempts to capture an important union, for example, are often conducted with a ruthless determination to use any means, including the most unscrupulous and the most violent, which they can command. Democratic socialists who are leaders, local leaders or active members of such unions, have had to engage in the most bitter, sustained and arduous struggles, if they did not wish to see themselves pushed aside, and the organisation put under communist domination. Even when such resistance on the part of democratic socialist trade unionists succeeds—as it succeeded in a key British union, the Amalgamated Engineering Union, for example—it leaves a deep and permanent scar upon those who have had to engage in it. It is very difficult for such men to resume their former struggle with the conservative forces. Their real emotions are now only aroused when they scent —or think that they scent—communist influence.

The same process only too often takes place within the local branches of the political parties of the Left—the local Labour Parties in the British case, for example. Here the effect of communist attempts to press policies which are rooted in basic misconceptions of the social environment is often to kill the whole spirit and life of the unit of the democratic socialist organisations concerned. Discussion becomes impossible; animosities lead to the most violent personal accusations; soon the sole way of conducting the branch or local party appears to its staunchest members to be that of excluding all who even appear to take anything resembling, not merely a communist, but even a generally "left-wing" point of view. Yet, when once that is done, the resultant conflict and split leaves the "right wingers," who have usually remained in possession of the field, bereft of much, if not all, of their original zeal and social purpose. They, too, are only too apt to have been turned, whether they are conscious of the fact or not, into extremely conservatively minded personalities.

This process, however natural, is an almost wholly disastrous one for a party of the Left. The historical function of such a party can never be anything else than to transform the economic and social system in the interests of that 90% of the population who have until recently received about half of the national income. Once its leading figures no longer feel in their hearts that this is their mission, virtue will have gone out of them.

Nothing would be more barren than to try to assess the blame for this development. In one sense, of course, it is the direct and inevitable result of the original communist error as to the whole character of the contemporary situation. But the communists will never admit that—even to themselves. Therefore the only remedy lies in democratic socialists succeeding in rising above their only too natural reaction to the communist assault upon them. They must indeed reject the communists—almost as a matter of course—yet they must contrive to remain at the same time determined democratic socialists, devoting themselves wholeheartedly to the struggle for socialism. This is a most difficult psychological adjustment. It is all the more difficult thus to "maintain the aim" of socialism, because it is perfectly true that the native conservative forces are, in Britain and America, far more humane, civilized and, for that matter, democratic than the communists have shown themselves to be. Therefore the first impulse of a democratic socialist will often be to put all his real heart into fighting the communists. But to do so is naïve; to do so is to neglect the very nature of the task of social transformation which our times impose upon us. That task is to transform, ultimately completely, the present economic system. The conservative forces by their very nature stand in the way of that task being accomplished. For, if they give way here and there before democratic pressure within their own ranks, that will in the end turn them into bitter anti-democrats. Therefore the preservation of democracy and all the infinitely precious things that go with it will largely depend upon such parties of the Left as the British Labour Party, retaining their original "direction of march." It depends on such parties refusing to be turned right round by the shock of the communists' onset. It depends upon such parties refusing to be made into bulwarks of the *status quo*.

Such parties must, if they are to survive, exhibit the boldness, the hardihood, the moral and intellectual courage, themselves to undertake the task of social transformation by democratic methods. And that means keeping the "point" of their political effort steadily directed against the conservative forces. Indeed this, paradoxically perhaps, is the sole way in which the communists themselves can ultimately be defeated. The communist programme for the revolutionary reconstruction of contemporary society cannot in the nature of things be defeated by standing statically against it in the defence of what is. For nothing is more certain than that contemporary society must be, and will be, reconstructed. The sole way in which the communists can ultimately be defeated is by effecting that indispensable reconstruction by democratic means. The democratic forces can, in fact, only defeat the communists by themselves opening up the alternative way to social reconstruction. That is why even those leaders of the British Labour Party, for example, whose only strong remaining impulse is anti-communist, should, even from their own point of view, still concentrate their attention upon the struggle with their opponents on the Right. For their opponents on the Left cannot be directly overcome; the only way of defeating *them* is to show that the job can be done in the democratic way.

Those leaders of the democratic forces in the West who have become obsessed with the communist menace upon both the national and the international plane are involuntarily playing directly into the communists' hands. For their total preoccupation with the communists partakes, whether they know it or not, of the rabbit's preoccupation with the snake. They have been immobilised and prevented from performing their own essential function of carrying through the process of social transition, by democratic means. Such leaders should take to heart a story of the Duke of Marlborough told by Sir Winston Churchill in the volume of his life of his ancestor dealing with the Battle of Blenheim. It is recalled that at one point in the engagement the Duke saw some squadrons of his cavalry streaming back in confusion after being repulsed by the French line. Seizing the bridle of their commander's horse, he admonished the discomforted officer as follows:

> "Mr. ———, you are under a mistake; the enemy lies that way; you have nothing to do but face him and the day is your own."
> (*Marlborough: His Life and Times*, Vol. IV, p. 104.)

It may be objected that this amounts to saying that democracy must do the communists' work for them. If that work is defined as the eventual establishment of socialism, then it must be agreed that this is the task which faces not only the democrats but humanity itself in our epoch. But if we have learnt anything in our epoch, it is that the means and methods profoundly condition the goal. A socialism achieved by democratic means will inevitably be a basically different thing from a socialism achieved by dictatorial coercion.

DEMOCRACY MAY GO FURTHEST

All this is by no means to say that the final transformation which democracy, if it can preserve itself in existence, will effect in our societies will be less far-reaching than the transformations of revolution. No one can say in advance just what kind of society the British people, for instance, will create if they are able to continue, over the decades, freely to remould and remodel their existing economic and social structure. But it would be rash to think that they may not in the end write "thorough" upon their banners. Democracy, although it works so much more slowly and unobtrusively, may prove a more complete solvent of every species of privilege than ever revolution has been. For the very rapidity of their action has always led the revolutionaries to overstep what proved to be the bounds of the possible for their time and place. It may be that modern democracy alone, just because it is equipped with rudimentary sense organs which, as it were, enable it to feel its slow way forward along the line of the objectively possible, will not have to retrace its steps. If so, it will be found at the end of the day to have journeyed furthest.

PARTICIPATION OR CONTROL?

We must now return from this excursus upon the actual workings of contemporary democracy in mid-twentieth-century Britain to a resumption of our discussion of the interactions of an oligopolistic society and democratic institutions. It is a commonplace that the increase in size and decrease in number, which characterizes the institutions of contemporary society, poses acute questions for democracy. But the general tendency is not usually linked with the specific mutation of the economy into its oligopolistic phase. And for this reason there is a failure to distinguish between two separate aspects of democracy which are affected in different ways. It is true that democracy, if it is to fulfil its function of diffusing power, must seek in one way or another to draw an ever-growing proportion of the population into active participation in the running of the country. And the growth in size, and the centralisation, of our institutions undoubtedly creates serious problems in this respect. Nevertheless, even for the purposes of participation a growth in size may not be all loss. A small master may be a great tyrant. And a large organisation may by careful arrangements secure very real possibilities of participation on the part of its members.

But, after all, participation is only one aspect—although no doubt it is the highest aspect—of democracy. The more immediate task for democracy is to secure ultimate *control* over the main national institutions. Such control has been fairly effectively secured in the case of our political institutions. It is a most rough-and-ready sort of control. Nevertheless, because of the competitive political process discussed in Chapter 8 it is a very real thing. One way of describing the first purpose of socialism is to write that it is an attempt to secure the same kind and the same degree of overall democratic control in the case of our major economic institutions, the oligopolistic firms. And for this simpler purpose of democracy the growth in size and scale is by no means wholly adverse. True, it may threaten the very existence of democracy, in the ways we have described, *if* that overall democratic control is not progressively achieved. But at the same time it makes such overall democratic control possible, as well as necessary. In spite of sustained attempts to deny it, the fact that the administrators of a publicly owned corporation are ultimately responsible to elected representatives of the whole population, instead of to a motley, ever-changing, but relatively very narrow, group of shareholders, is of crucial importance. It may, or may not, make much visible difference to the day-to-day conduct of the concern, but it will, in the end, if it becomes the predominant form of ownership in the economy, condition the whole character of society.

Thus the essence of the matter which we are discussing is that it is not so much the growth of size and scale in itself, as that growth combined with the ownership of the great corporations by wholly irresponsible shareholders, which menaces democracy. Capitalism in its latest stage, when it is progressively outgrowing the forms of ownership which were once appropriate to it, threatens to turn upon what was once its own political counterpart, namely, democracy.

THE TRANSFORMATION OF BOTH DEMOCRACY AND CAPITALISM

Thus the interaction between capitalism and democracy is seen to be exceedingly complex and dynamic. The character of both has been, and continues to be, transformed. On the one hand, democracy has ceased to be the method by which different sections of the ruling class, such as the landlords and the industrialists in nineteenth-century Britain, fought out, and compromised over, the question of which should rule, with the, at most, partial and intermittent intervention of the wage earners. It has become, in the advanced, latest-stage capitalisms, a method by which, on the one hand, the wage earners as a whole and, on the other, the property owners as a whole, seek to fight out, and to compromise over, the question of which of them shall control the economy.

Simultaneously, the structure of the economy has become modified in such a way that it imperatively requires a central regulating authority in order to function at all. It has lost its automatic, self-regulatory characteristics and has become far more centralised and concentrated. It has become latest-stage capitalism. This simultaneous transformation of the natures of both democracy and capitalism is causing the tension within our societies to mount. For the transformation of capitalism makes it indispensable that *someone* should regulate it. And the transformation of democracy sharply poses the question of which class, or as we traditionally say in British public life, which *interest*, is to do the regulating. It is a most ambitious attempt to decide such a question as that by democratic means. And yet at the mid-point of the century it is possible to say that, on the whole, at least in Britain and America, the democratic method is showing possibilities of being able successfully to undertake this critical task.

SPATIAL LIMITATIONS OF DEMOCRACY

". . . At least in Britain and America." But how vast is that qualification! It means that the contemporary attempt at *democratic* regulation and control is being made by little more than the 200 million inhabitants of America and Britain, and, to a greater or lesser extent, by a comparable number of other kindred peoples in Northwest Europe, Australasia, and in a few other areas of the world.* Such are the

* The daring Indian experiment of attempting to develop a predominantly pre-capitalist society by democratic means will be discussed in a later volume of this study.

narrow spatial limits of contemporary democracy. It is true that democratic *forms* exist in other important capitalist societies, some of them not yet in the latest stage—in Brazil, in Japan, and in some others, for example. But it would be a bold man who would claim that democratic forms and institutions in these societies had as yet been made effective, in the specific sense in which we have defined that term, namely, that they exercise a significant effect upon the balance of the economy by modifying the distribution of the national income. There is little sign that in these countries their democratic institutions are raising the standard of life of the wage-earning, or peasant, masses appreciably above what it "naturally" would be if the "laws" of capitalism were allowed to operate freely, namely, a subsistence level. For, let it be repeated, in those capitalist societies in which democracy is either non-existent or ineffective, there is no reason to suppose that the basic Marxist diagram, and its Leninist extrapolations, are incorrect. It is effective democratic pressure, in all its forms, and nothing else, which has caused the real development to diverge from the diagram in the case of the two or three leading capitalist societies. Remove that pressure and we are back in the world which Marx observed and elucidated.

Moreover, in most of the contemporary capitalist societies, except those of Northwest Europe, North America and Australasia, it is not a question of *removing* democratic pressures; the question is whether democratic pressures, which never have existed and do not yet exist, can arise. And for them to arise those complex capacities for public life, which we mentioned in Chapter 8, must appear among the mass of the population. They must somehow learn the subtle and at first sight contradictory techniques of loyal, and yet real, opposition: of national solidarity, and yet diversity. They must learn that "the Queen's, or the King's, or the President's, Government must be carried on," and yet that "the

business of an opposition is to oppose." They must learn that
the Government must be neither omnipotent nor impotent;
that power can be real, and yet limited; that social antagonisms are better expressed than repressed. They must learn
all this, and also all the other immensely difficult techniques
of democratic political life.

What possibility is there that the people of Brazil or Japan,
to take two large-scale instances, can learn these techniques?
The answer must be that no doubt it would be foolish to
suppose that they could learn them *quickly*. After all, even in
the "heartlands" of contemporary democracy, in America
and in Britain themselves, we do not practise them any too
perfectly. It would be unfair to suppose that communities
such as Japan or Brazil could successfully do so in the immediate future. Fortunately, they are not under the necessity. Their economies are at an earlier stage of development.
Property in the means of production, above all in land, is
still much more diffused than it is in Britain or America.
They are not nearly such high-geared, volatile, inherently
unstable economies, needing such effective central regulation, as do Britain, America and Germany. (Japan is, I take
it, on the way to becoming so, as are, for that matter, both
France and Italy.) Therefore they should have several decades at least in which to develop the social preconditions
in which alone contemporary democracy can become effective.

The nations in which democracy can hope to bit and
bridle latest-stage capitalism, and then to transform it, ultimately to the degree that is no longer capitalism, are, I
repeat, no more than brightly lit islands in the vast sea of
contemporary humanity. It is perhaps natural enough that
the communist social theorists, looking out at the world from
Moscow, should ignore the special characteristics of the
Western democracies. They constitute a most irritating exception to the main Leninist generalisation, spoiling the

sweep of its universality. The Leninist theoreticians note that there seems to be little to qualify the basic social and economic diagram which Marx and Lenin drew, so far as the hundreds of millions of inhabitants of Asia, Africa and South America are concerned. There capitalism seems to be working itself out on the whole, and allowing, as they are quite willing to do, for local circumstances changing the forms of the development, very much as might be expected. It is only amongst the three or four hundred million inhabitants of the societies in which democracy is effective that anything seems to have gone wrong with the great prediction. How tempting it must be to overlook this tiresome irregularity—to treat contemporary Western democracy as a fad and a foible, nay, as a hypocritical deception of the people, practised by the British, the Americans and the Northwest Europeans, to reserve, as they do, the word democracy for their own rule.

BUT CRITICAL IMPORTANCE OF WESTERN DEMOCRACY

How tempting it must be to do just this and how unreservedly the Leninists have yielded to that temptation. And yet how misleading a guide to action their whole theory becomes the moment that they do so. For the fact is that these few hundred millions of eccentric British, Americans and Northwestern Europeans comprise the most highly developed economies of the non-communist world. Outside Russia it is they, and they alone, who are capable of supplying the apparatus of modern industry. They are the prime producers of the means of production, and upon that fact is based, as the Leninists should be the first to recognise, an economic and military power entirely out of proportion to the number of their inhabitants. Thus to overlook the special characteristics of such societies is an error of the first magnitude. It is indeed the error of errors which the Leninists have committed ever since the founding of the Communist International in 1921.

A NEW STAKE IN THE COUNTRY

This volume is not the appropriate place for an adequate discussion of contemporary democracy as it really works, and as it may be expected to work in the future, in the major latest-stage capitalisms. Here it is possible to do no more than to illustrate by one further example how far more complex those workings are than is allowed for either by the Leninists or, for that matter, by orthodox political theorists.

The main tendency of an unmodified latest-stage capitalism is deeply antagonistic to democracy. But if democratic institutions are strong enough, as they have been in Britain and America, to modify the "set" of the economy, then these modified economic tendencies begin, in turn, to help democratic institutions to maintain and extend themselves. If, to put the matter more specifically, the democratic countervailing pressures can once become strong enough to make the distribution of the national income significantly more favourable to the mass of the population than it would "naturally" have been, then the wage earners and farmers begin to acquire a vested interest in democracy. They find that democratic institutions really can be valuable to them. Moreover, their improved economic position, rising as we have seen much above a subsistence level, instead of falling below it, gives them access to those educational and cultural facilities which are almost indispensable to the effective exercise of democratic rights. Not only materially, but in every way, they begin to have, and to feel that they have, what is often called "a stake in the country." They become, in Marxist terminology, increasingly de-proletarianised.

Both Marxist and conservative observers have insufficiently noticed that this process of acquiring "a stake in the country" need not necessarily, and indeed will not typically, consist in acquiring a nest egg of property. A right to an Old Age Pension, to adequate Unemployment Benefit, to a Free Health Service, and to the other main features of the Welfare State, plus a right to normally uninterrupted employment at trade-union rates of wages, plus satisfactory educational facilities provided by the community, plus publicly developed housing, all amount to a substantial stake in the country, even if the wage earners in general have no significant quantity of investments.* Once such "rights" as these have been acquired, democracy becomes much more strongly entrenched than before. For then the struggle to maintain and extend democracy can be undertaken as a struggle to preserve known, tangible and valued rights, and not merely as a struggle to achieve theoretically desirable ideals. Thus it is vital that democratic institutions should have been established, and effectively used, at a relatively early point in the development of latest-stage capitalism. For then only will they have the opportunity to become strong enough to withstand the antidemocratic pressures to which they will sooner or later be subjected.

THE PROSPECT OF DEMOCRACY

Contemporary democracy must live and develop amidst the complex and violent social forces of our century. What are its chances of survival? Even to put such a question will seem strange and dubious to many in the West. For in

* See footnote p. 228 above for figures.

our societies the majority of even the politically conscious are quite unaware of any antagonism between the development of the economies of their countries and their democratic political institutions. They would be, for the most part, unwilling to admit the possibility of such an antagonism. The whole concept—the whole way of thinking—represented by an analysis of the interactions of economic and political factors is unfamiliar and unwelcome to them. Their countries are democracies, they feel; they sincerely intend to keep them so, and they see nothing in their economies to threaten their political institutions.

Leninist social theorists, on the other hand, take an exactly opposite view. Ignoring the real complexities (such as the above-described development of "a stake in the country" worth defending by the wage-earning masses), they see only the antidemocratic tendencies of the latest stage. They rate the prospects for the exercise of effective democracy within the latest-stage capitalisms as negligible. They see only too clearly the immense power of the great, integrated, highly organised, ably led capitalist interests. They see the relative dispersion and weakness of the forces and powers of the wage earners and farmers. They ignore the historical fact that, in spite of all the difficulties and all the obstacles, democracy, in our favoured corner of the world, has succeeded in profoundly modifying the course of social development. And they therefore adopt policies which again and again prove catastrophically inapplicable to the West.

When we remind ourselves of the way in which our democratic institutions really work; when we recollect how much by way of maturity, steadiness and insight the effective use of those institutions demands of the wage earners and farmers; when we recollect, also, that they must exercise those qualities amidst the screech and din of the counter-propaganda of capital, we also may sometimes be tempted to doubt the democratic cause. But such doubts are not only unworthy; they are also futile. No one can assess the true chances of democracy in the long struggle which lies ahead of it. Nor should we attempt to do so. The thing to do is not to speculate on the chances of the struggle; the thing is to engage in it. For if none can know the outcome, all can know that the preservation, development and final triumph of democracy offer the only tolerable future for societies such as ours. Even if democracy's chances were very small (which I do not believe), the experience of the first half of the twentieth century proves that it would still be our duty to devote ourselves to its preservation. For the struggle of democracy is in our type of society the decisive aspect of every other form of social struggle. It is true that we shall often find ourselves fighting for other causes: for peace, for liberty, for socialism, for equality. But the outcome of these particular struggles will depend on whether contemporary democracy can be preserved and made into an effective instrument of social transformation. Everything else will be won or lost on this battlefield.

14. SOCIALISM

TWO UNDISCUSSED FACTORS

We cannot make further progress with the argument of this study until two other factors have been brought into the picture. The first of these is the relationship of the latest-stage capitalisms with the rest of the world. Hitherto we have considered them almost in isolation, and that was necessary for purposes of exposition. But in fact they and their democratic political institutions are highly exceptional organisms in a world the greater part of which conducts its economic as well as its political life quite differently. Not only does some third of the human race conduct its life in the communist way, but also the greater part of the population of even the non-communist world lives under pre-capitalist, rather than under capitalist, "relations of production."

The fact is that nearly 80% of the living generation of mankind are peasants.* Moreover, this vast mass of peasant farmers, with its still mediaeval poverty, its prejudices, its inexorable stability, its whole immemorial way of life—with all its liabilities and assets—stretches right across the split in

* This calculation, necessarily a most rough-and-ready one, depending on the definition of the peasant, is made by Professor Toynbee in Vol. VIII of his *Study of History*. See p. 684 of that work for the estimates upon which it is based.

the world between communism and capitalism. From this point of view both communism and capitalism are merely rival methods of industrialisation; they are systems still emerging from the peasant ocean of mankind. The whole future of the capitalist democracies is bound up with their relationship, not only to their rivals, the communist societies, but also, and above all, with their relationship to the peasant masses in the precapitalist areas of the non-communist world. That relationship used to be summed up in one word: Imperialism. A section of this study will be devoted to that subject. For an unforeseen transformation has, undeniably, been taking place, in the past ten years especially, in the imperial relationship. This very transformation, however, has brought us face to face with an acute economic problem. We have to find a method, alternative to the imperial one, by which the latest-stage capitalisms can transfer across their frontiers those masses of capital which will be necessary to the development of the peasant 80% of the world. For such a transfer is indispensable not only to the development of the peasant world, but to their own stability also.

After that we shall endeavour to give an account of the actual attempts which were made in the first half of our century in each of the three major latest-stage capitalisms (America, Britain and Germany) to transcend the capitalist relations of production by democratic means. We shall discover, I repeat, that there is a specific economic stumbling-block to this process, which did more than anything else to frustrate the democratic attempts, and in so doing helped to produce the unparalleled tragedies of the first half of the century. It will be shown that this specific stumbling block will ruin us again unless the democratic forces become fully conscious of its existence and learn how to circumvent it.

TOO EASY—OR TOO DIFFICULT?

In this volume we have been concerned to draw the outline of capitalism in its contemporary form; to trace its innate tendencies; to chart "the set of the system"; to see whither its tides would take us, if they were allowed to flow unchecked; and then to study the interaction of these tides with the other principal actor upon the twentieth-century stage, namely, contemporary democracy.

The question arises: have we in all this been dealing in the economic problems of the day before yesterday? All this concern with instability and crisis, this anxiety over the ability of democracy to hold its own with the social forces generated by contemporary capitalism—all this sort of thing, it may be said, is out of date. These, it may be said, may have been the troubles of the nineteen-thirties; today they are surmounted both in theory and in practice. Capitalism, it may be claimed, has now solved its problems and will sail on serenely through the second half of the century.

I do not believe a word of it. As the argument of nearly every chapter has implied, I do indeed suppose that the experience of the last twenty-five years, combined with its intellectual advances, should make these problems soluble. But I am convinced that they will only in fact be solved by mobilising every ounce of economic knowledge, political insight, wisdom and practical skill, which we can command; and then only by means of transforming the very nature of the system, until in the end, it is no longer capitalism.

Indeed, the continuing necessity to concern ourselves with these matters is illustrated by what is in fact the opposite objection. Other readers, far from supposing that we are now out of the wood, will surely feel, either consciously or unconsciously, that the world of the nuclear weapons is too desperate a place in which to be able to concentrate our attention on such issues as these. But if the first objection is a counsel of complacency, the second is a counsel of despair. In the short run, it is true, a comprehension of the workings of contemporary capitalist societies may not do much to help us to keep the peace; what matters for that is political wisdom rather than any sort of political economy. In the longer run, however, the range of considerations herein discussed may be of decisive importance for the supreme issue of peace or war also. It is true that that issue can never be more than partly within our own control. If, for example, in the mid-twentieth-century situation, the communist powers were to commit general and unprovoked aggression, no development of the economies of the Western powers, however successful, could keep the peace. But such general and unprovoked aggression on the part of the communist powers is most unlikely, provided that we in the West keep both our strength and our heads. And in order that we may do so, the progressive solution of, precisely, our economic and social problems, is all-important. In history it has been those powers which have failed to solve the problems of their own internal development which have either turned deliberately towards war as the sole remaining solution, or, if they have not gone so far as that, have failed to show the judgment, the strength, the self-confidence, the poise, which are the qualities needed to keep the peace. Thus it is no more than an oversimplification to say that, if the highly developed societies of the West can continue to modify their economies so as to avoid anything comparable to the instabilities which they suffered in the first half of the century, then, but then only, will they do all that is in their power, at least, to keep the peace.

IMPORTANCE OF ECONOMICS

For all these reasons the problems of political economy, that humble and humdrum science of social housekeeping, still seem to me to be of immense importance. For breakdown in this field can wreck all else. Moreover, its problems are so immensely difficult, not because of any innate complexity, but because the growth of our knowledge in this field faces uniquely formidable psychological and emotional disturbances. Here blind and violent class prejudices and passions fill our minds and block our understanding.

Even in this sphere, however, such great men as Smith, Ricardo, Marx and Keynes have made a beginning. Each has laboured faithfully, according to his lights. At the time and to themselves their work seemed almost wholly antagonistic. But to us it is becoming apparent that, slowly and by a dialectical process of contradiction, they have been building up the economic component of a sociology which may at length enable us to control the workings of our societies. It may be that a sociology sufficiently realistic to be, at any rate, a better guide to action than our prejudices and our passions is no longer very far beyond our grasp. It is true that the profound inhibitions of class interest will prevent many of the most influential members of our societies from recognising the existence of such sociological discoveries. For their instincts warn them that these discoveries point towards conclusions which must be painfully unwelcome to them. Nevertheless, there are now enough educationally equipped men and women whose interests will be promoted rather than prejudiced by the conscious and democratic control of their societies, to make it realistic to believe that the thing may yet be done.

THE CONSERVATIVE ICONOCLAST

And in all sobriety it does seem as if nothing less than everything is now at stake. Think of all that there is, not only to achieve, but also to preserve! Now that the very existence of our societies has been put in question we have all found that there is as much in them which we passionately wish to preserve as to eliminate. We value the intellectual and cultural achievements of the West with a new intensity, since the possibility of losing them has become real to us. (The traveller, for example, goes through Europe today with a certain naïveté, seeing its great familiar monuments as if for the first, because he feels that it may be for the last, time.)

But one thing is certain: the riches, complexities and marvels of the Western heritage can only be preserved by being developed. One of the few things that we may confidently assert about human societies is this: A society which does not develop, which does not continue to unfold ever new and richer potentialities, decays, or, if it does not at once decay, freezes into sterility. For these reasons the true conservatives will seem to be, and in a sense really will be, ruthless innovators and iconoclasts. For they alone can clear the way for the continuing life and growth of their societies. Moreover, in the fullness of time those things which in the first half of our century have proved to be illusions will come within the sphere of the possible. The factors upon which the health, strength and growth of society, and the happiness of its members, depend are far more complex and far less understood than we once supposed. But that does not mean that they are incomprehensible. One day these things also will be understood.

THE CRASH AND THE DEBRIS

The breathtaking claim of Marxism was, and is, nothing less than to have discovered an exact science of human society, capable of providing an infallible guide to action. Lenin was asserting this claim when he said that, although of course communists made mistakes, yet their mistakes were of the order of two and two make five, while the mistakes of their opponents were of the order of two and two make tallow candles. He meant that communists, being fallible human beings, might apply their basically infallible doctrine incorrectly. But non-Marxists, he believed, were bound to make not merely mistakes, but to make nonsense: to make nonsense of their efforts to understand social reality, for they lacked the key to it. It has not proved so. It has proved possible indeed to found human societies which are likely to show great economic vigour upon Marxist theory and Leninist practice. But the character of such societies, after almost forty years of experience of the principal one, has convinced us that the all-embracing social theory upon which they are founded must be an extreme oversimplification. The failure of Marxism to provide an account of latest-stage capitalism sufficiently accurate to avoid being gravely misleading is equally marked.

The crash of this vast claim to have solved the problems of human society at one stroke reverberates through our century. Consequently men are now inclined blankly to reject the whole of Marx's in fact indispensable contribution towards a useable sociology. But not only so: the discovery of the fallibility of Marxism threatens to discredit the rational and scientific method * as a whole and to plunge us back

* I repeat that the verdict of history upon Marxism is likely to be that the truly valuable thing about it was its *method*—its approach—to the problems

into an intellectually dark age. At such a moment we must summon up all our resources of mind and will and passion in order to renew the attack upon the social problem. It is, above all, for intellectual courage that this is a time. It is a time for faith in our ability to solve, in the end, those problems of the control of our social environment which are proving far more intractable than the control of our physical environment. We would be poor creatures if we allowed either the intellectual or the physical catastrophes of our times to dismay us. We cannot know whether the second half of our century is to be terrible like the first, or a period of recovery. But we do know what the mind of man, given even the barest opportunity, can accomplish. Therefore, within the limits of the possible for our time and place, our principal duty is to show intransigence towards those gross evils and irrationalities of our societies which still threaten to destroy us.

SOCIALISM

This is still to put the matter negatively. But some positive and deeply felt ideal, some sustained sense of social purpose, will alone make us even desire to master the complexities of our contemporary societies. The breath of life will not be in the social and economic concepts in which these pages have dealt unless we come to them with a positive ideal be-

---

of human society. No doubt even in this respect it will prove to have been no more than a beginning, but who can really doubt that, compared to what had gone before it—and what still exists today without it—it marked an immense advance?

Contemporary Marxists themselves pay lip service to this conclusion and speak of Marxism as a marvellously flexible method. That is what it *should* be; what it has become in the hands of the communists is a cast-iron system. It is that intellectual system which has crashed.

fore us, no matter whether we give that ideal the name of democratic socialism or some other. For if we come to the study of what exists empty of social purpose we shall find that, like Ezekiel, we have come to a valley of dry bones.

"And behold there were very many [bones] in the open valley; and, lo, they were very dry." But Ezekiel was commanded to "prophesy unto the wind." When he did so he prayed, "Come from the four winds, O breath." Then the breath of life came into the dry bones and they lived. An analysis of existing society will only live if it is informed by an aspiration for what society may become.

That aspiration can be expressed in the religious or in the secular idiom. We may echo the original Christian challenge to the ancient world: the challenge that there was a sense in which men were all of an equal worth, and that this underlying human equivalence was incompatible with slavery, the master institution of that world. In our epoch we reaffirm that revolutionary message in the wider context that the basic equivalence of human beings is incompatible with the division of our communities into social classes. For slavery itself was only one, although the most extreme, of the social classes into which all developed human societies have hitherto been divided.

On the other hand, we may find inspiration in the great secular formulations of our ideals; we may see our task as one of seeking a second time to realise on earth the trinity of concepts—liberty, equality and fraternity—which men put before themselves at the beginning of the modern epoch. It is easy for us now to see how naïvely it was supposed, a hundred and fifty years ago, that it was only necessary to knock away the old tyrannies in order to realise all three of these ideals in combination. The men of 1798, when they expected to produce Arcadia, simply by giving free rein to every form of individualism, produced, in fact, capitalism. In our own century the men of 1917, believing that they would fulfil the prophecies of socialism, produced the iron-clad regimes of rigid, coercive communism. We live in the period of this double disillusionment. We have learned *both* that the child "trappers" in the mines of early nineteenth-century capitalism, choking their lives away in the eighteen-inch coal seams, were mocked by the assurance that they could no longer be thrown into subterranean dungeons at the will of tyrants, and equally we have learned that the prisoner incarcerated in the twentieth-century Soviet labour camp, because he knew a man who knew a man who spoke against the Government, is mocked, as he dies from his enforced toil, by the assurance that he is guaranteed the right to work. We cannot help knowing all this. Yet so much social experience is dangerous; in destroying our illusions it is only too apt to destroy our ideals also. Our danger, in the countries of the West, which have seen so much, is to sink into an acceptance of what is—to sink into that mood of acceptance into which the far older civilizations of Asia sank long ago (and from which, ironically, they appear to be emerging at this very moment): that mood of acceptance which is the invariable precursor of decline and decay.

Moreover, how foolishly premature such social disillusionment would be. In fact, our Western societies are still extremely dynamic. They are still changing and evolving far more rapidly than any previous societies known to history. Within thirty or forty years the worst features of early capitalism were beginning to be mitigated. In the nineteen-fifties, again thirty to forty years after its establishment, the Soviet *régime* appears to be modifying its most barbarous characteristics.* The verdict of history will not be that either the eight-

---

* While these pages were being printed, the February, 1956, Congress of the Communist Party of the Soviet Union met in Moscow. The Russian leaders went far towards admitting the terrible deceptions of the Russian people which had occurred in the Stalinist period. It became possible to conceive that a new and far more hopeful period might be beginning in Russia.

eenth- or the twentieth-century revolutions were abortive.
The *régimes* which they respectively established have proved
themselves to be formidable engines of material advance-
ment. But what neither the liberal nor the socialist revolutions could do was to establish societies which would bear
comparison with the aspirations of the men who made
them.

The ideal of democratic socialism may be thought of as the
attempt at length to realise those aspirations in combination,
to realise a liberty that will not turn into the liberty to exploit, an equality that will not contradict variety, and a
fraternity that will not become its opposite by striving to
impose co-operation by force. It was Lenin who said that
Soviet power plus electricity would equal socialism. The
equation has proved to have had too few terms. But it may
yet prove more true to say that present-day techniques, plus
the standard of life that can be founded upon them, plus a
reasonable distribution of the national product, involving
new forms of ownership for income-bearing property, plus
the democratic diffusion of power throughout the community, will equal socialism.

What, then, will socialism be? Will socialism, reached by
such means, fulfil at last the dreams, the longings, the prophecies of all the men and women who have lived and died for
it? Will the world foretold by its secular saints, by More*
and Morris and Owen, to name only our three Englishmen,
come into being amongst us? Perhaps we can now see that
these things—that even the abolition of poverty, the achievement of classless social equality, together with genuine self-
rule—are the prerequisites, the necessary material and social
furniture, of socialism, rather than the thing itself.

Inevitably, after all that has happened, we ask ourselves
with a new insistence the old question of whether human nature is inherently capable of realising the socialist vision. But

* Official Saint of his own Church also, for that matter.

again, how childishly premature it would be to answer that question in the negative. The first thing that the infant sciences of psychology and anthropology are beginning to teach us is that we know practically nothing about human nature, except, indeed, that it is incomparably more various, more complex and therefore, it seems probable, more capable of development (both for good and ill) than had been supposed. The human race is only just reaching the point of material and intellectual development at which it can consciously raise the question of the character of its societies. How ridiculous we, the early adolescents of racial development, shall look in the eyes of posterity if we pose as disillusioned elders who have seen and suffered all the experiences of which humanity is capable.

What democratic socialists should, surely, be ready enough to admit is that so far we possess no proof that our human nature, even given the favourable environment that we can now see to be an objective possibility, will be capable of developing those characteristics which will alone realise a society worthy of the name of socialist. Moreover, we shall, surely, agree that our twentieth-century experience indicates that the early socialist thinkers, from the most idealist to the most materialist, from More to Marx, all paid too little attention to this subjective, moral, active side of the matter. The indications are that they were wrong in so far as they implied that given the establishment of the right material and social environment, the necessary subjective developments would more or less automatically take place. The real interaction of the objective and subjective factors are so close and so reciprocal as to form an indissoluble complex, which, however much we have to take it to pieces for description and analysis, must in practice be tackled all together and as a whole.

If, however, non-socialist, and in particular moral and religious, opinion, meets us with an immense historical "I told you so" in this respect, the socialist has, perhaps, two answers. In the first place, the utopian overoptimism of the pioneers of socialist thought is likely to prove at least less wide of the mark than the traditional doctrine that human nature is a rigidly fixed factor, and a factor fixed for that matter in original evil. And second, the socialist pioneers lived at a time when any real attempt to ascertain by means of psychology and anthropology what human nature was like, and what were the possibilities of its development, had hardly begun.* Now, however, that a certain amount of evidence, at least, is coming to hand from these fields, the most urgent theoretical tasks for socialists may well lie in the assimilation of contemporary psychological and anthropological discoveries. Thus, until we know far more about our own natures than we do now, service to the cause of democratic socialism requires, as does the service of every other great cause, an act of faith. It requires an act of faith, not indeed in the perfectibility of human nature, but in its capacity for development in step with the development of man's command over his material environment. The need for that act of faith raises acutely all these supreme moral issues of social purpose which, as was said at the outset, lie far outside the scope of this volume.

Perhaps just this may be said, however. What else but the realisation of a society of liberty with co-operation, of equality in diversity and of fraternity unforced, is worth living for today? In the past men have lived and died for many other ideals. In recent times they have, above all, lived and died for their nation, their race or their class. And these ideals still have immense power over us. But nation, race and class are merely fragments of humanity. It is natural, and

---

* Engels is often scoffed at for seizing on Morgan's early attempts at anthropological theory. But, however much this work can now be corrected, was he not absolutely right in realising how vital a factor anthropology would become for socialist theory?

may be noble, to serve the fragment to which we belong; blindly to worship it is idolatry.

We pray before every sitting of the British House of Commons that we may "lay aside partial affections." That is surely one of the highest ideals to which a sovereign assembly can aspire. For today we may be betrayed not only by what is false, but also by what is incomplete, underdeveloped, and still morally adolescent, within us. What were even yesterday high ideals are coming, as the world changes and develops at its present headlong pace, to be precisely those partial affections which we pray that we may lay aside. In the first half of our century such partial affections, raised to frenzy in the blind worship of race and class and nation, have half wrecked the world. We have now equipped ourselves with weapons which ensure that if we repeat those idolatries, neither we, nor perhaps our world, will survive. Who at such a moment of time can give himself to anything less than the whole?

INDEX